TIM NOBLE & SUE WEBSTER

WASTED YOUTH

Rizzoli
NEW YORK

For all the members of our special friends club

THE MU

HAFUCKA

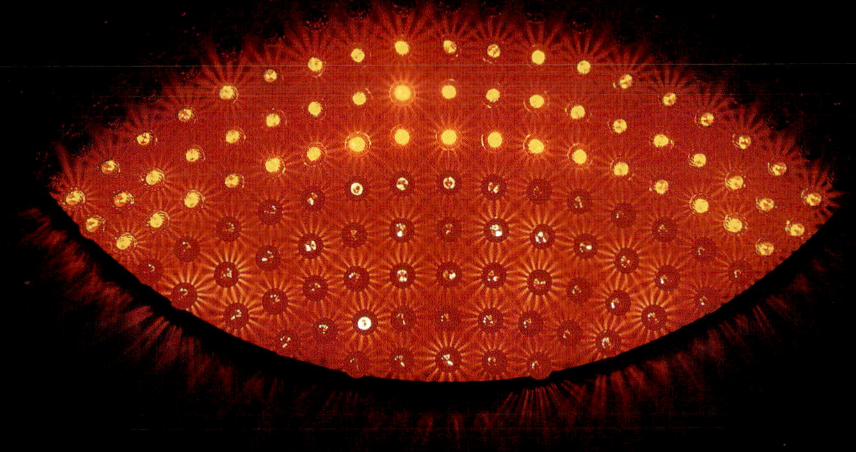

The Muthafucka, 2000

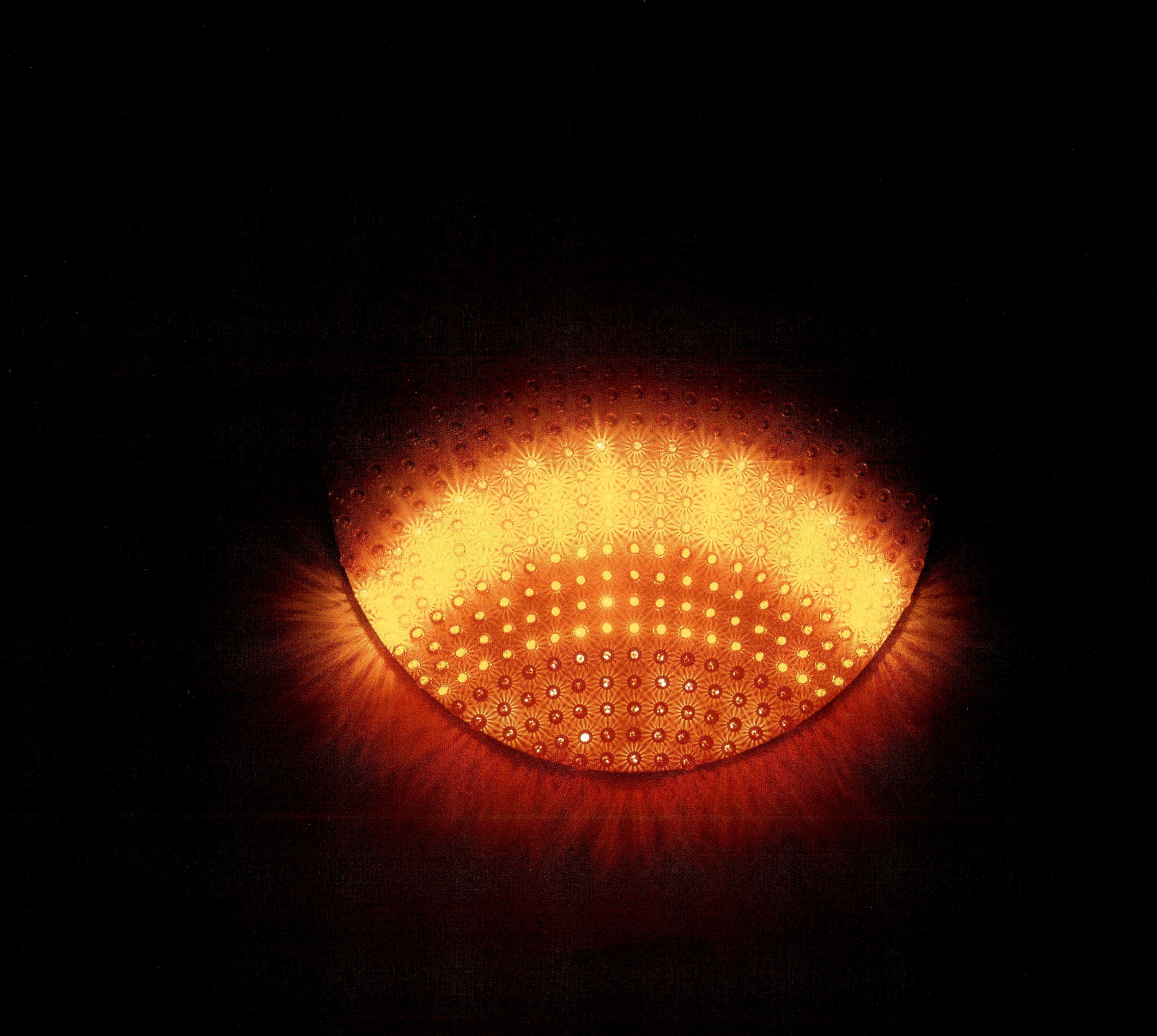

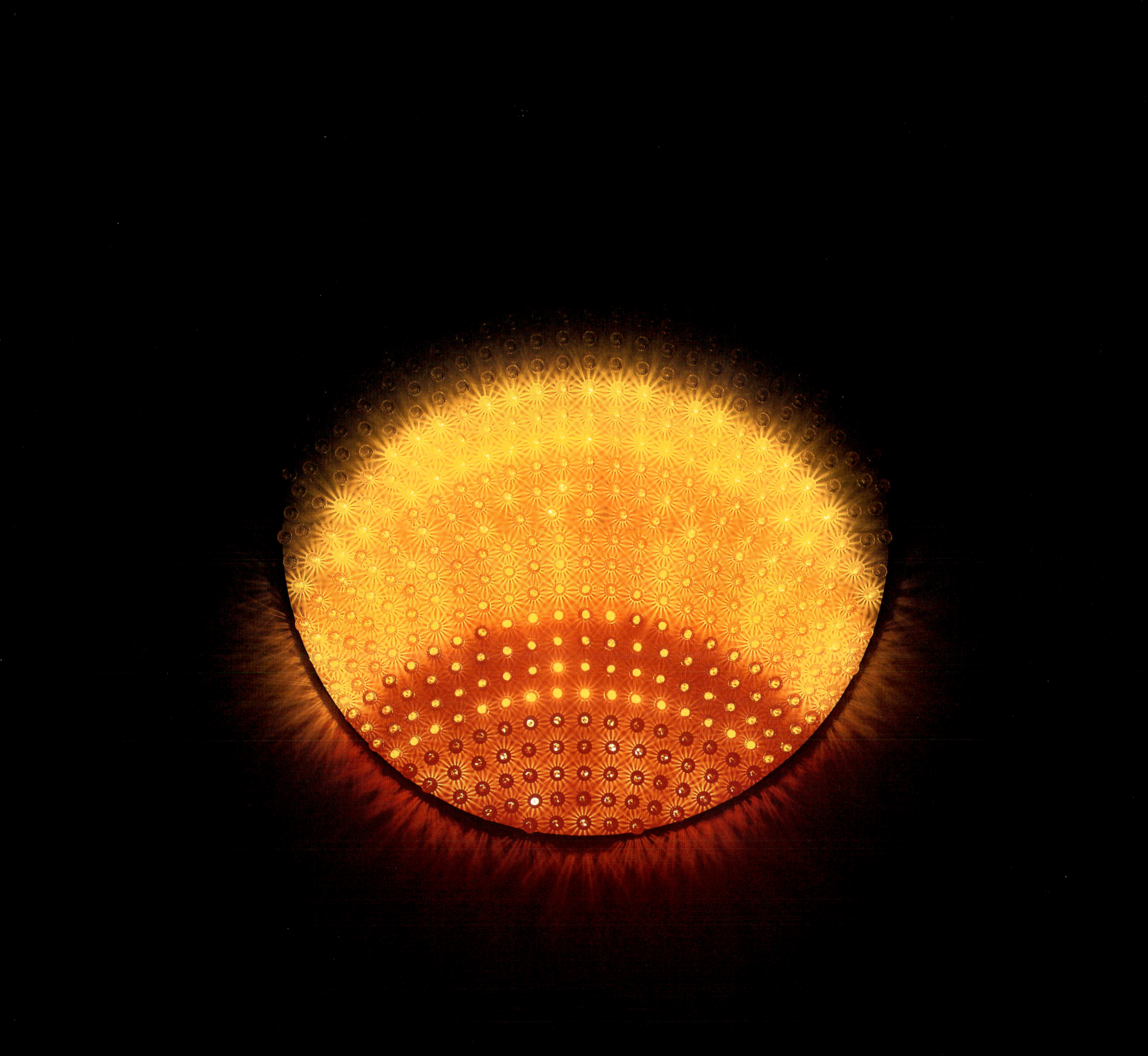

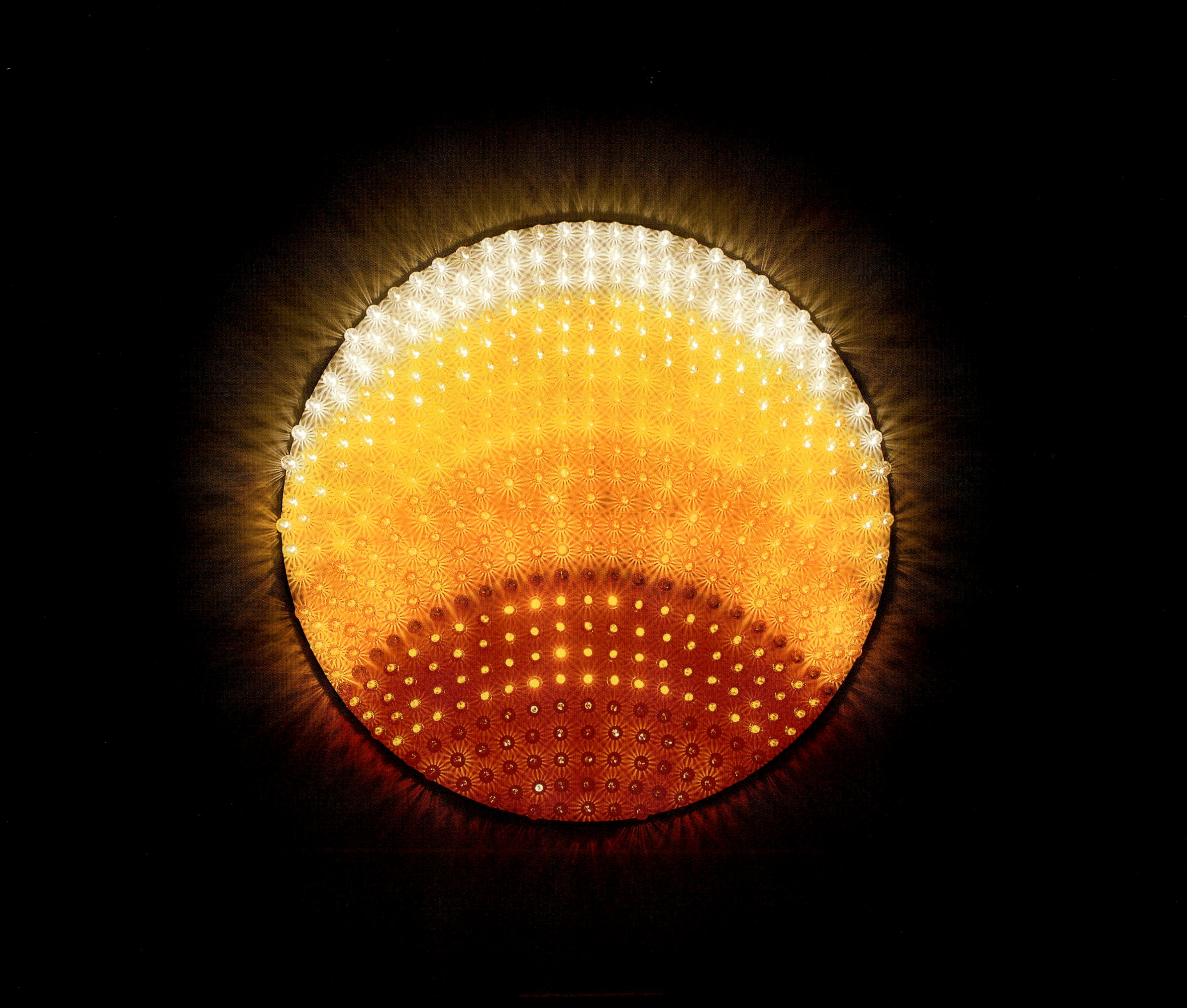

I ❤ YOU, 2000

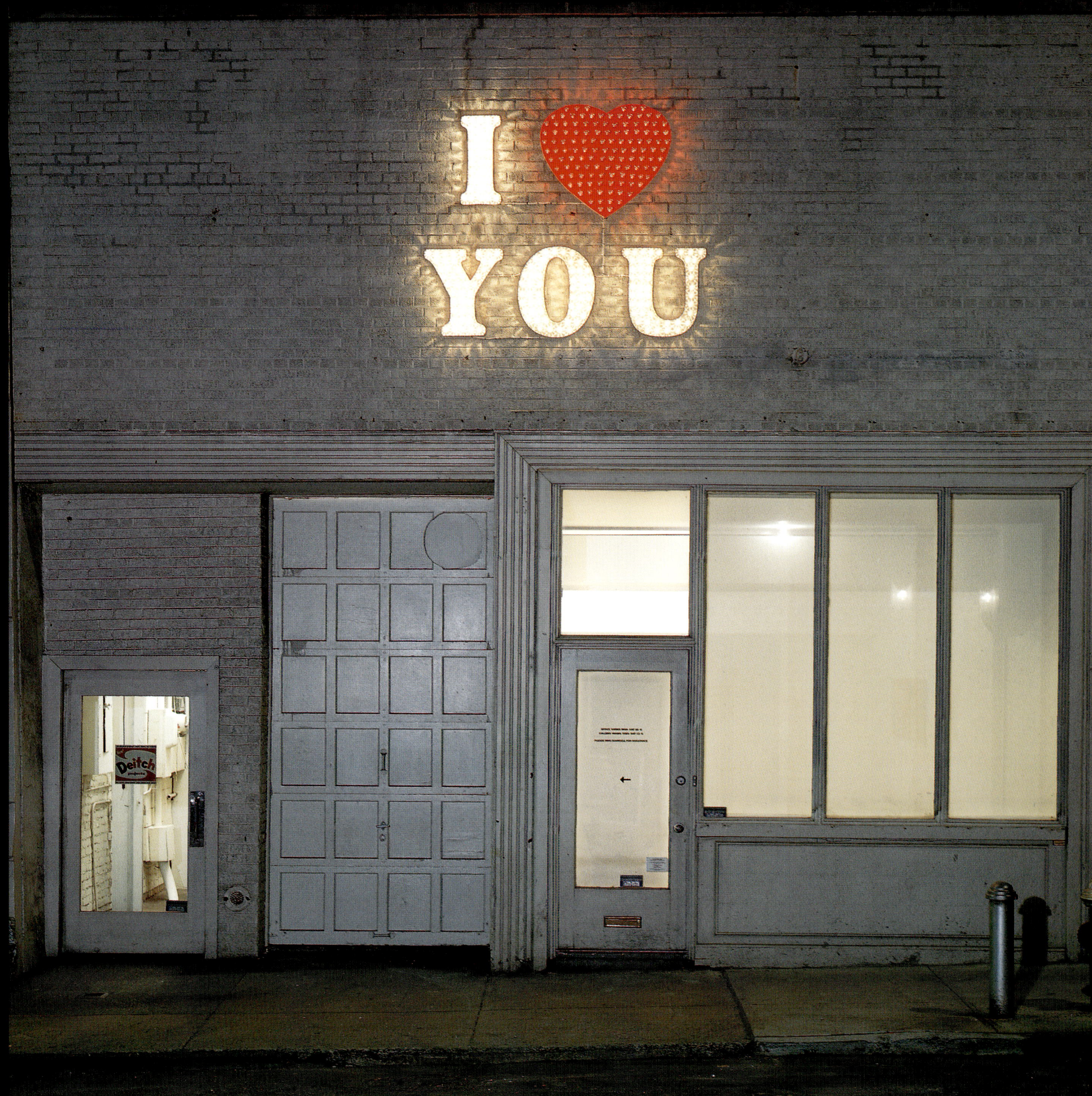
I ♥ YOU
Deitch projects

Forever, 1996

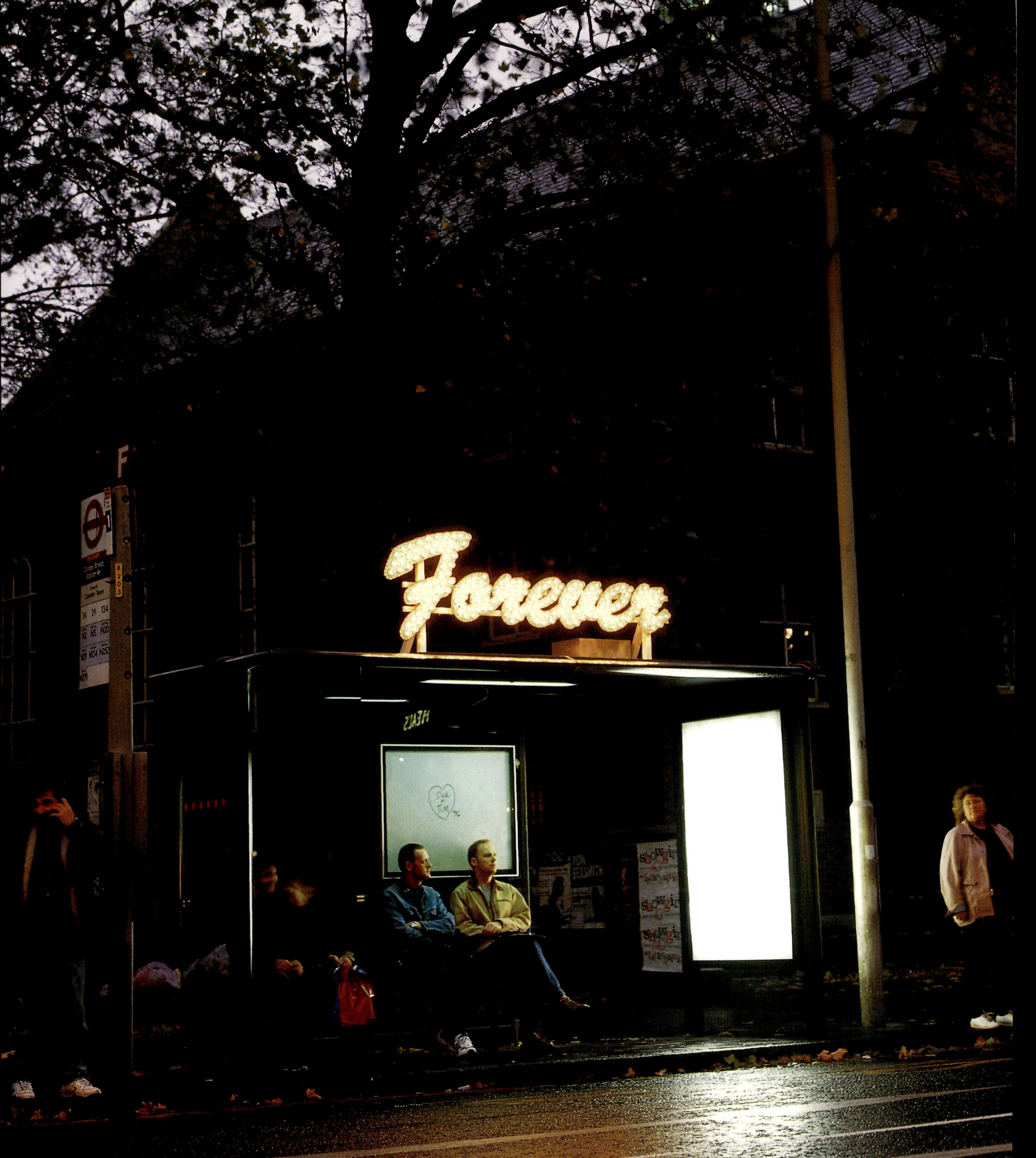
Forever
HEAL'S
Sue
+
TiM '96

Forever, 2001

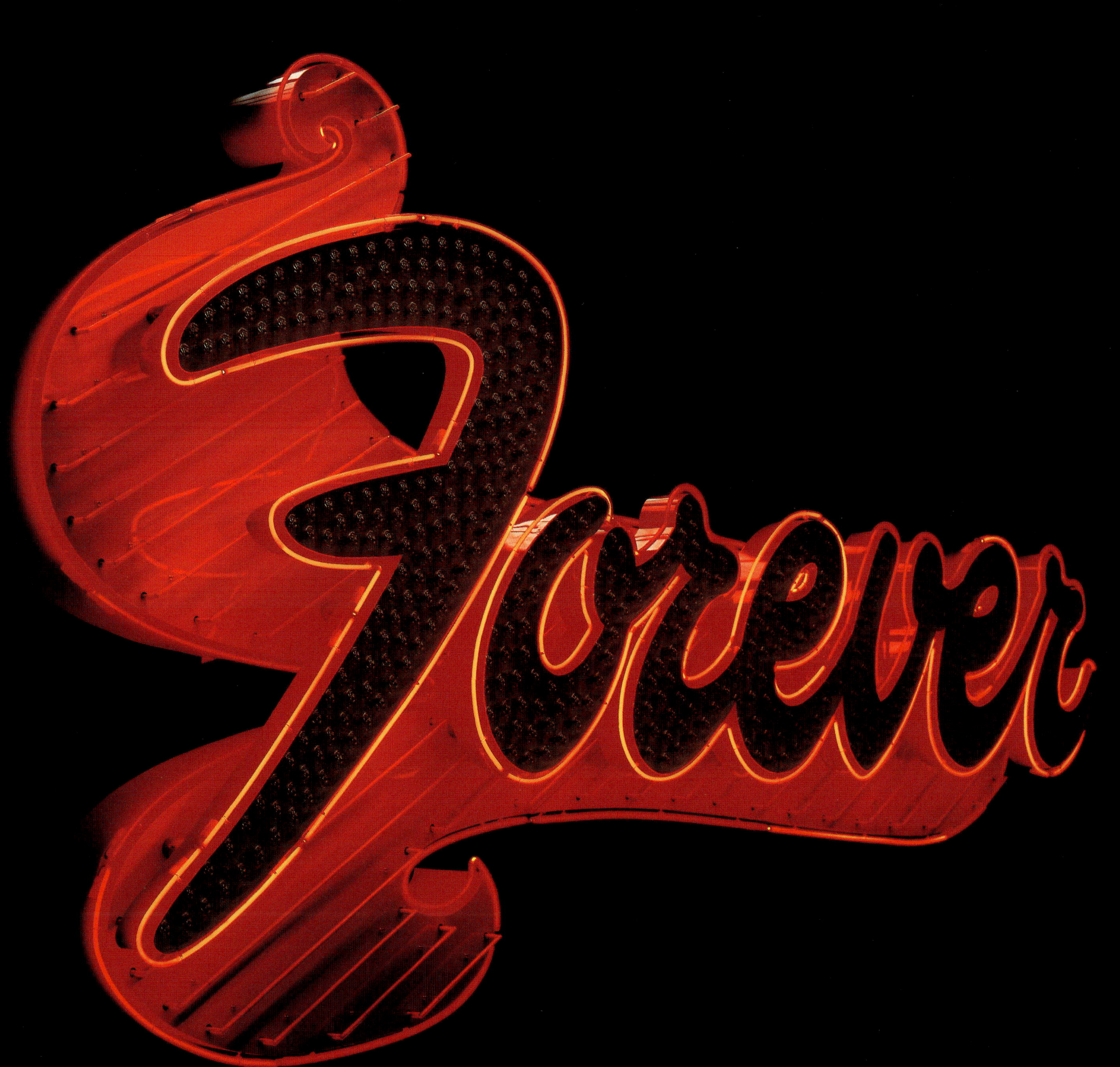

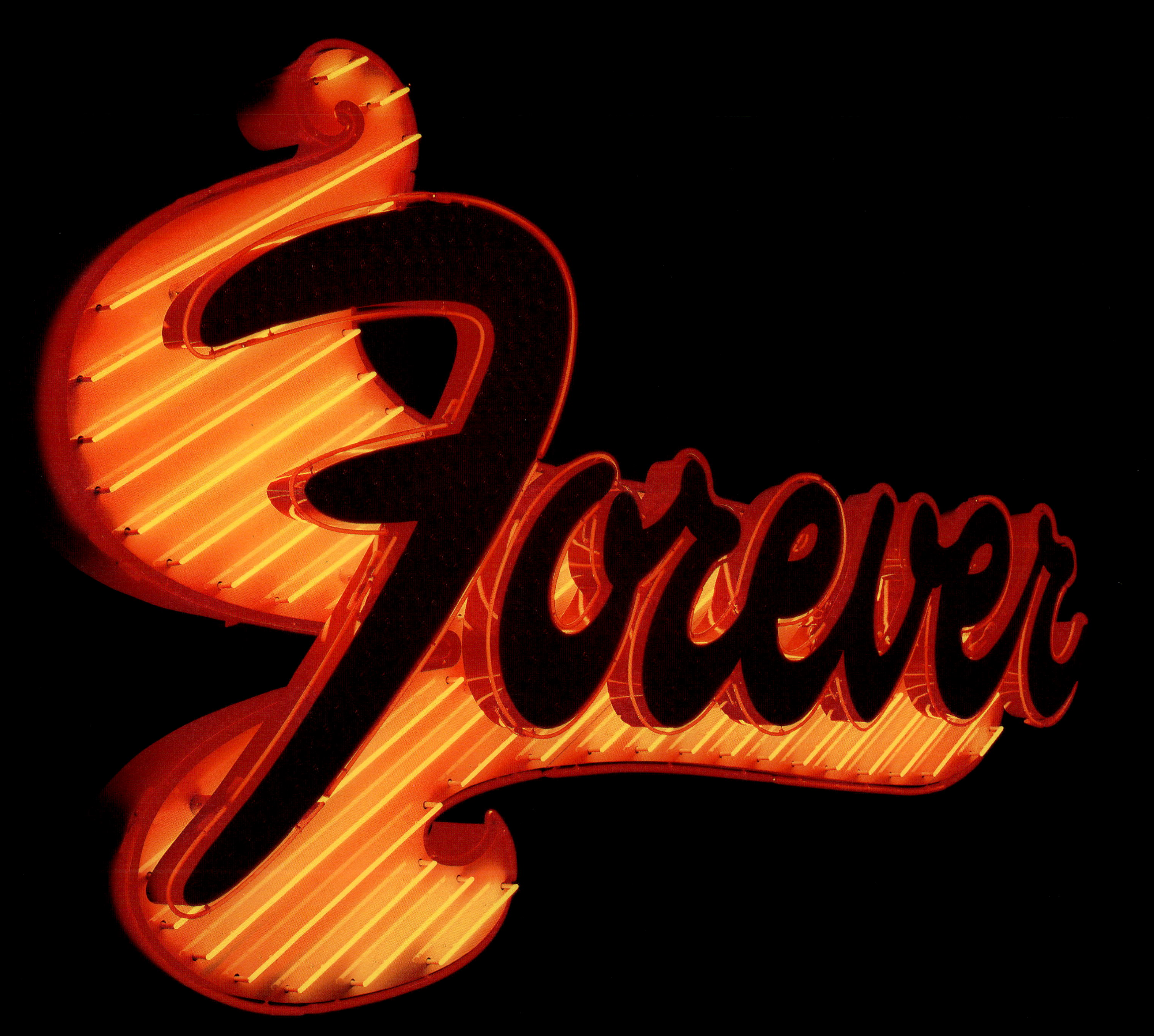
Forever

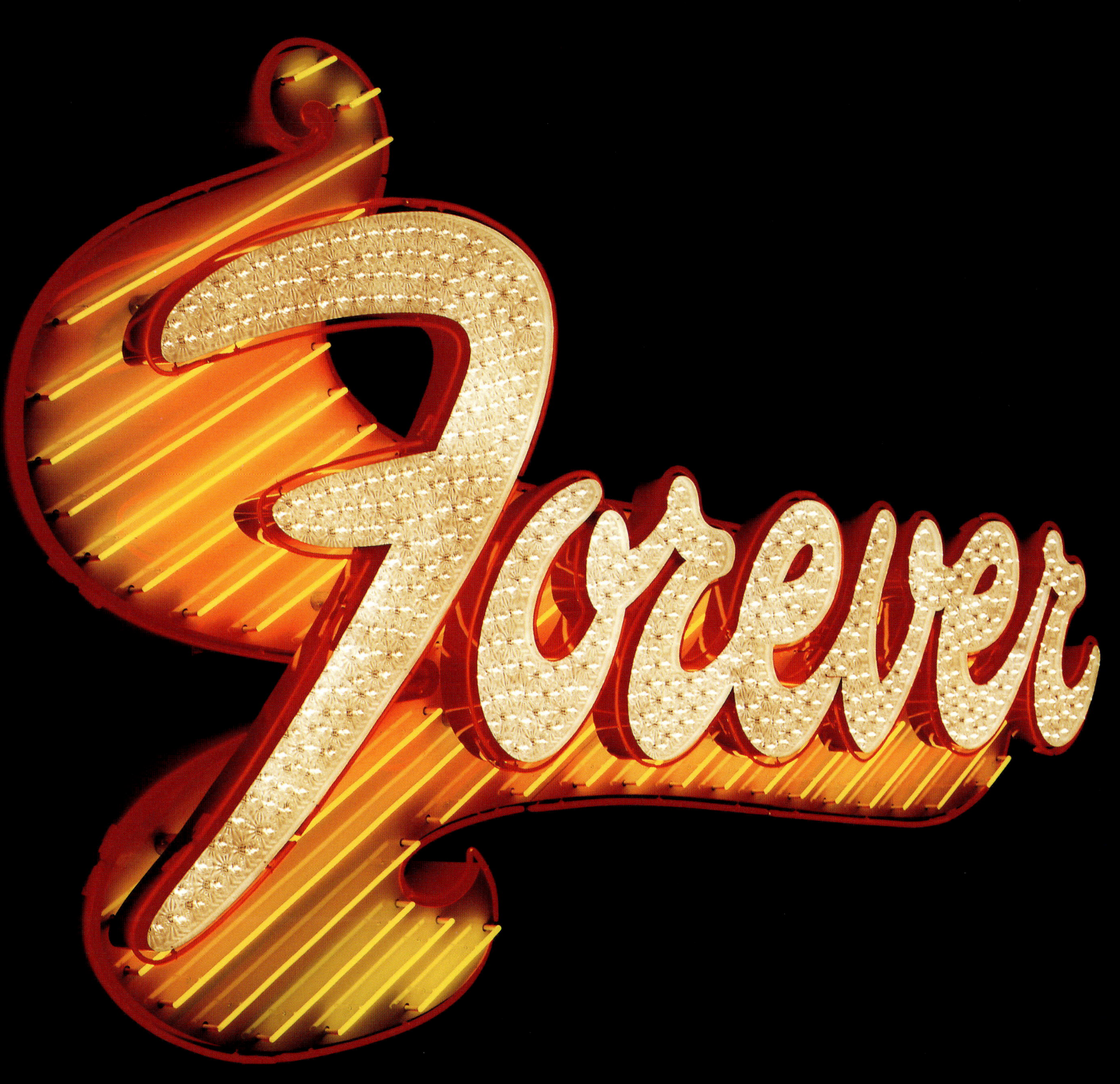
Forever

TO

SCHIZO

XIC

HRENIA

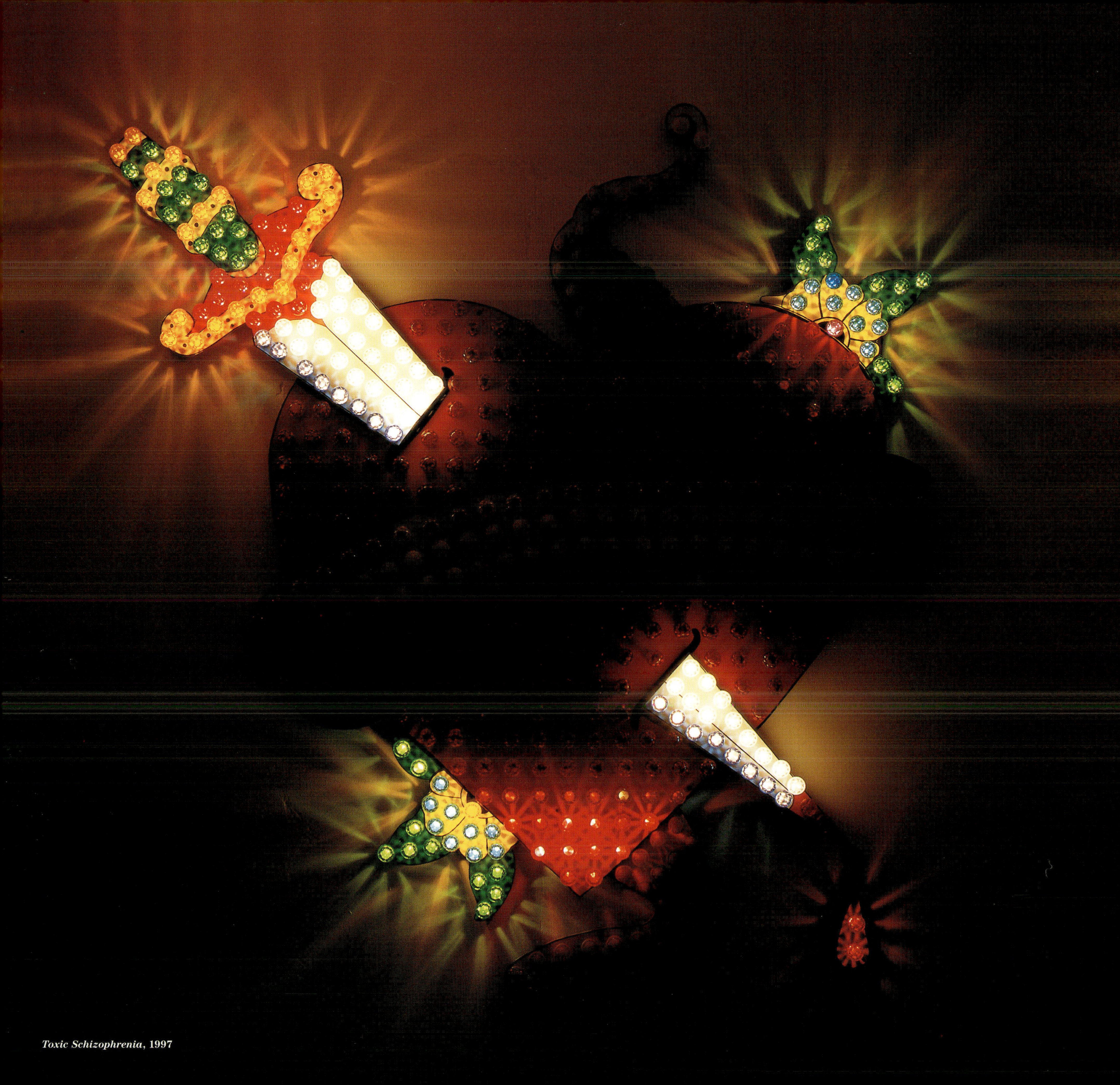

Toxic Schizophrenia, 1997

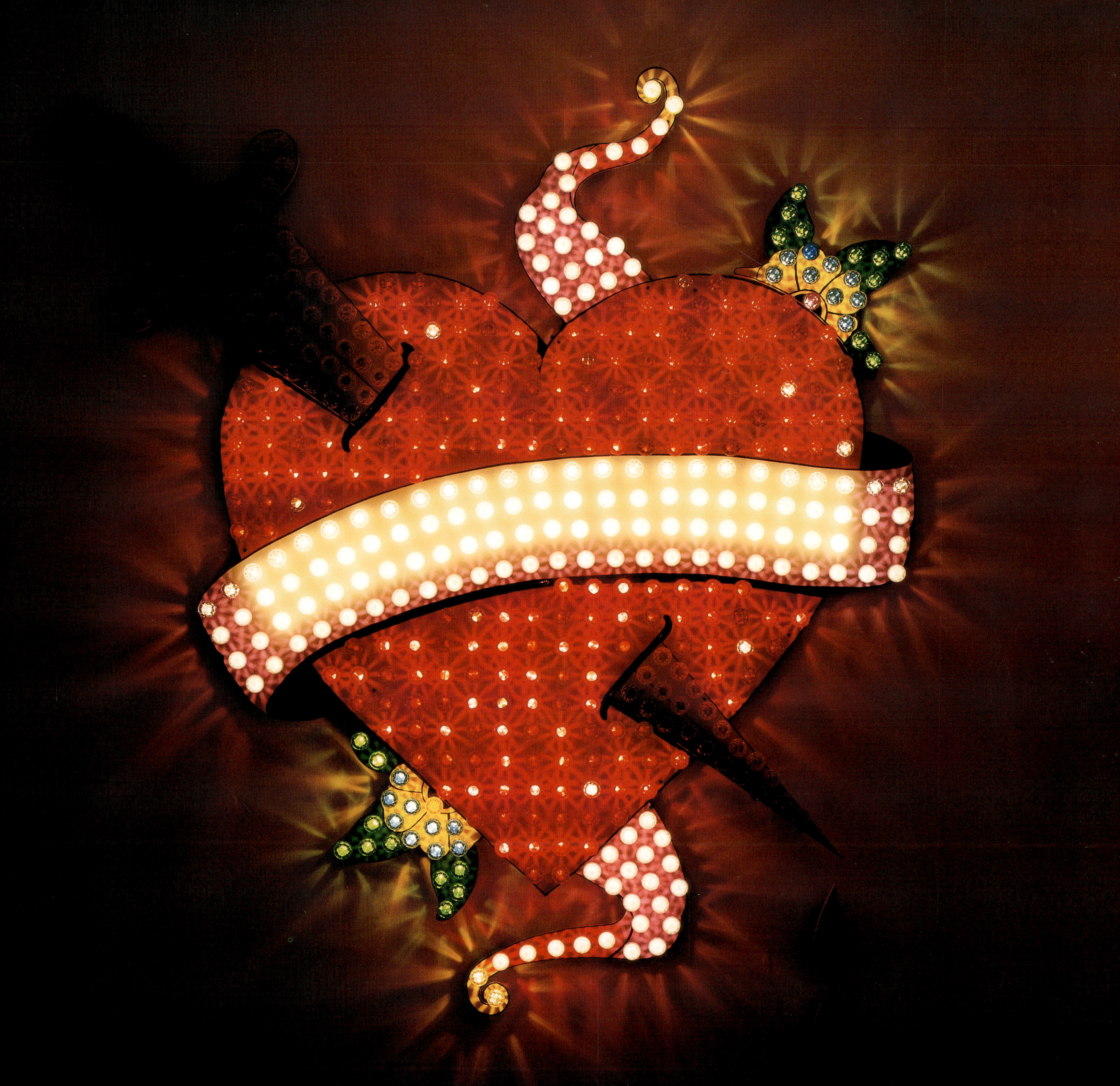

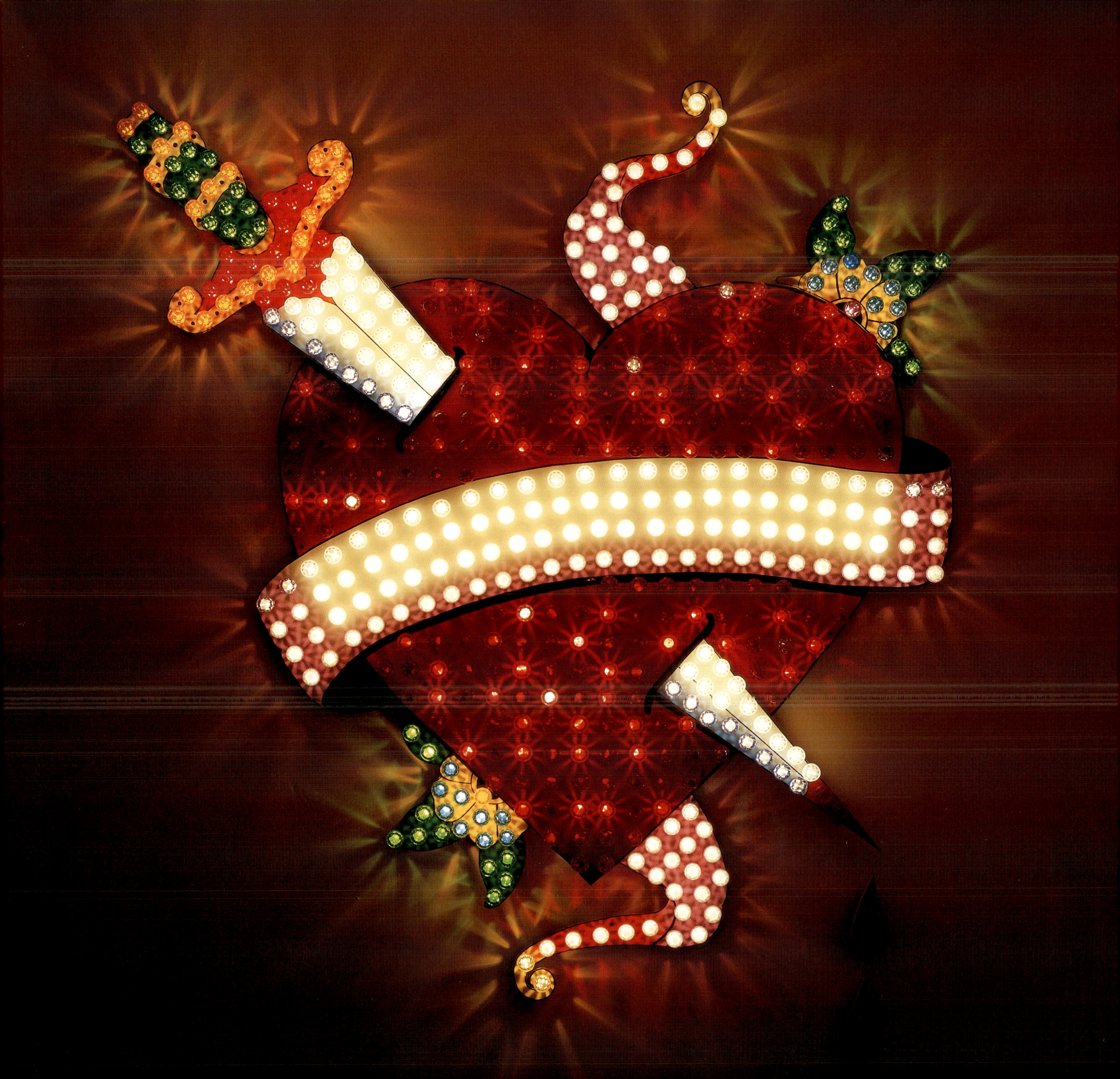

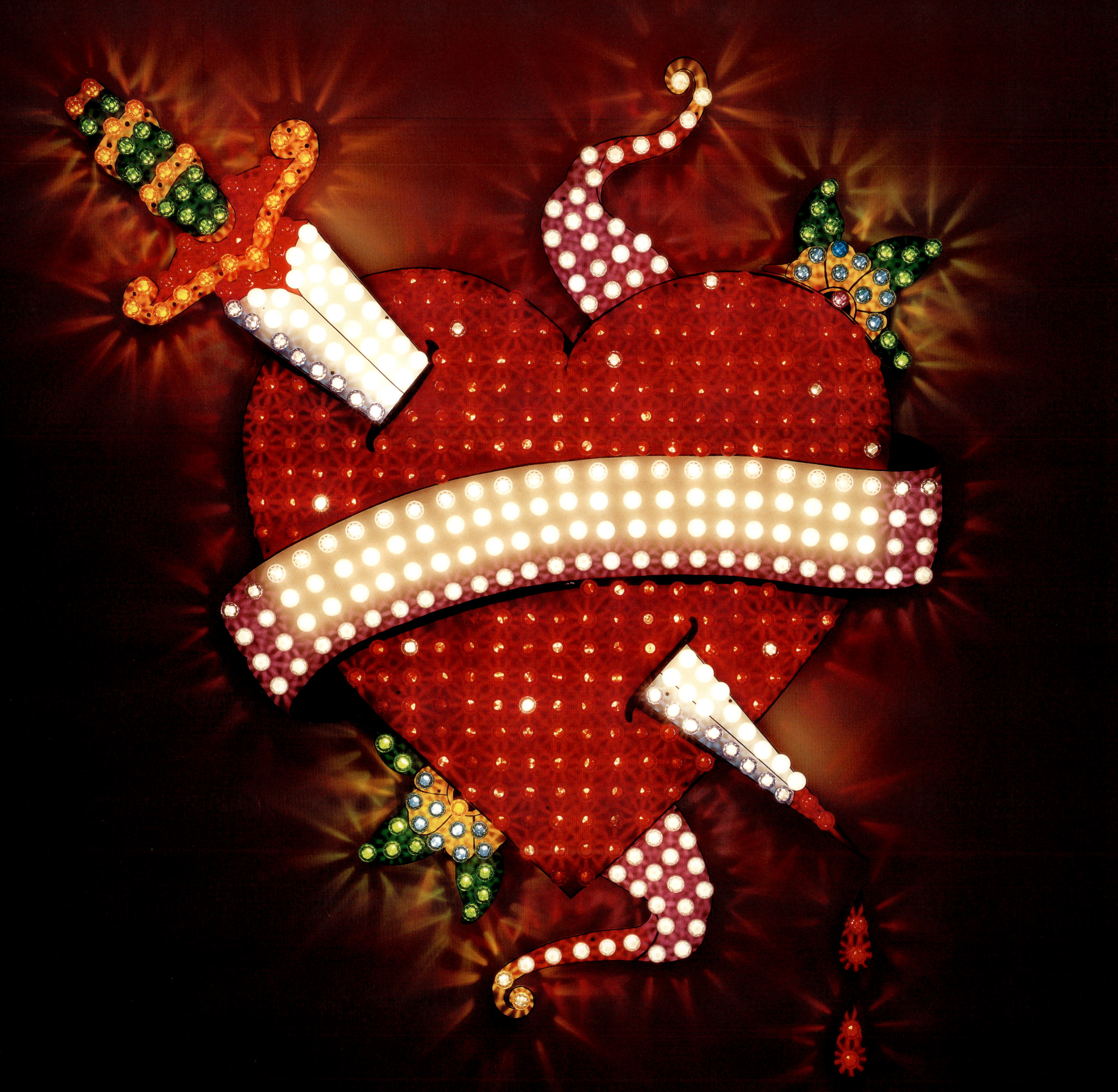

The Sweet Smell of Excess, 1998

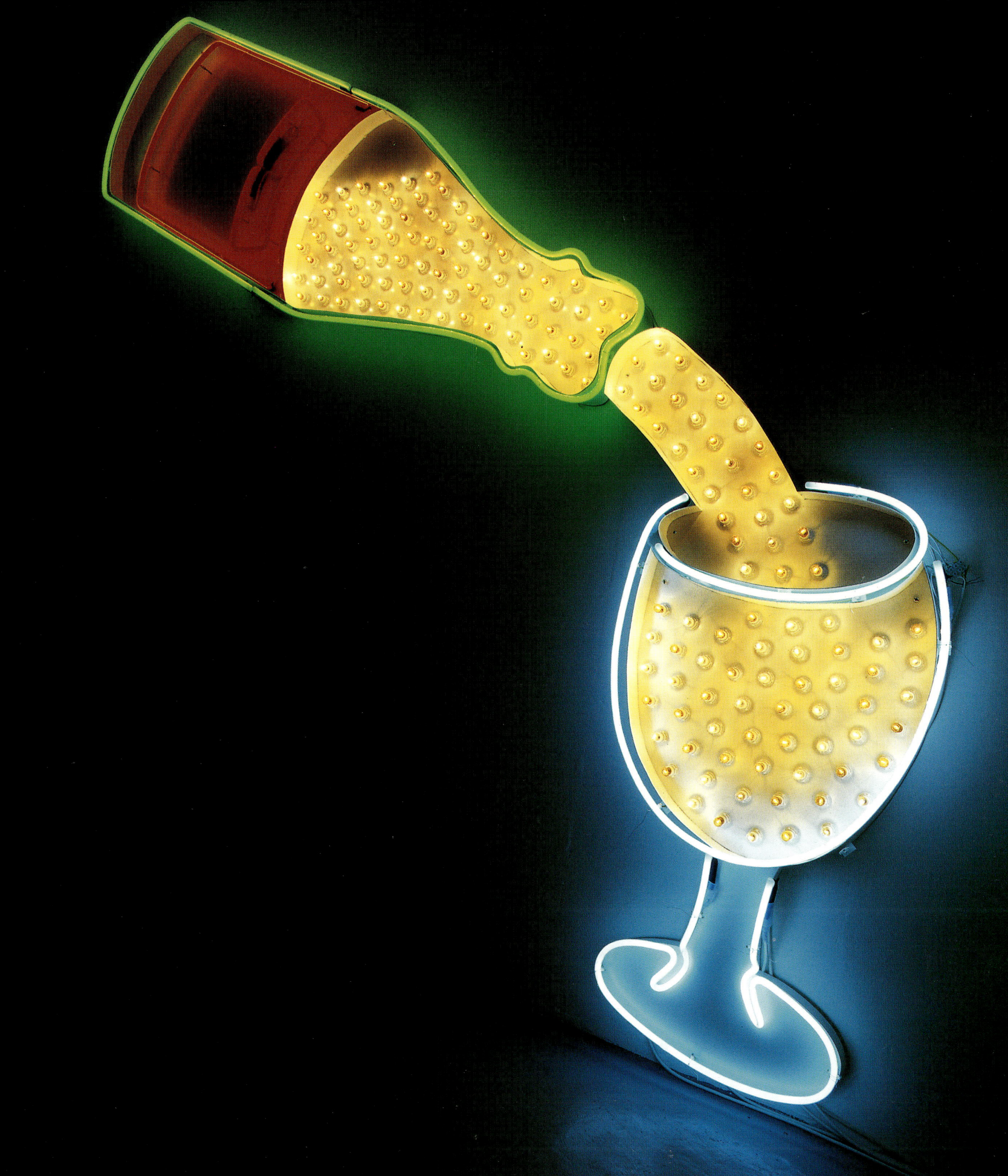

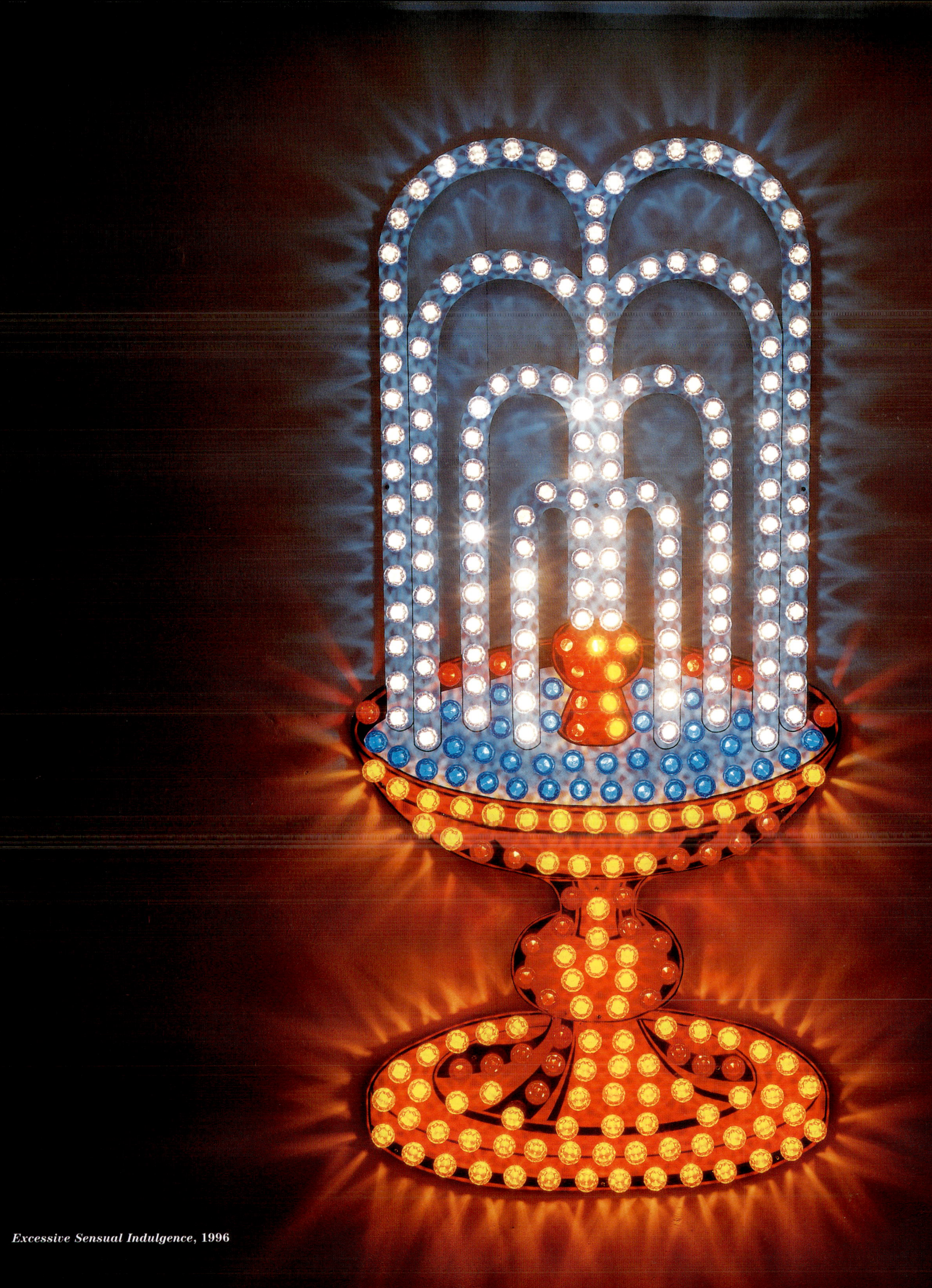

Excessive Sensual Indulgence, 1996

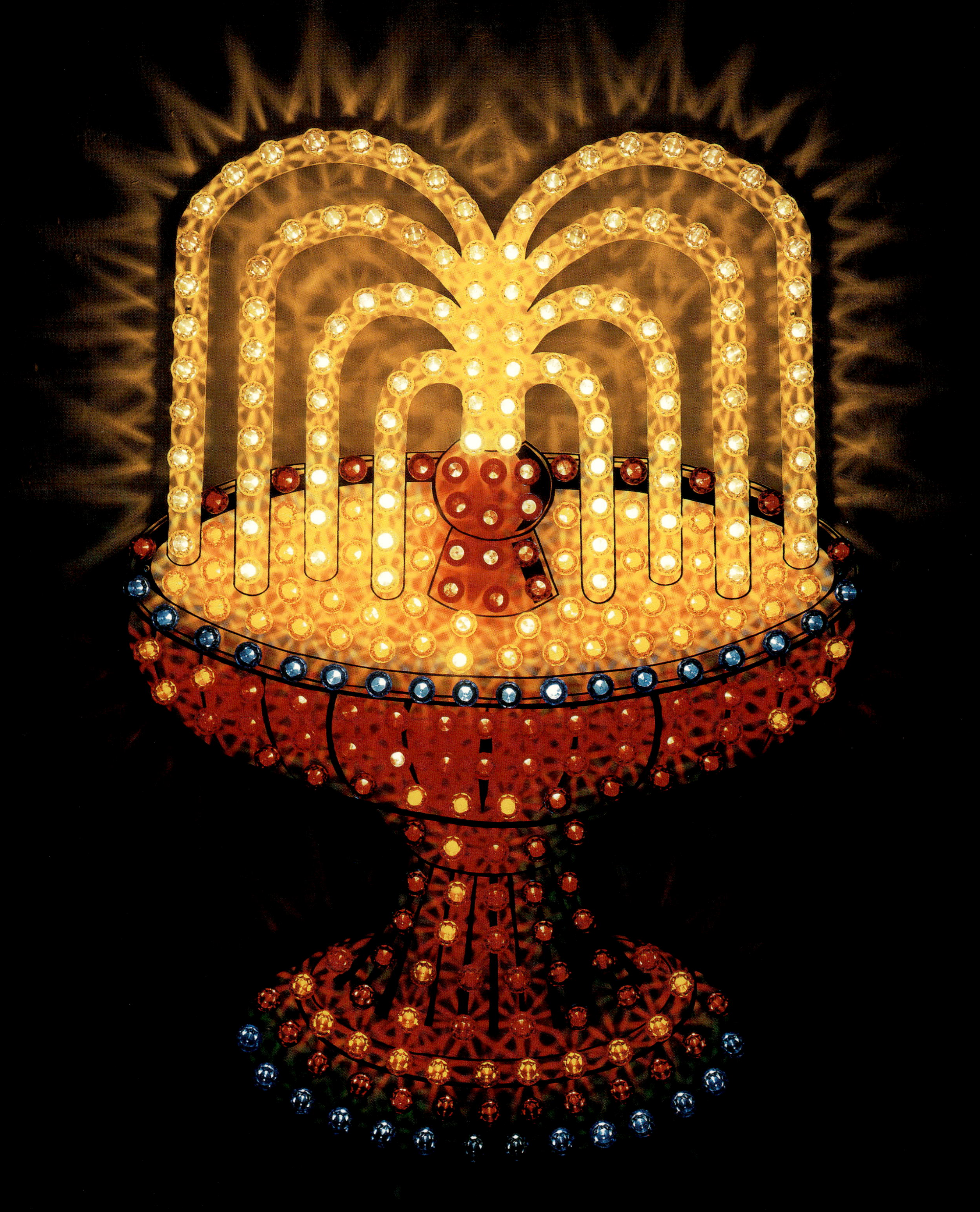

Golden Showers, 2000

GIRLF
FROM

RIEND
HELL

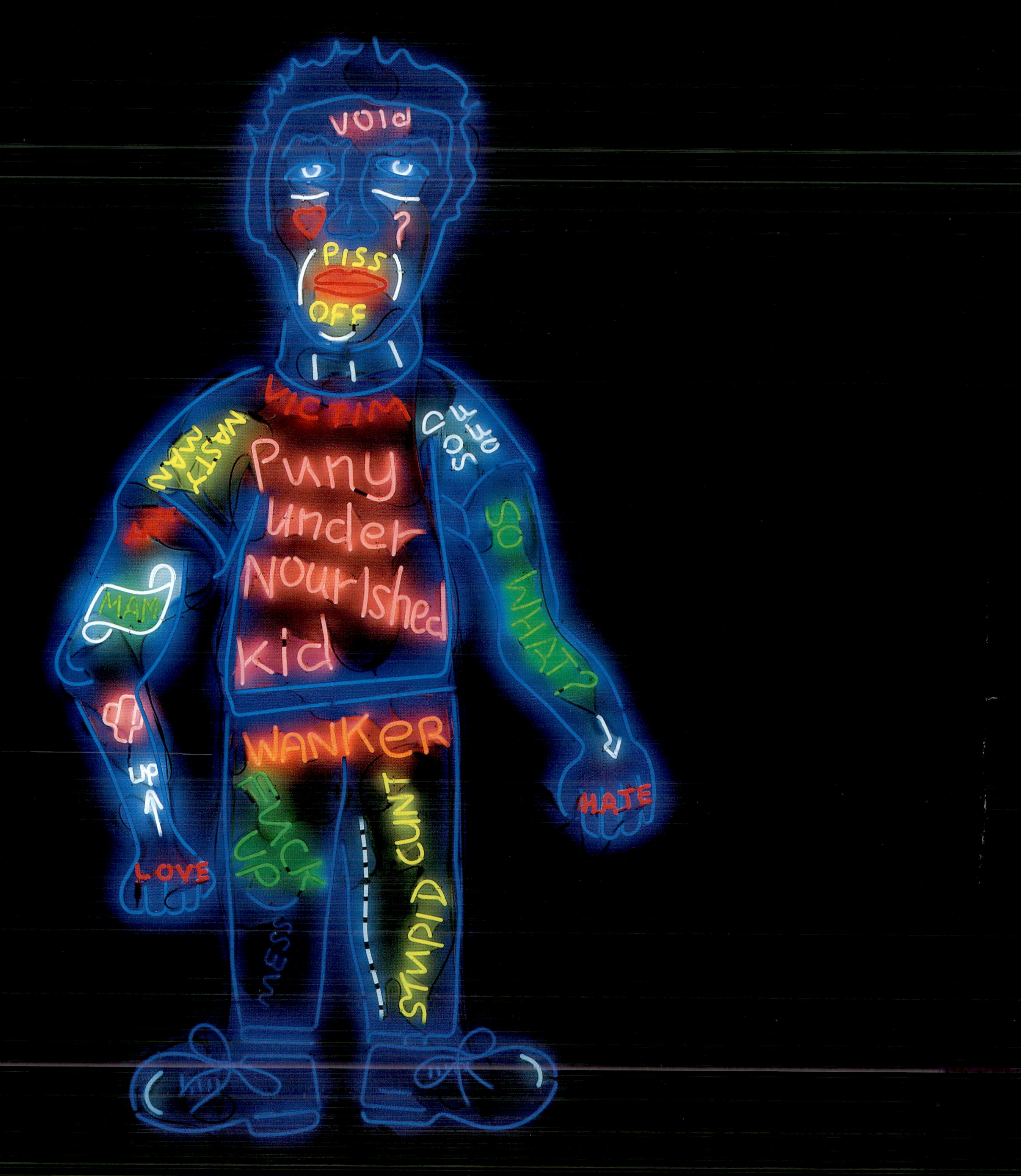

Puny Undernourished Kid & Girlfriend From Hell, 2004

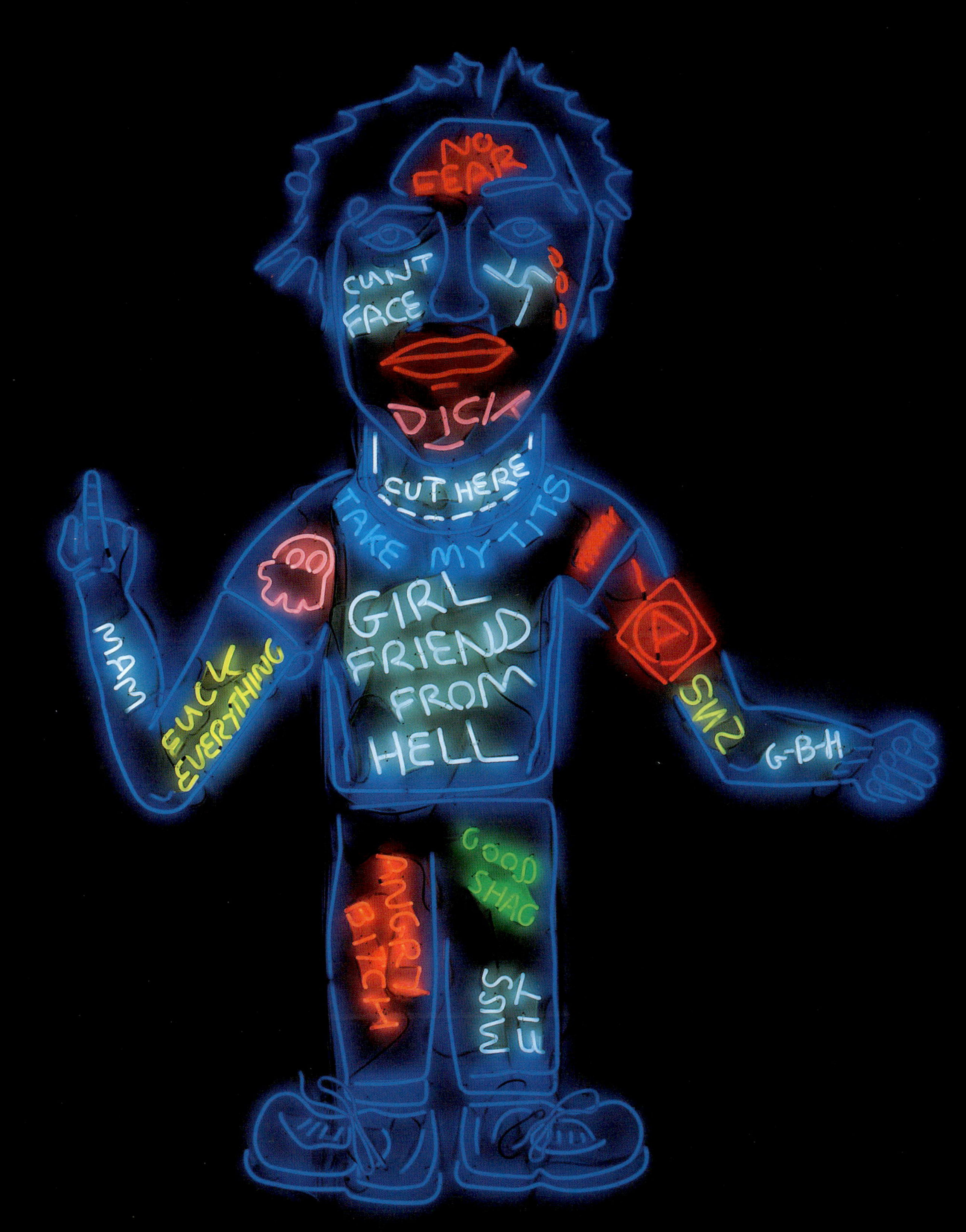

NO FEAR
CUNT FACE
DICK
CUT HERE
TAKE MY TITS
GIRL FRIEND FROM HELL
MAM
FUCK EVERYTHING
SUZ
G-B-H
ANGRY BITCH
GOOD SHAG
MISS IT

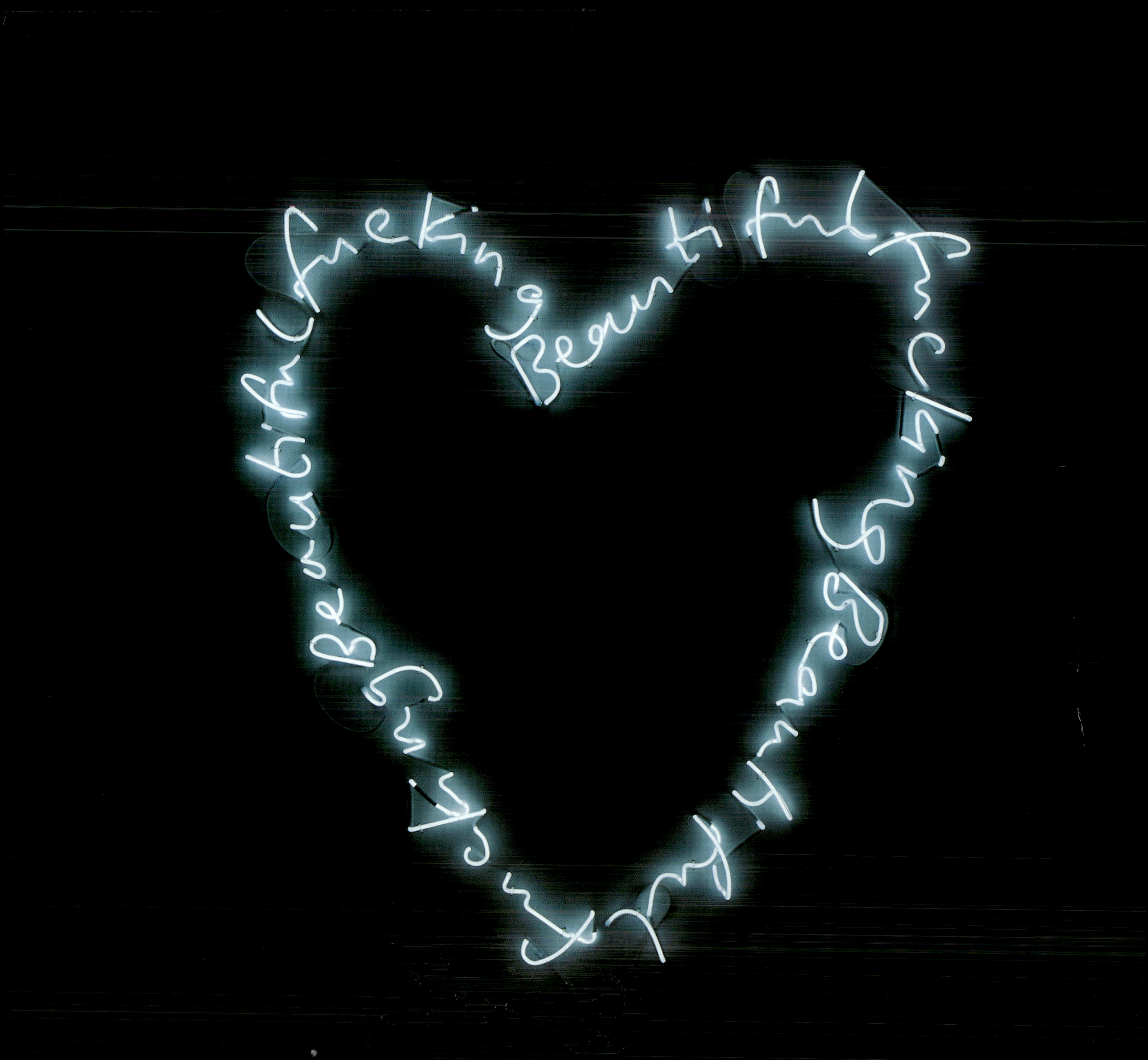

fuckingbeautiful (snow white/hot pink), 2000

fucking
Beautiful
fucking
Beautiful
fucking
Beautiful

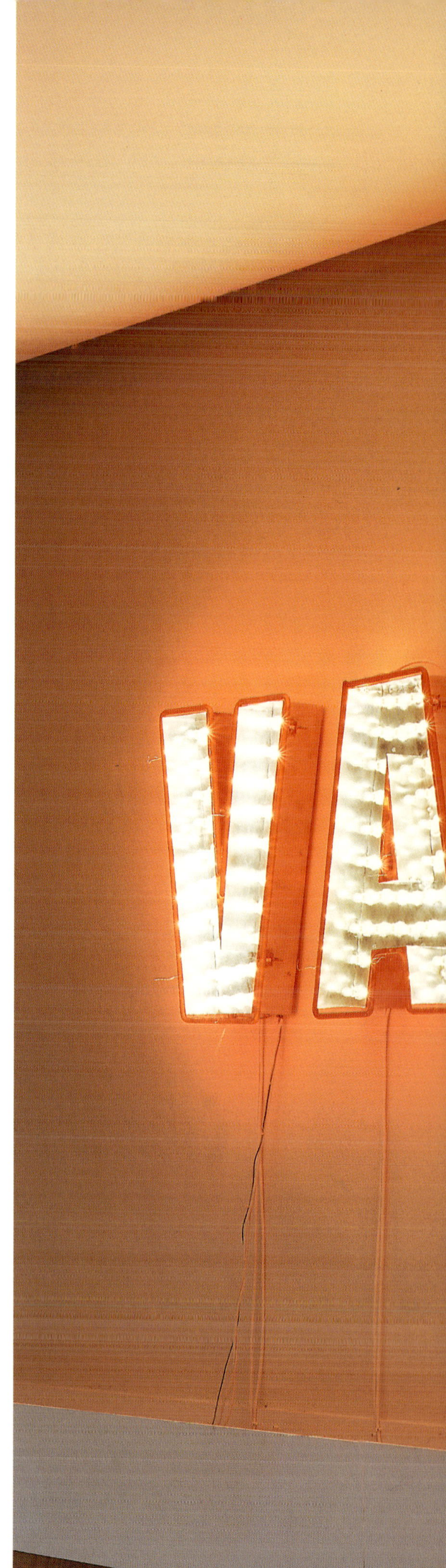

Vague Us, 1998

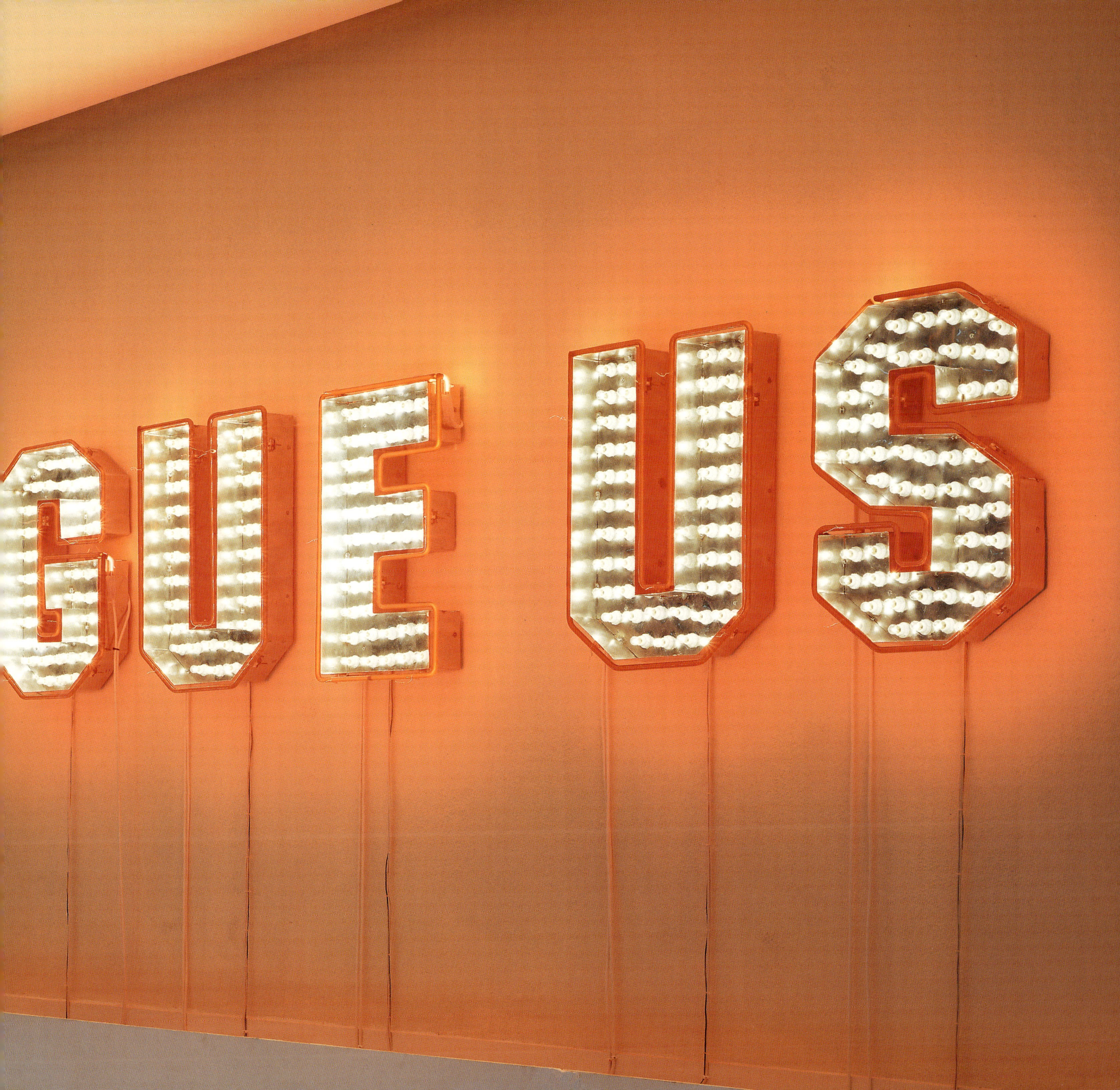

GUE US

YES, 2001

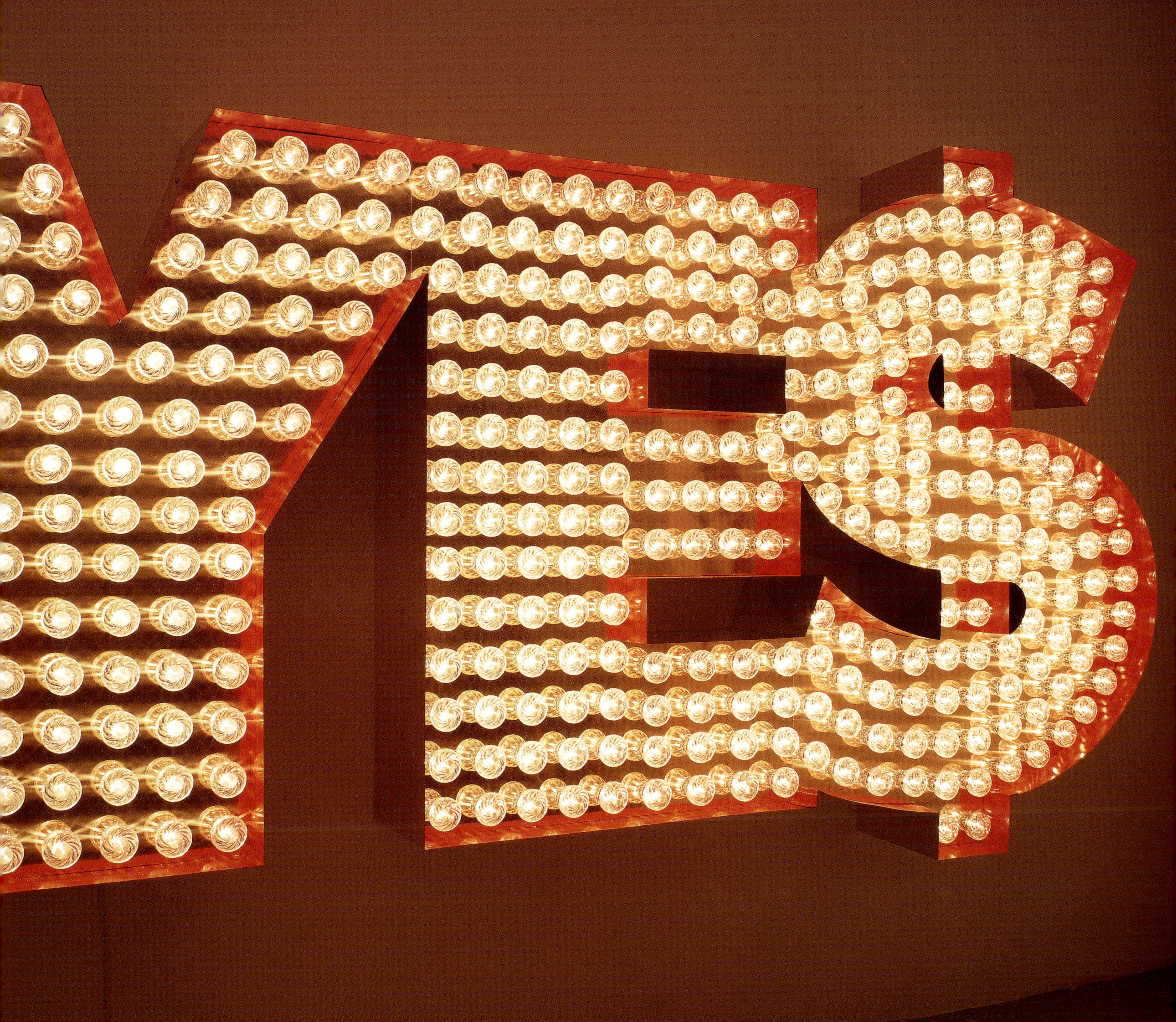

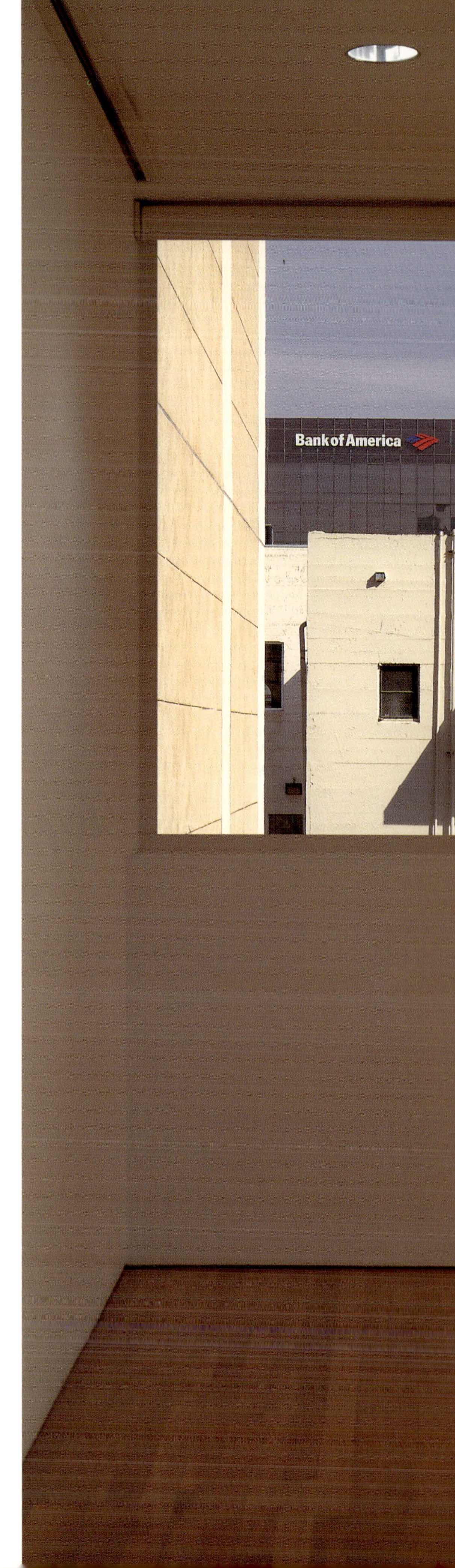

A Pair of Dollars (installation view), 2001

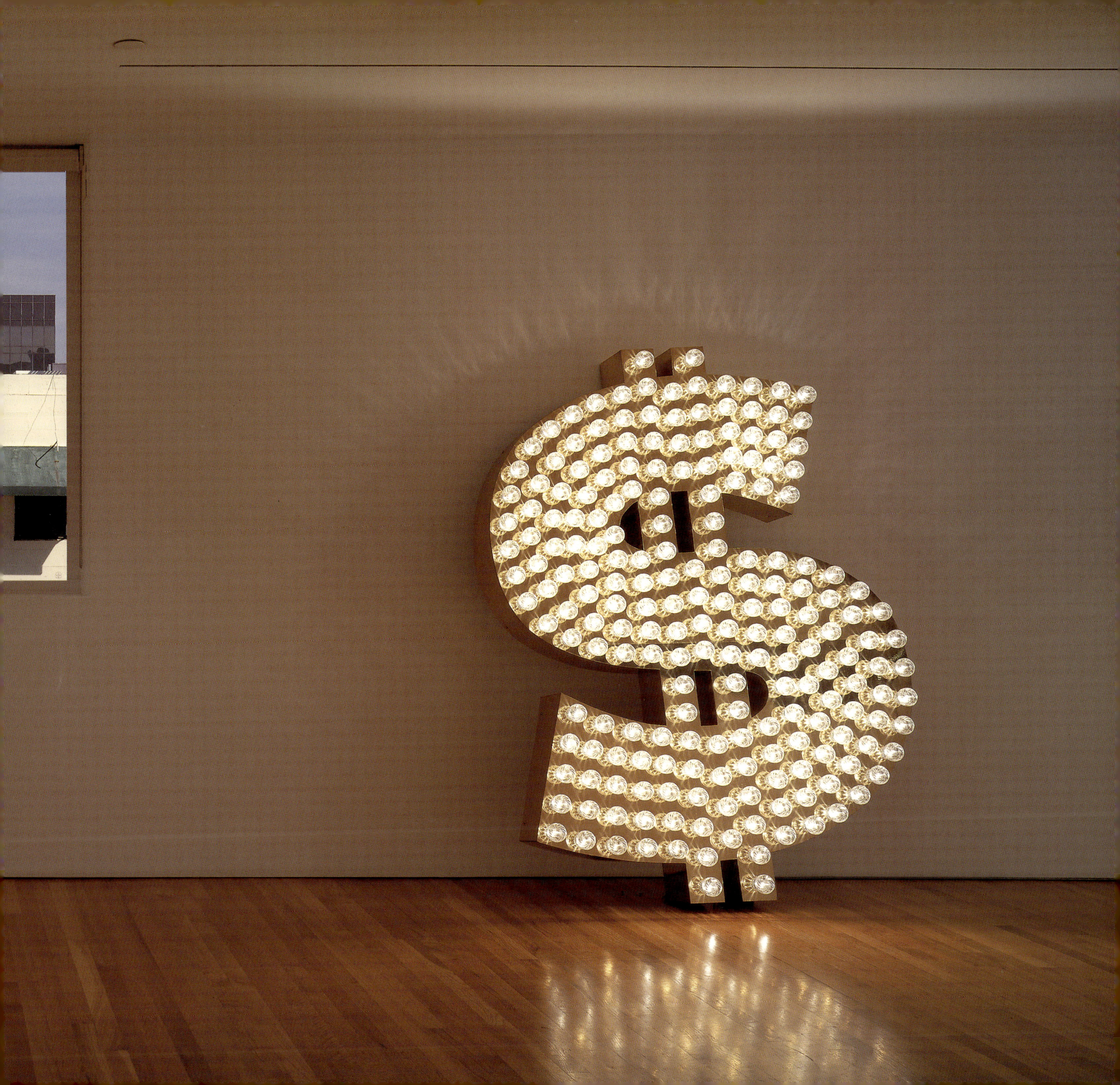

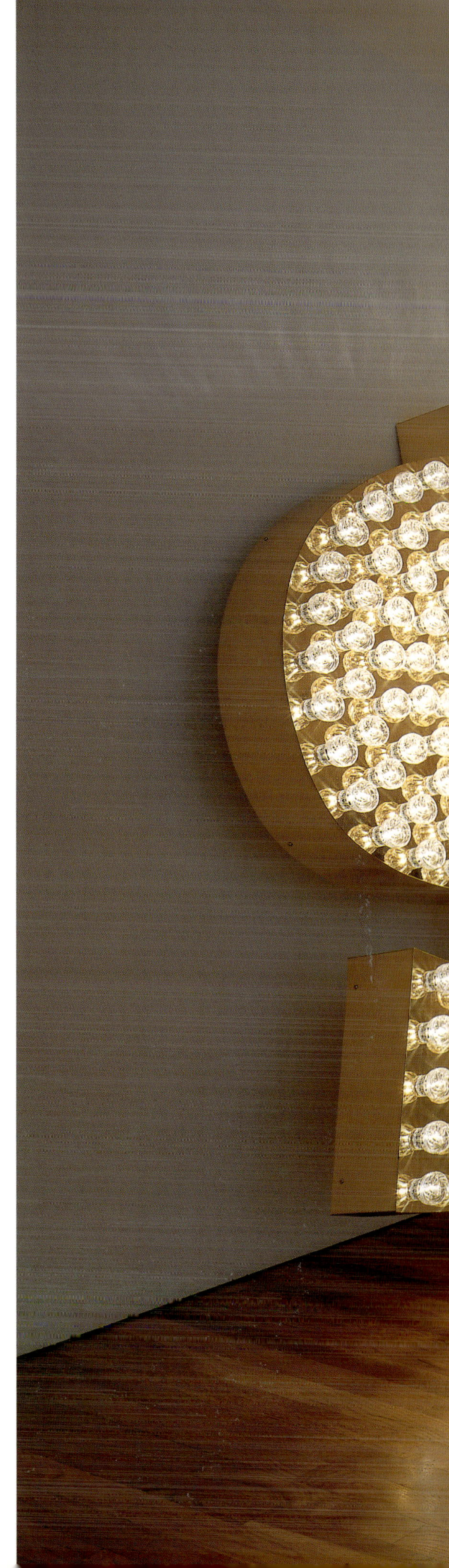

A Pair of Dollars (installation view), 2001

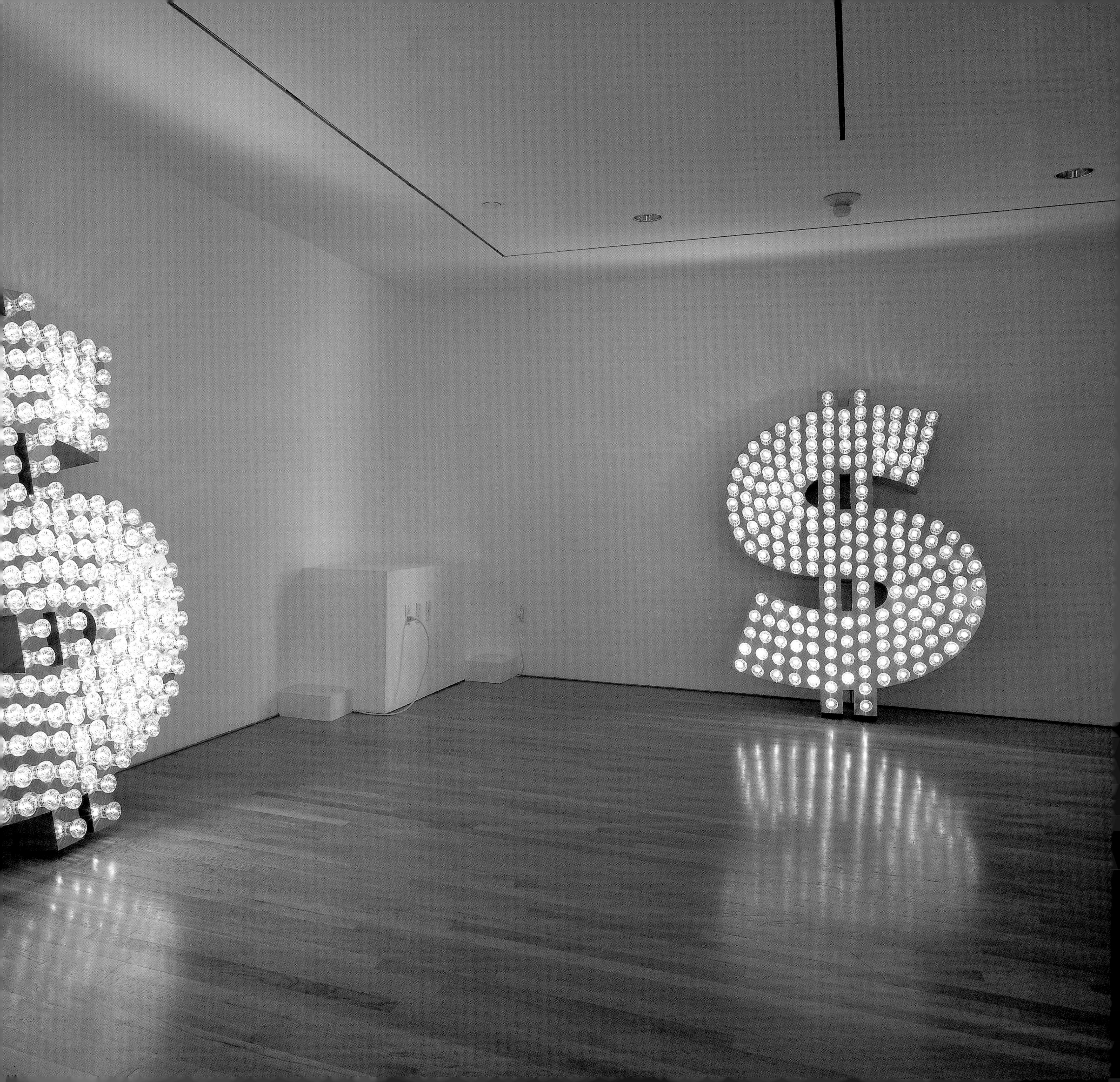

MADE O

MONEY

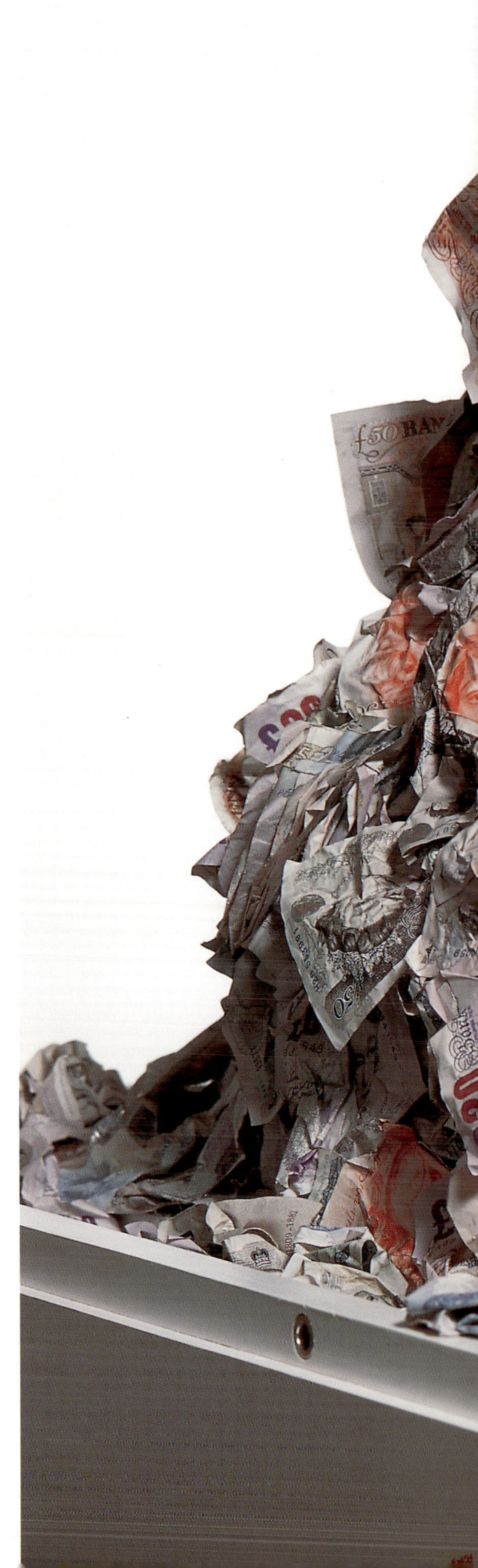

Made of Money (detail), 2002

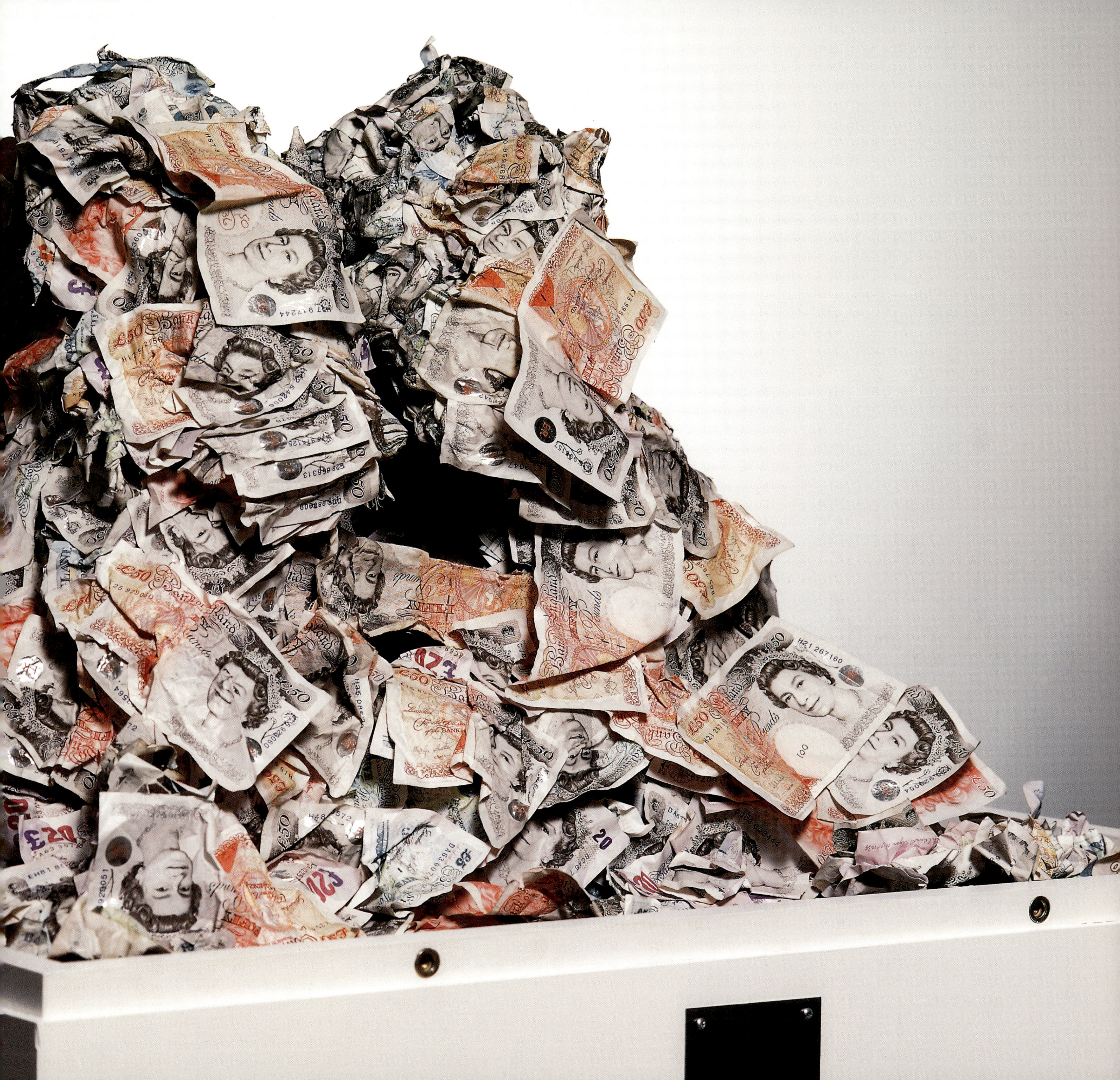

Made of Money, 2002

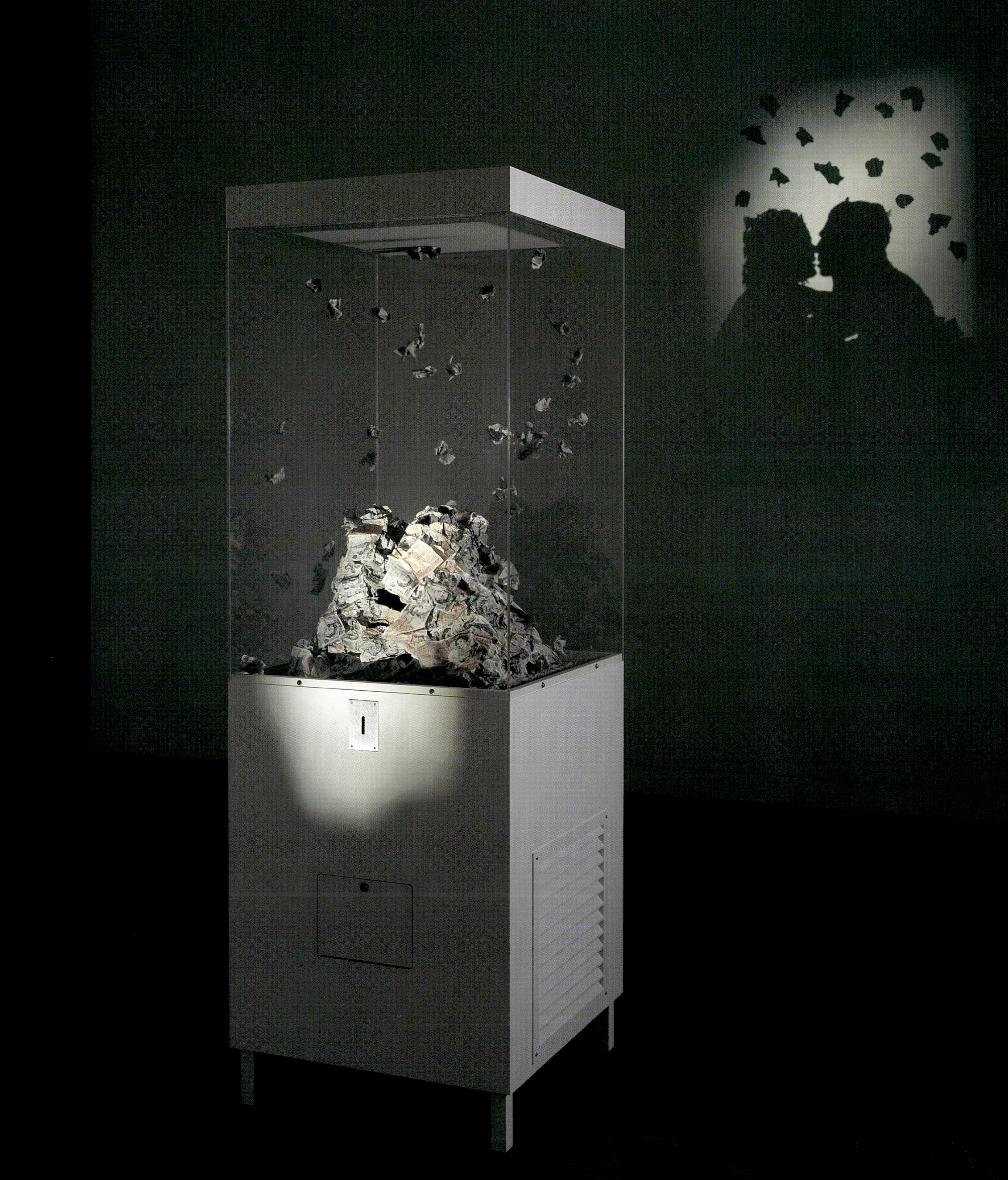

INST

GRATIF

ANT
CATION

Instant Gratification (detail), 2001

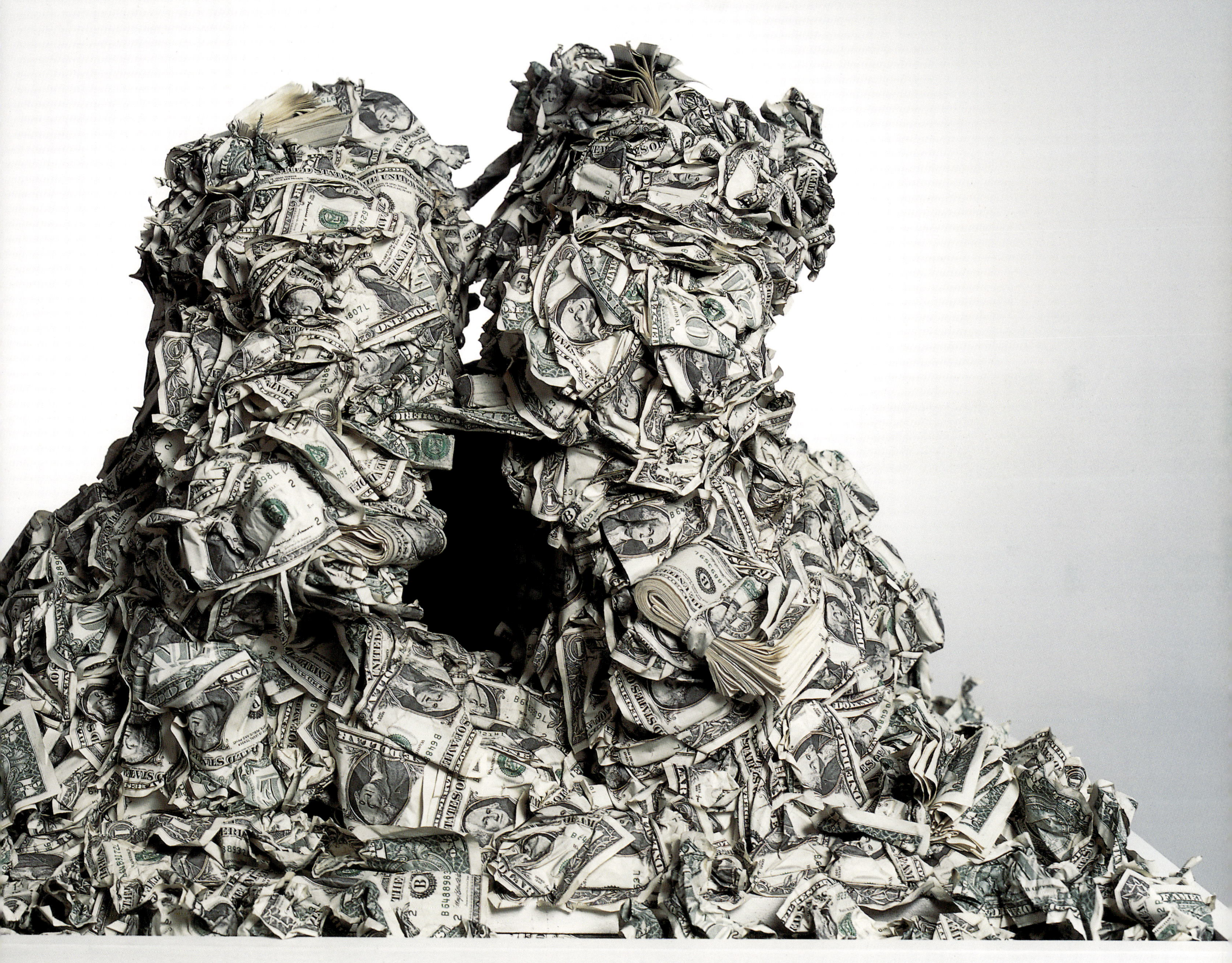

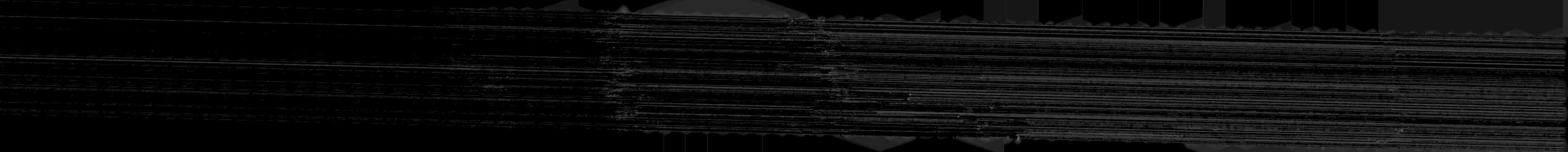

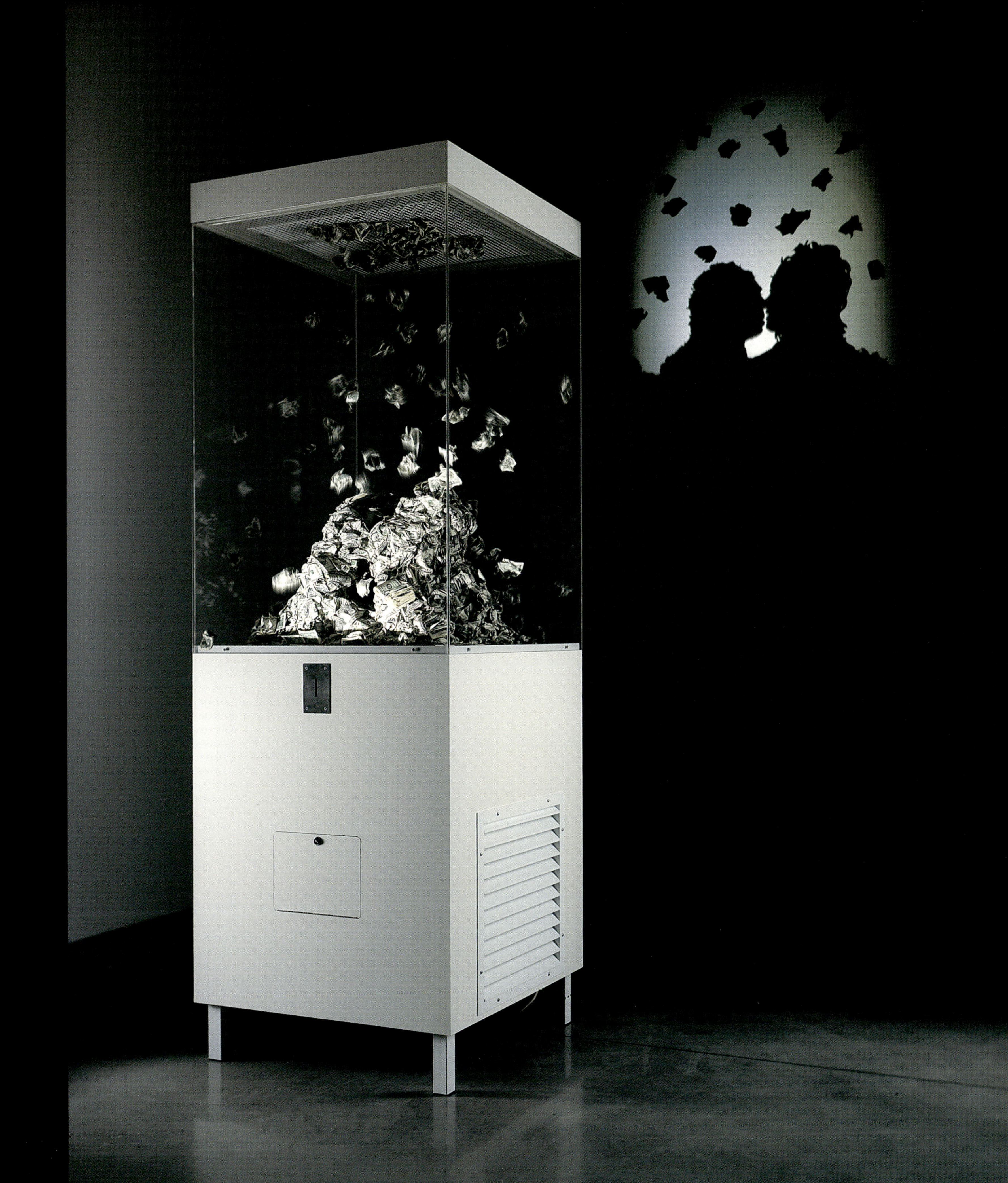

CHEAP 'N

I' NASTY

Cheap 'n' Nasty, 2000

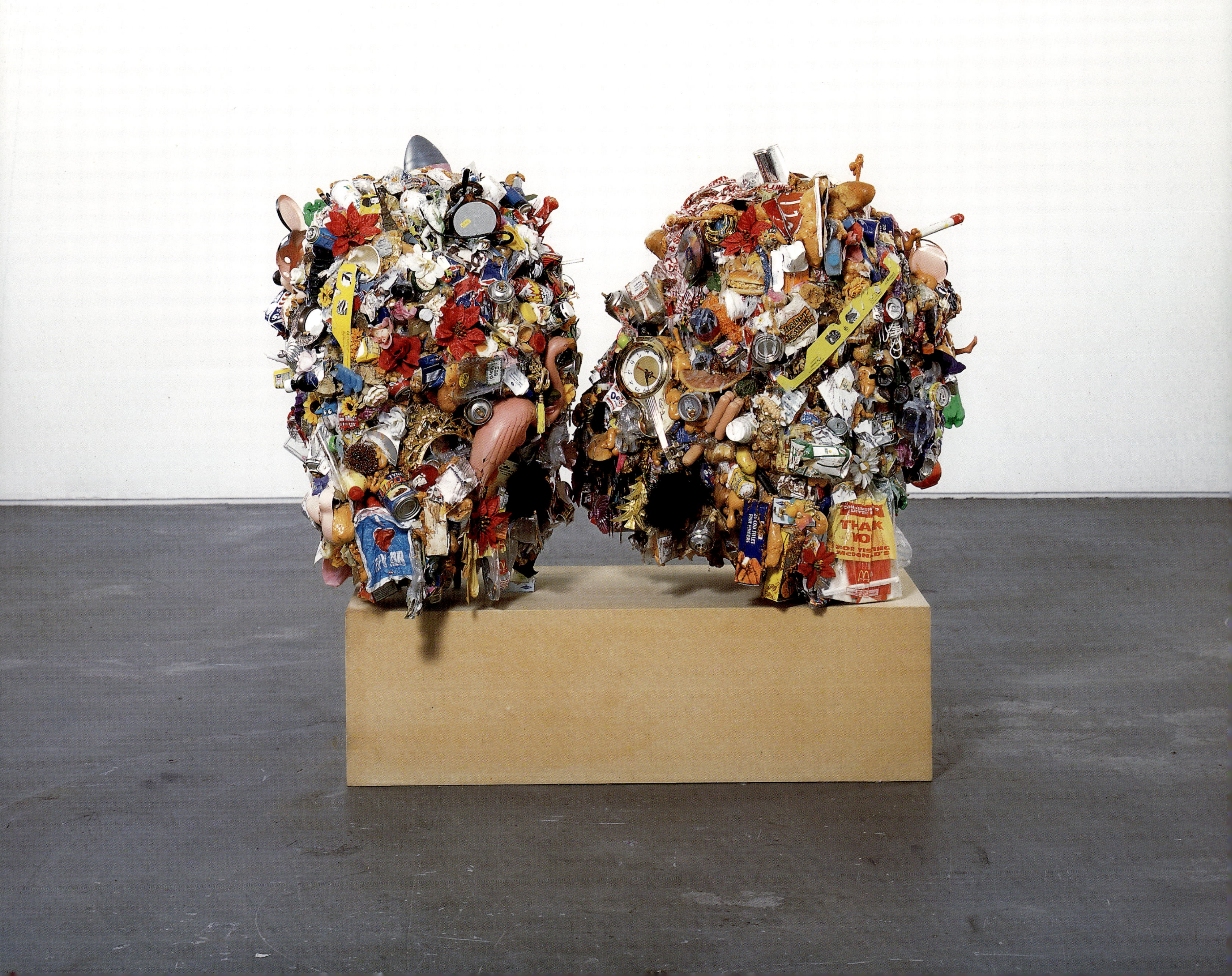

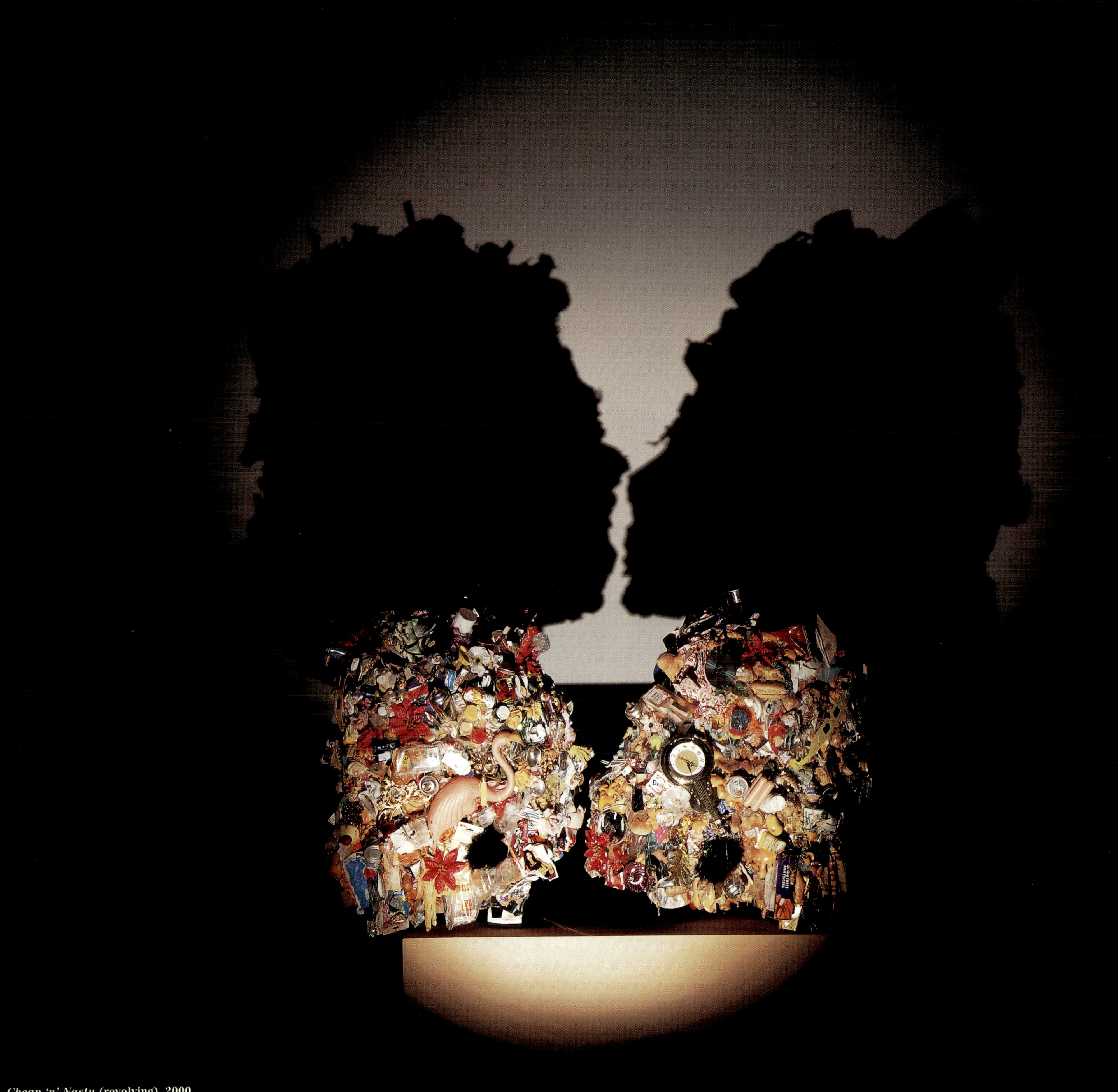

Cheap 'n' Nasty (revolving), 2000

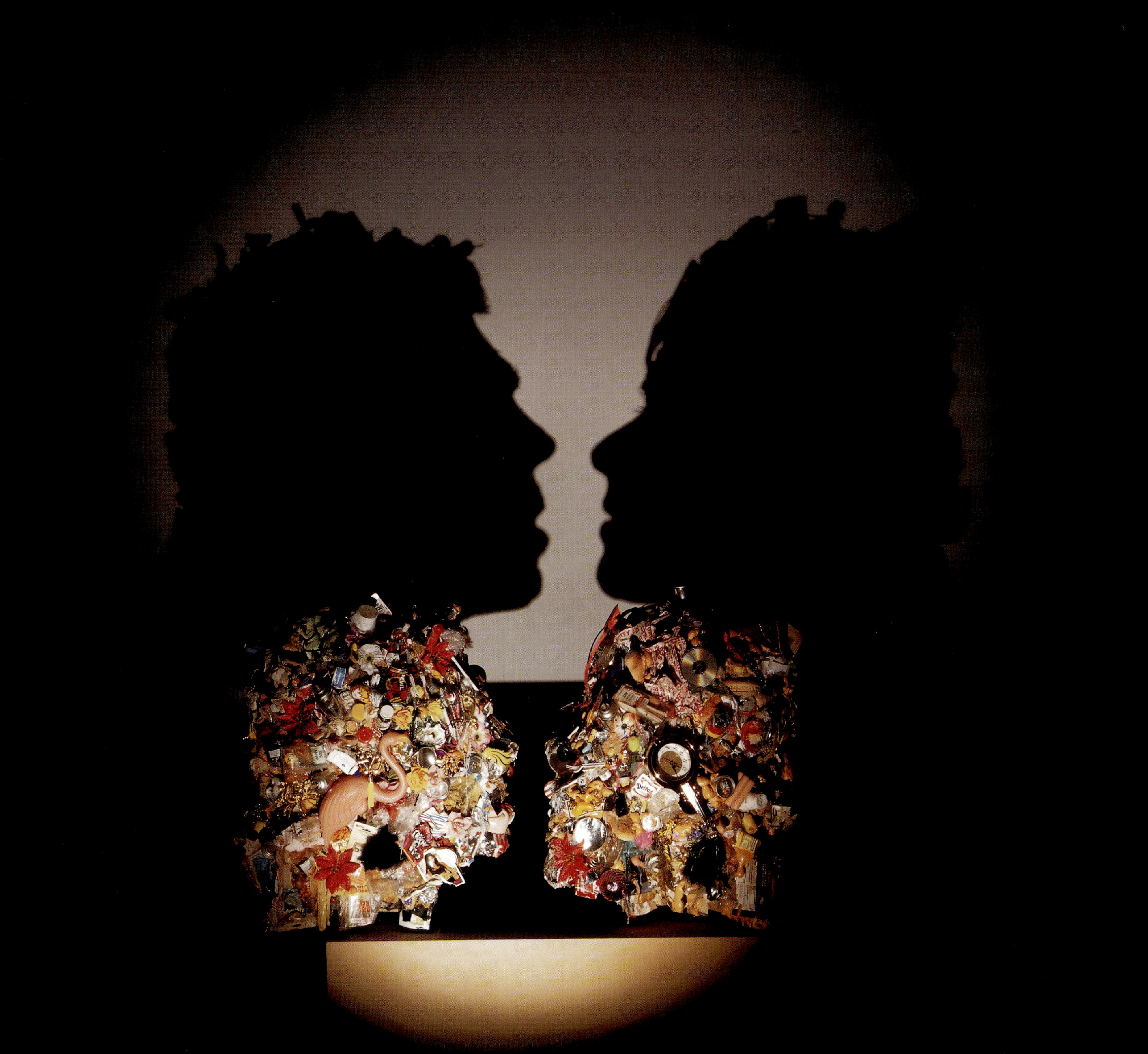

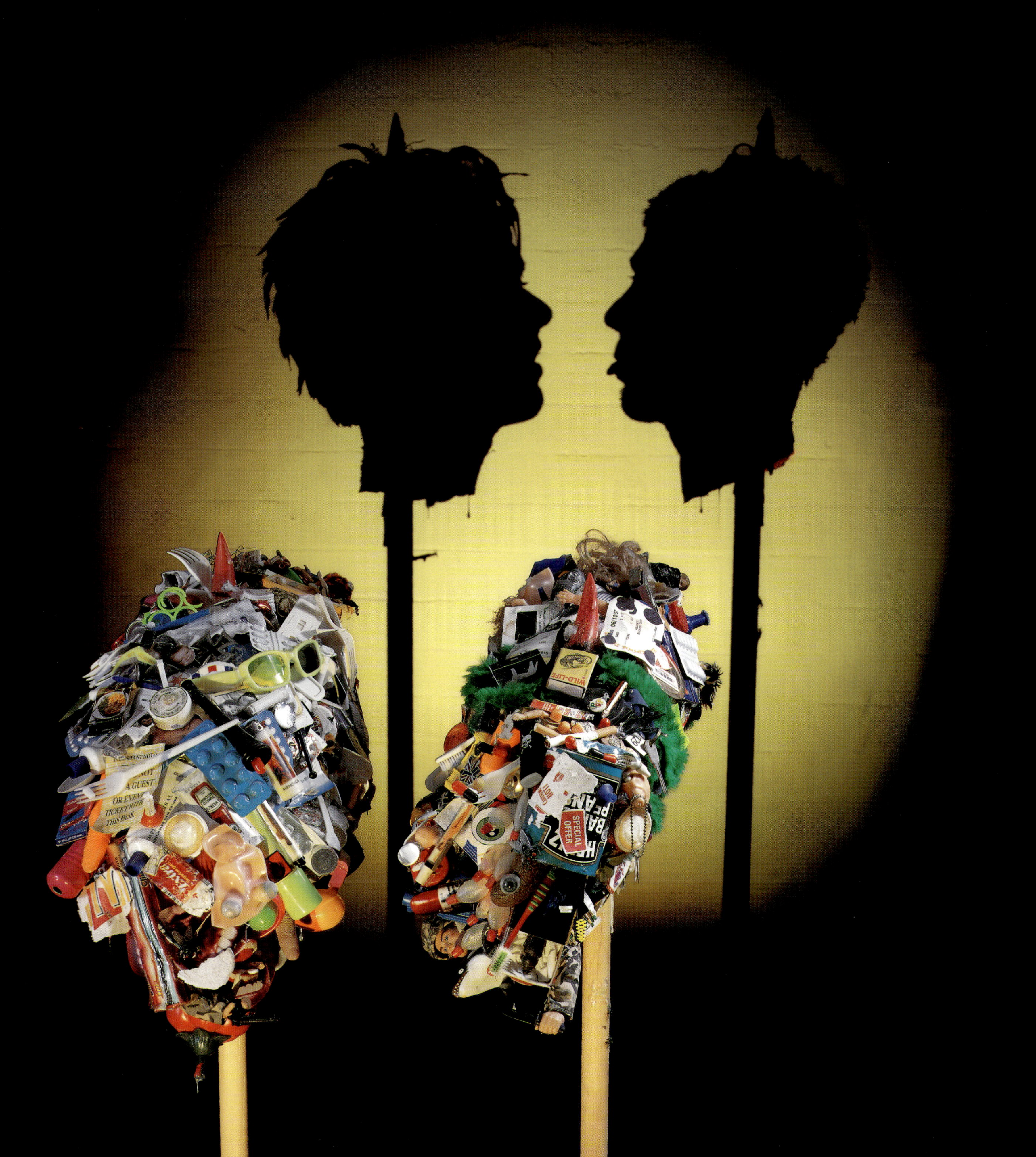

A Couple of Dirty Fucking Rats, 2000

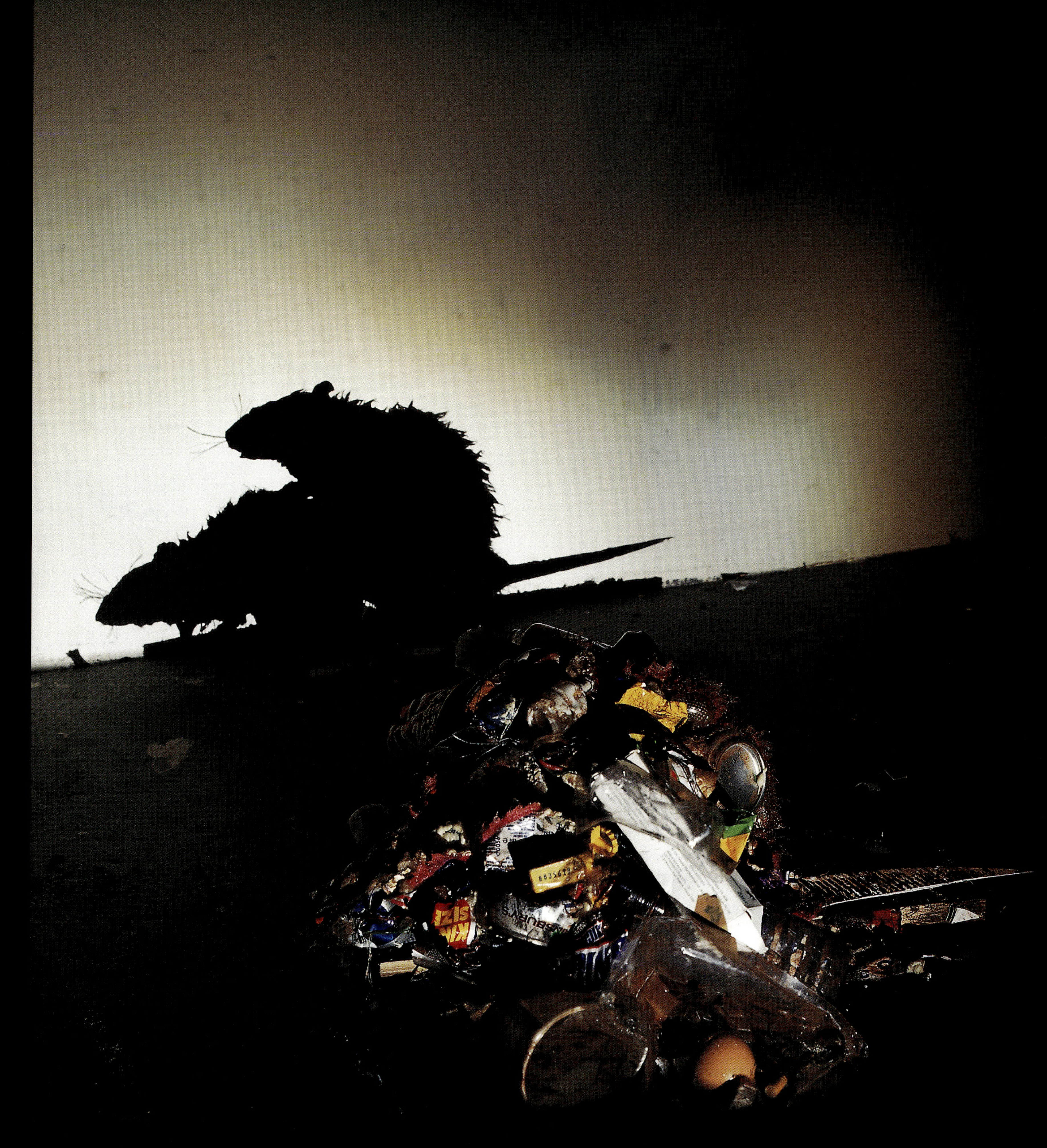
8835673
KIN
SIZE
SBURY'S

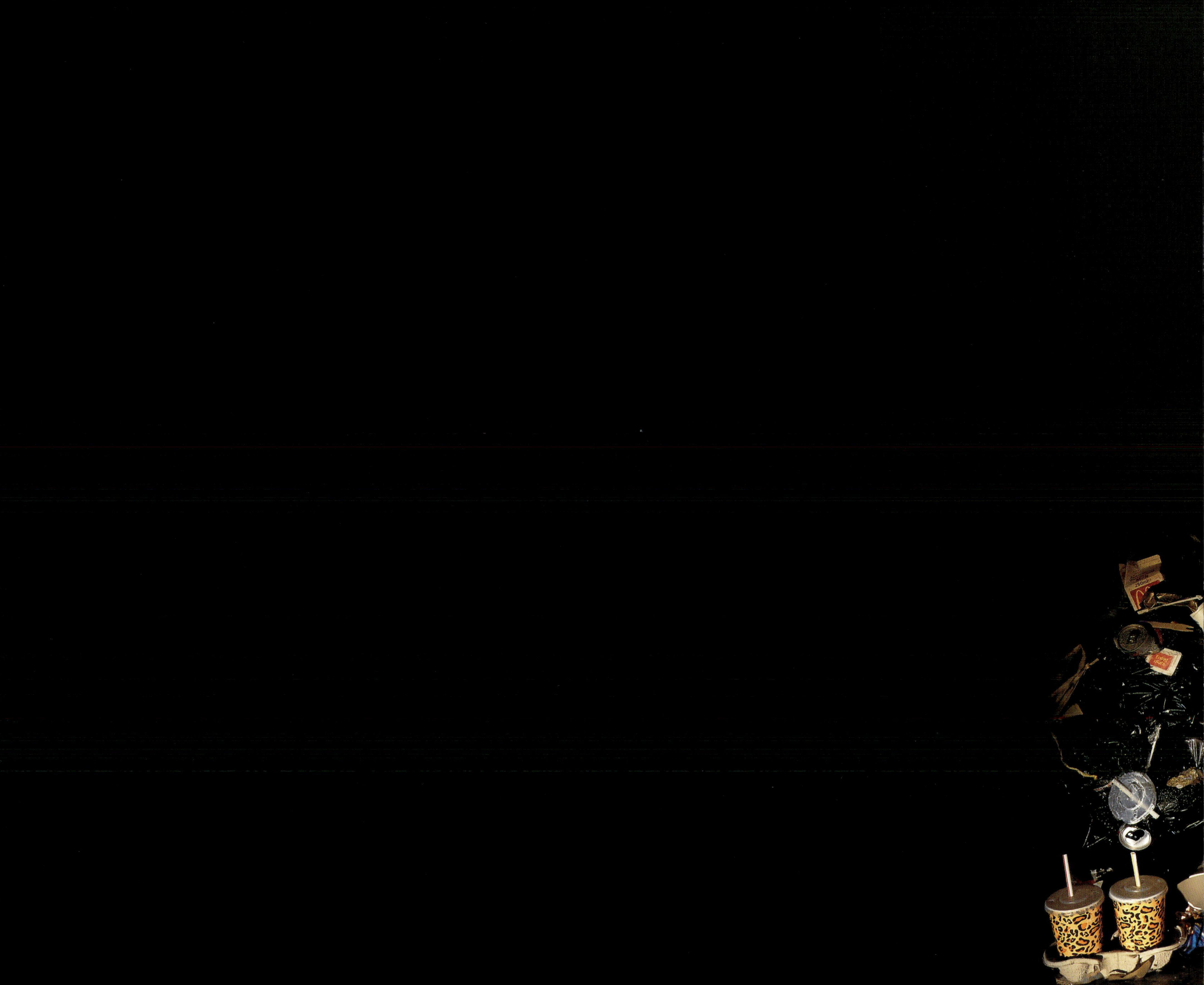

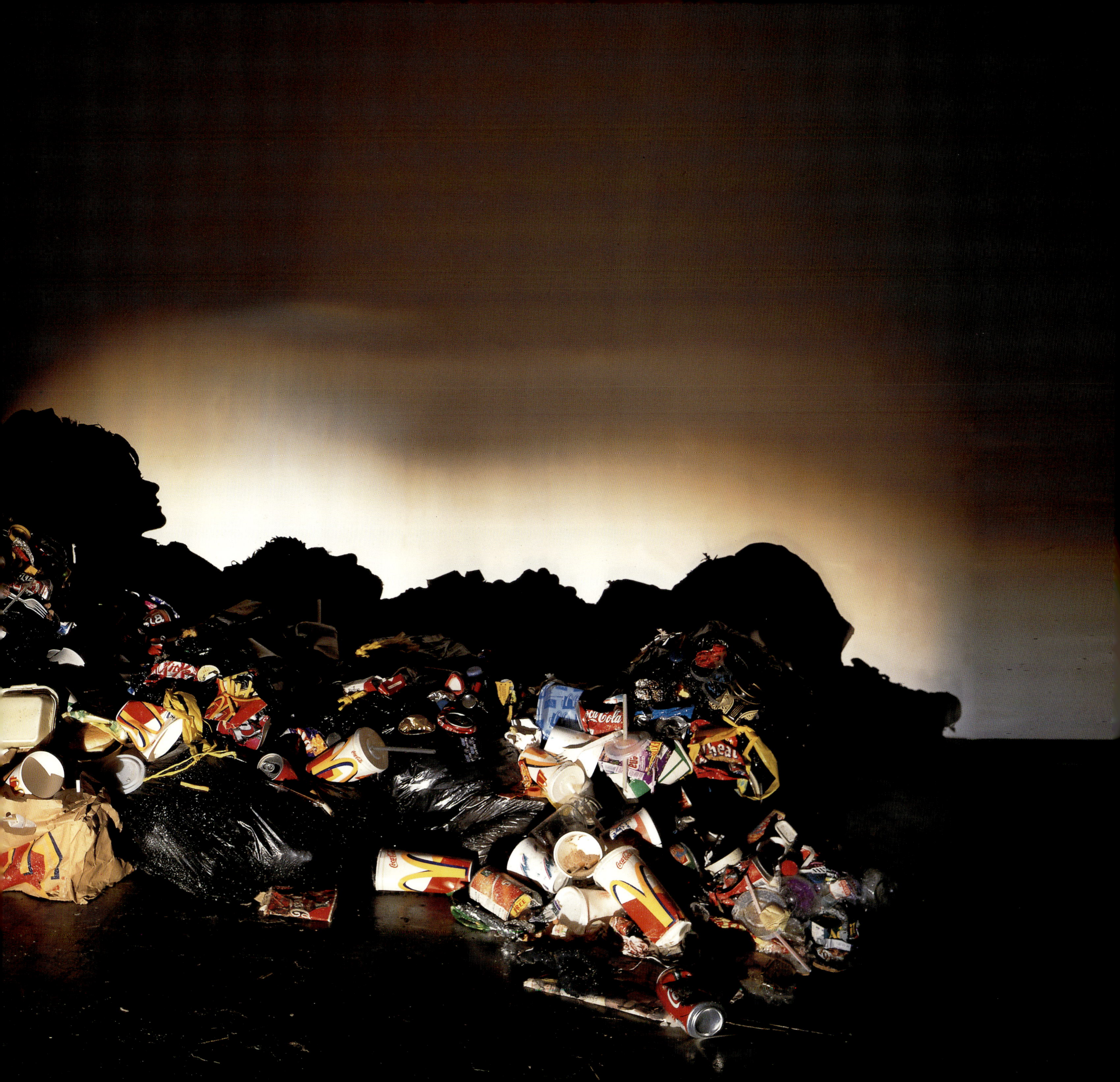

Dirty White Trash (with Gulls), 1998

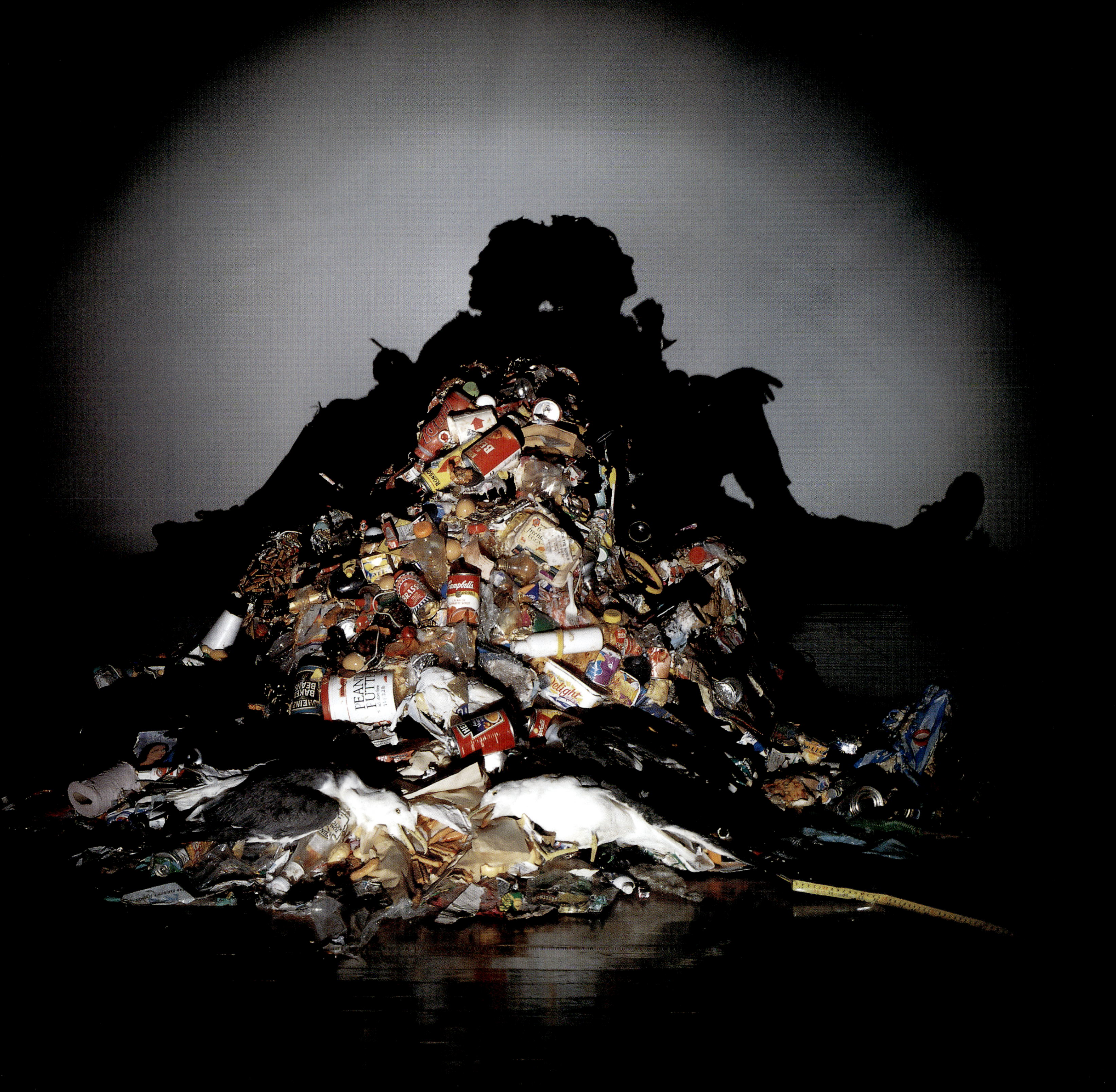

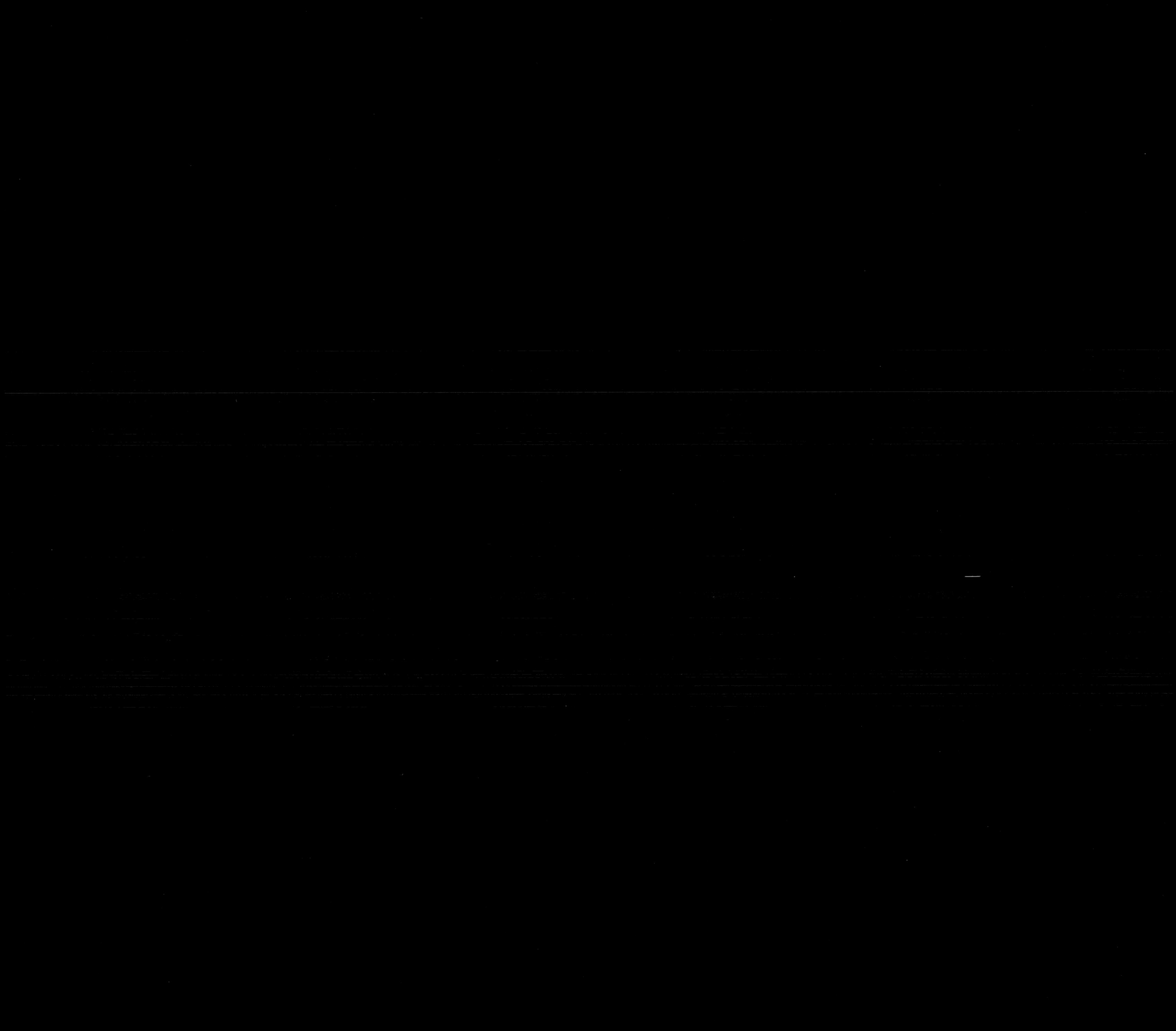

Dirty White Trash (with Gulls), 1998

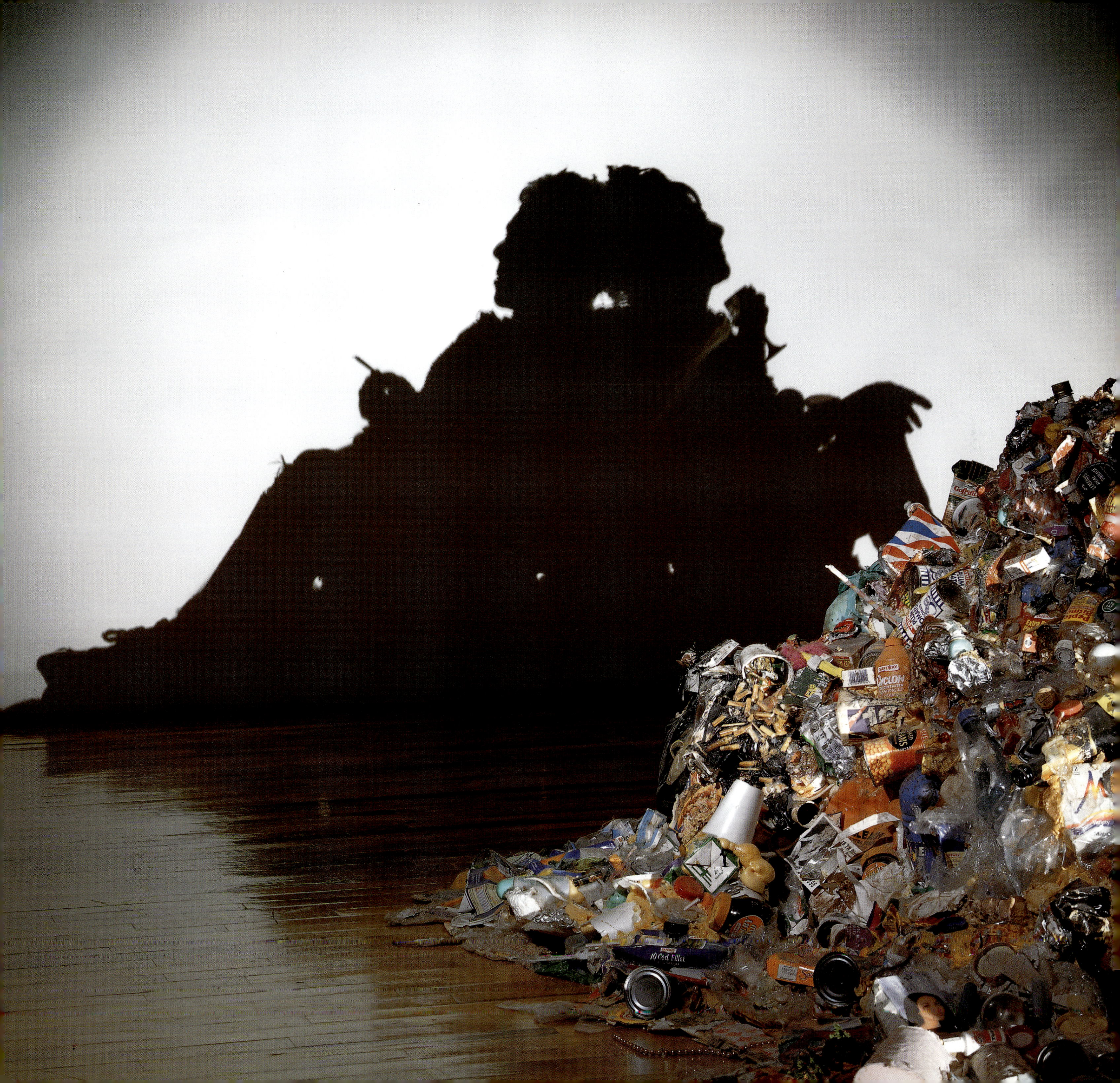

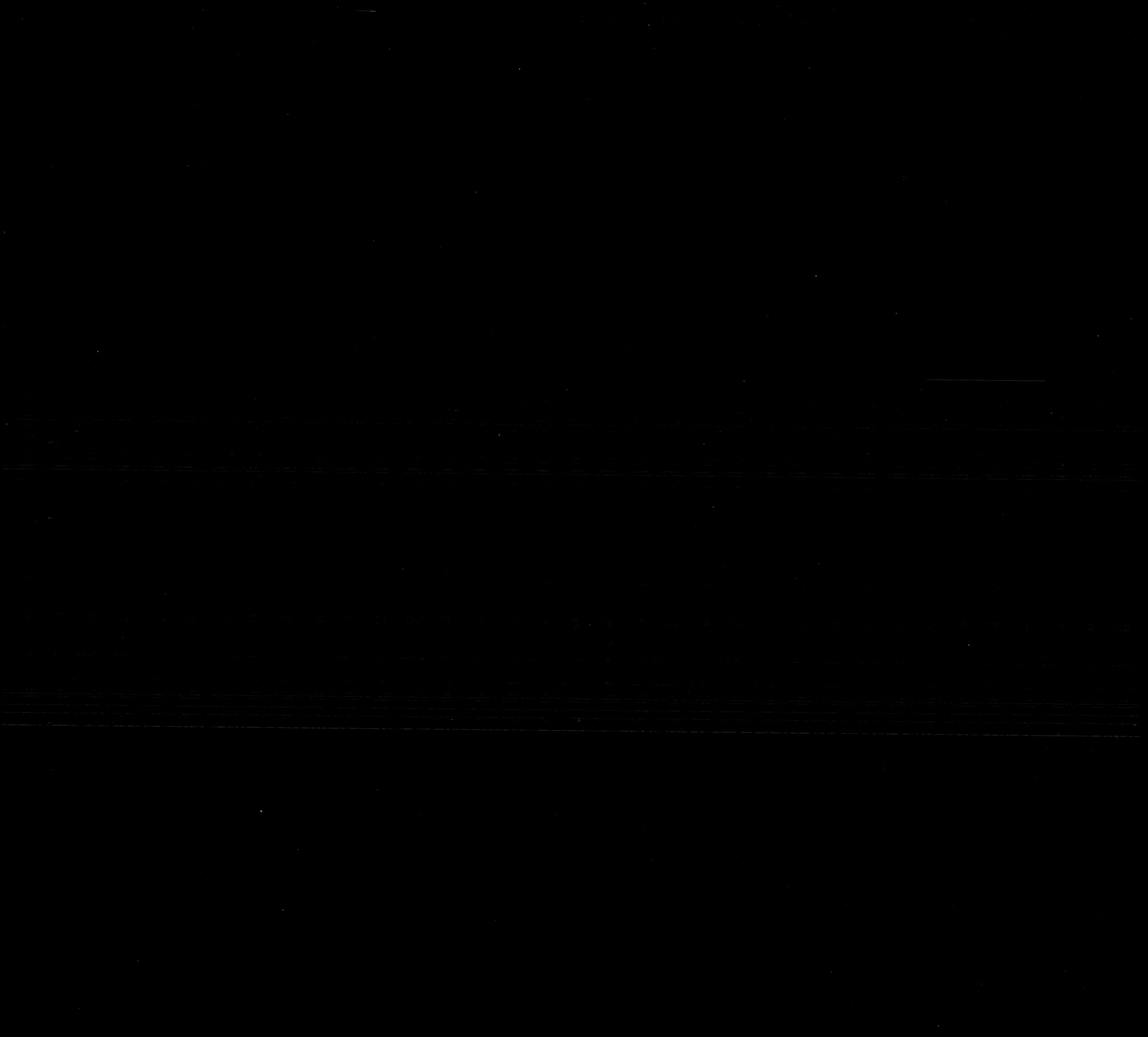

The Undesirables (detail), 2000

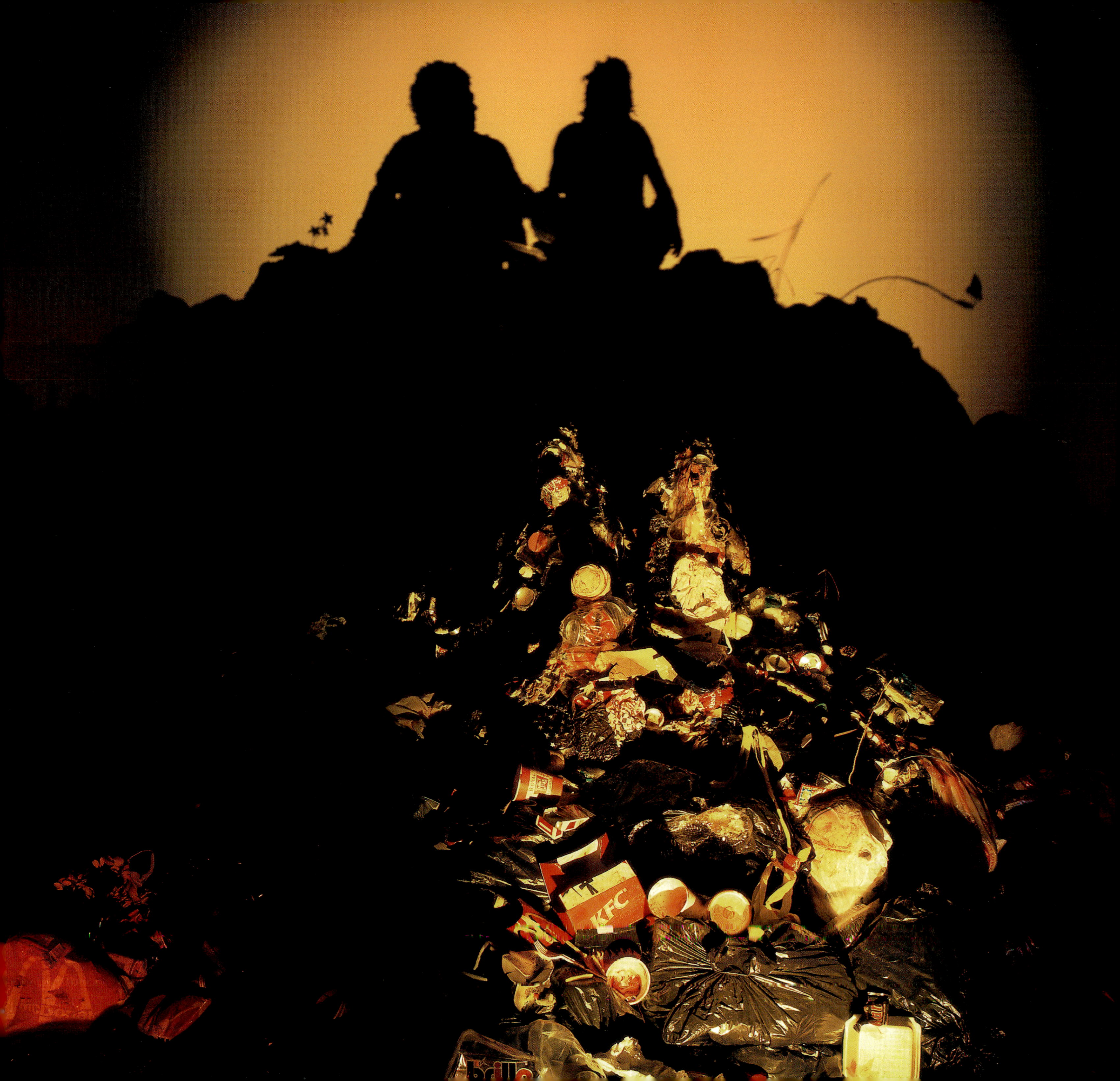

KFC
brillo

The Undesirables (installation view), 2000

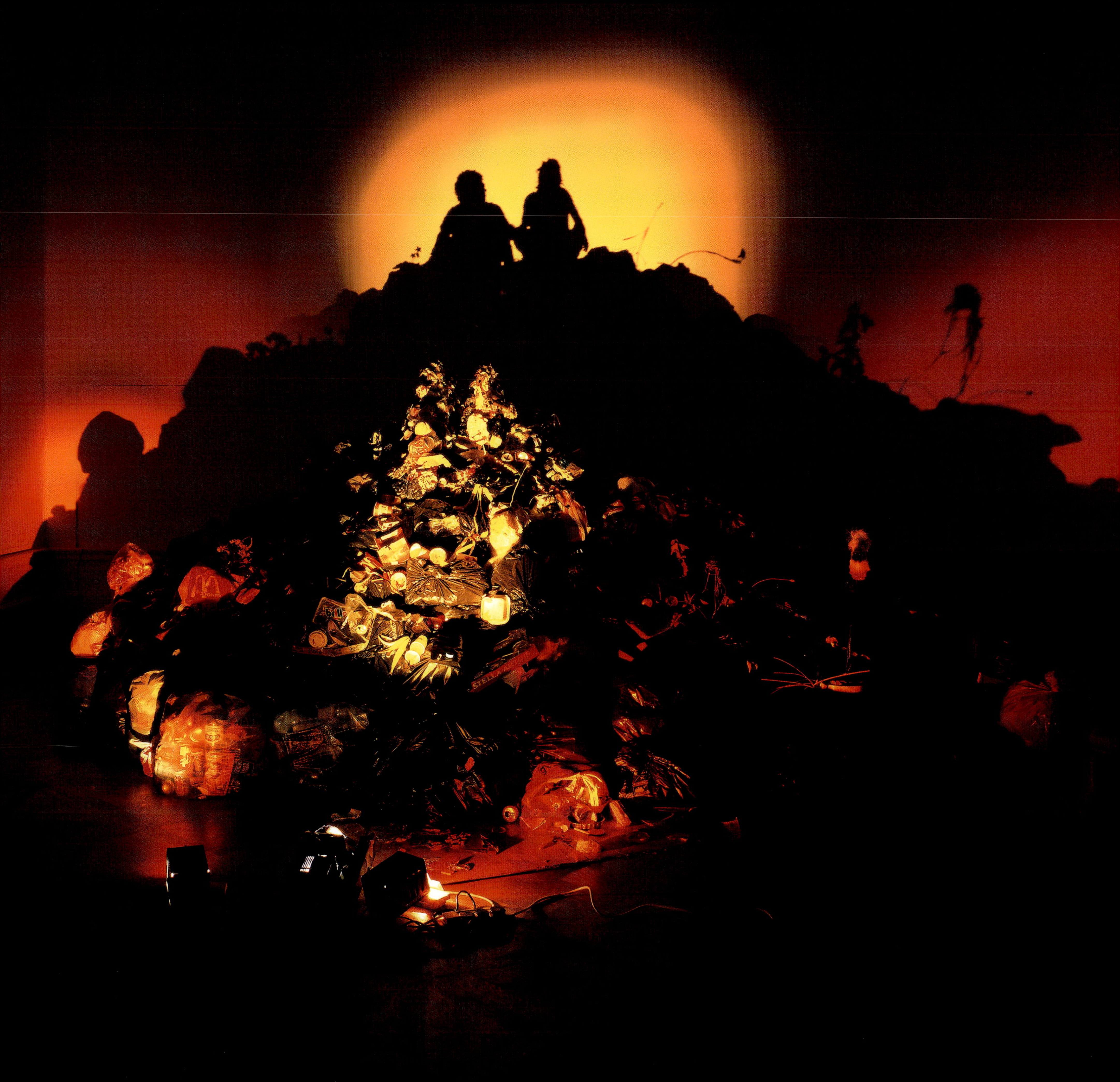

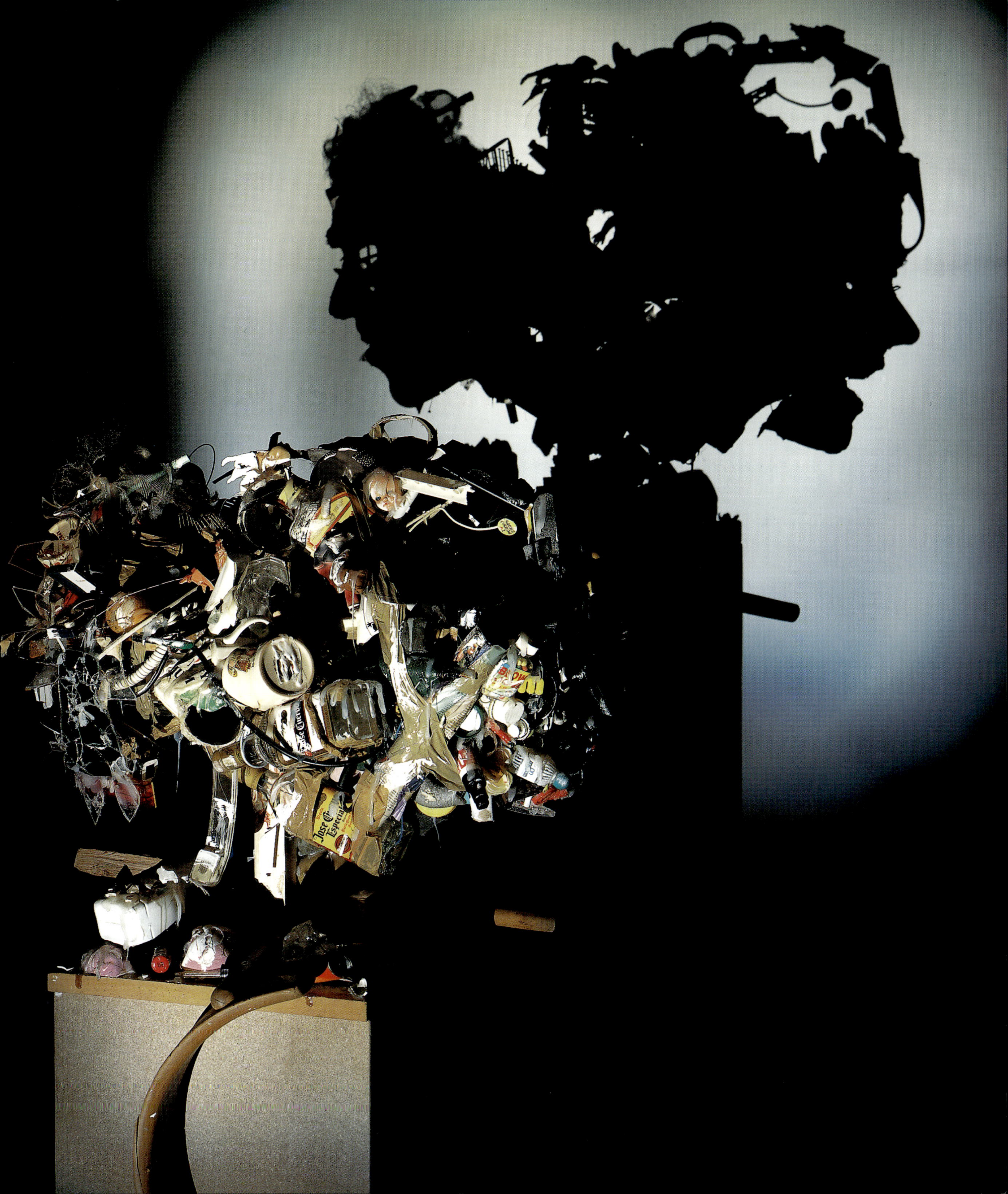

Sunset over Manhattan, 2003

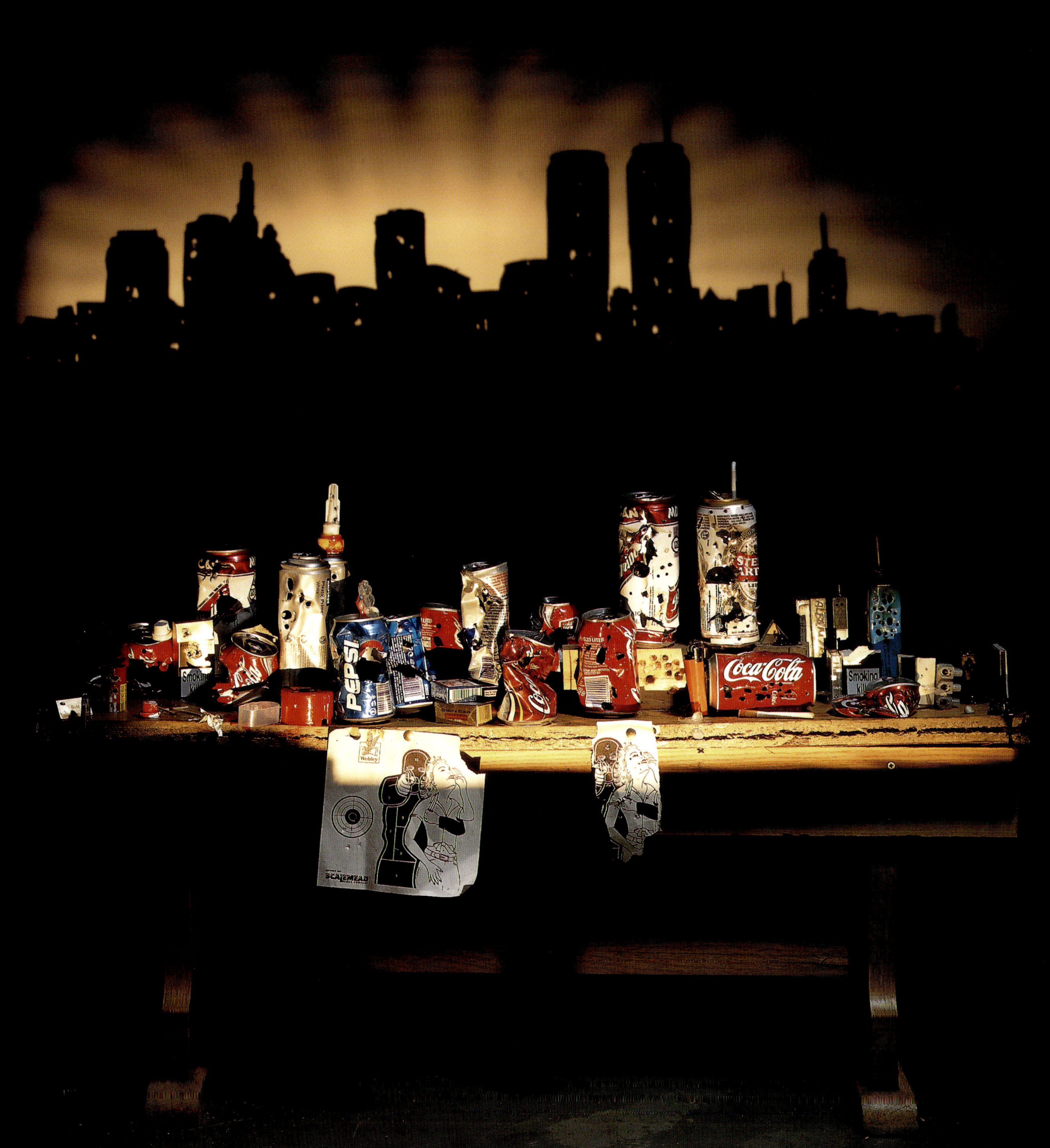

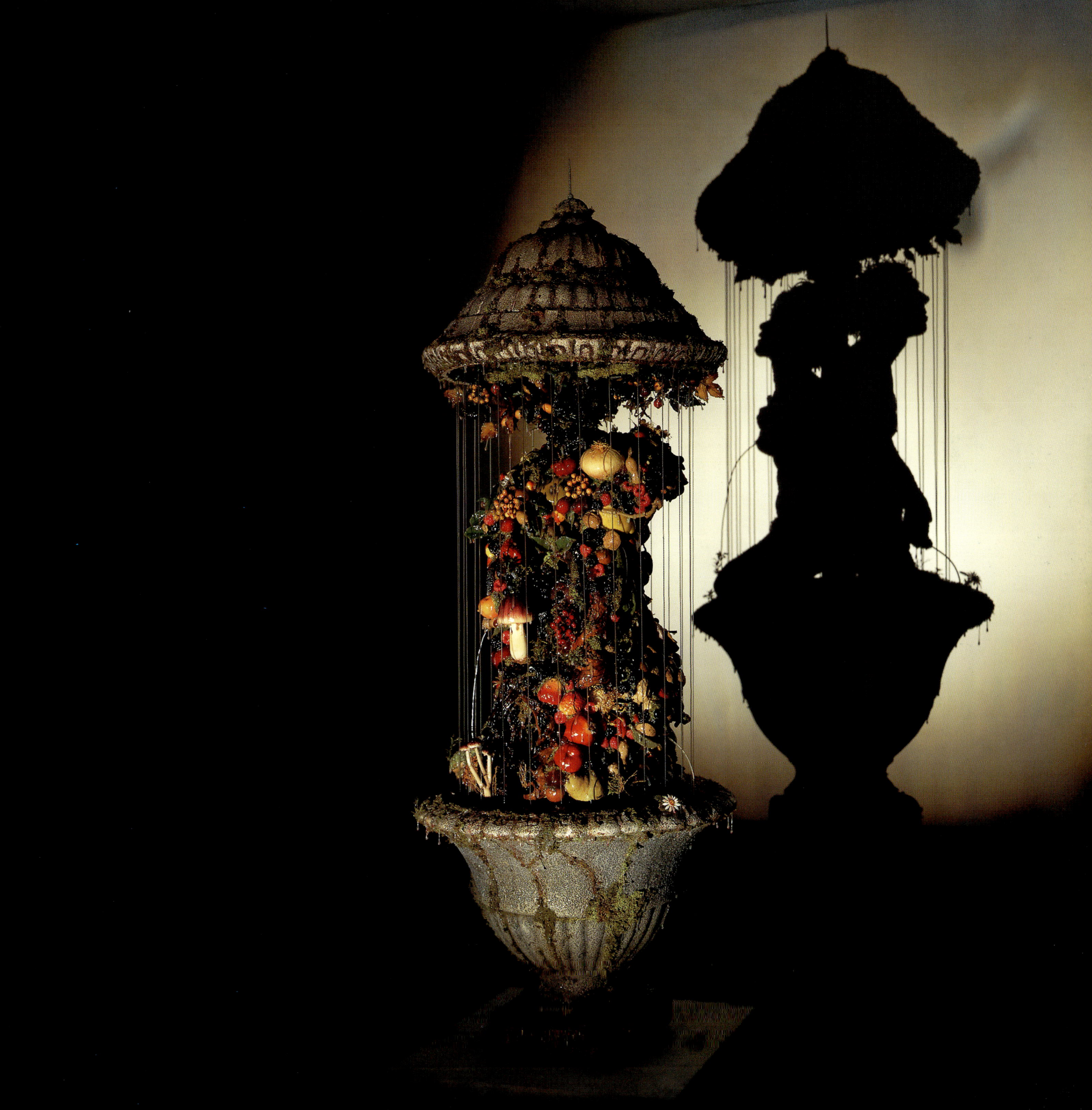

KISS OF

DEATH

Kiss of Death, 2003

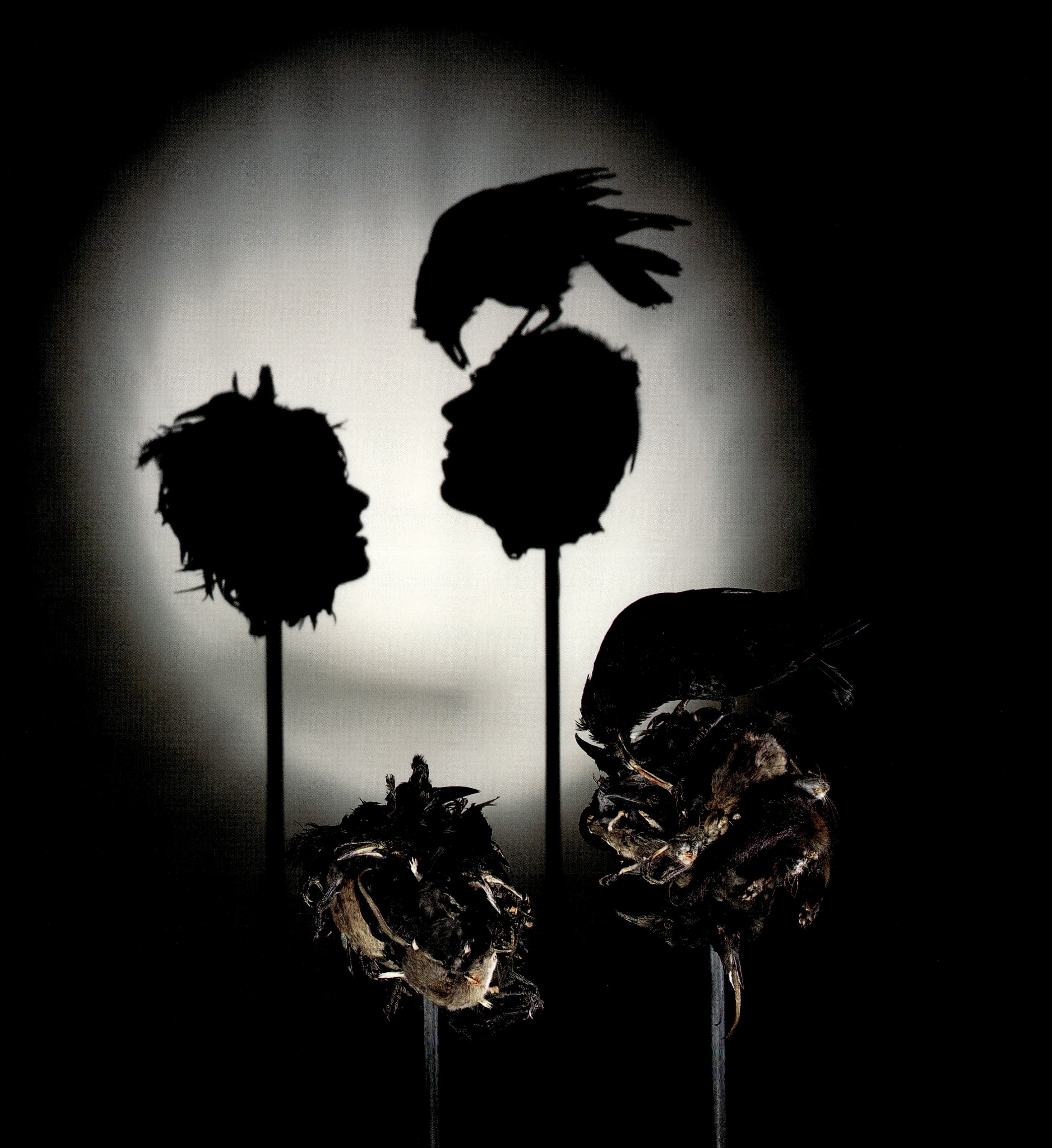

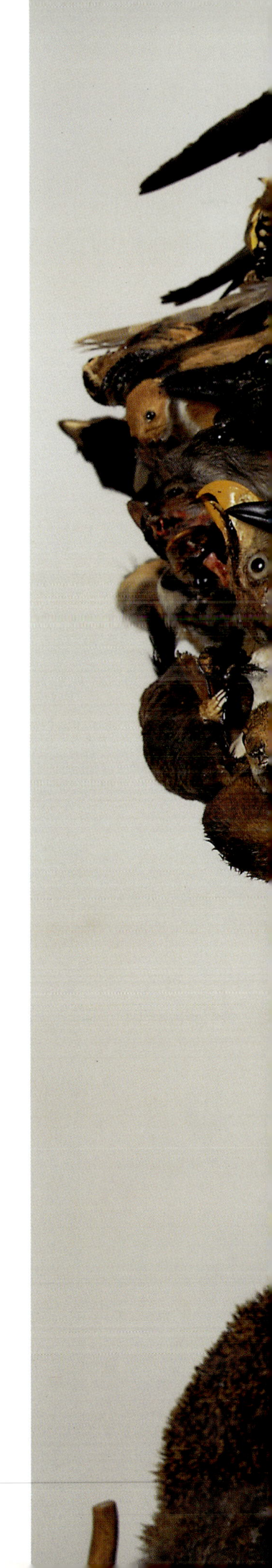

British Wildlife (detail), 2000

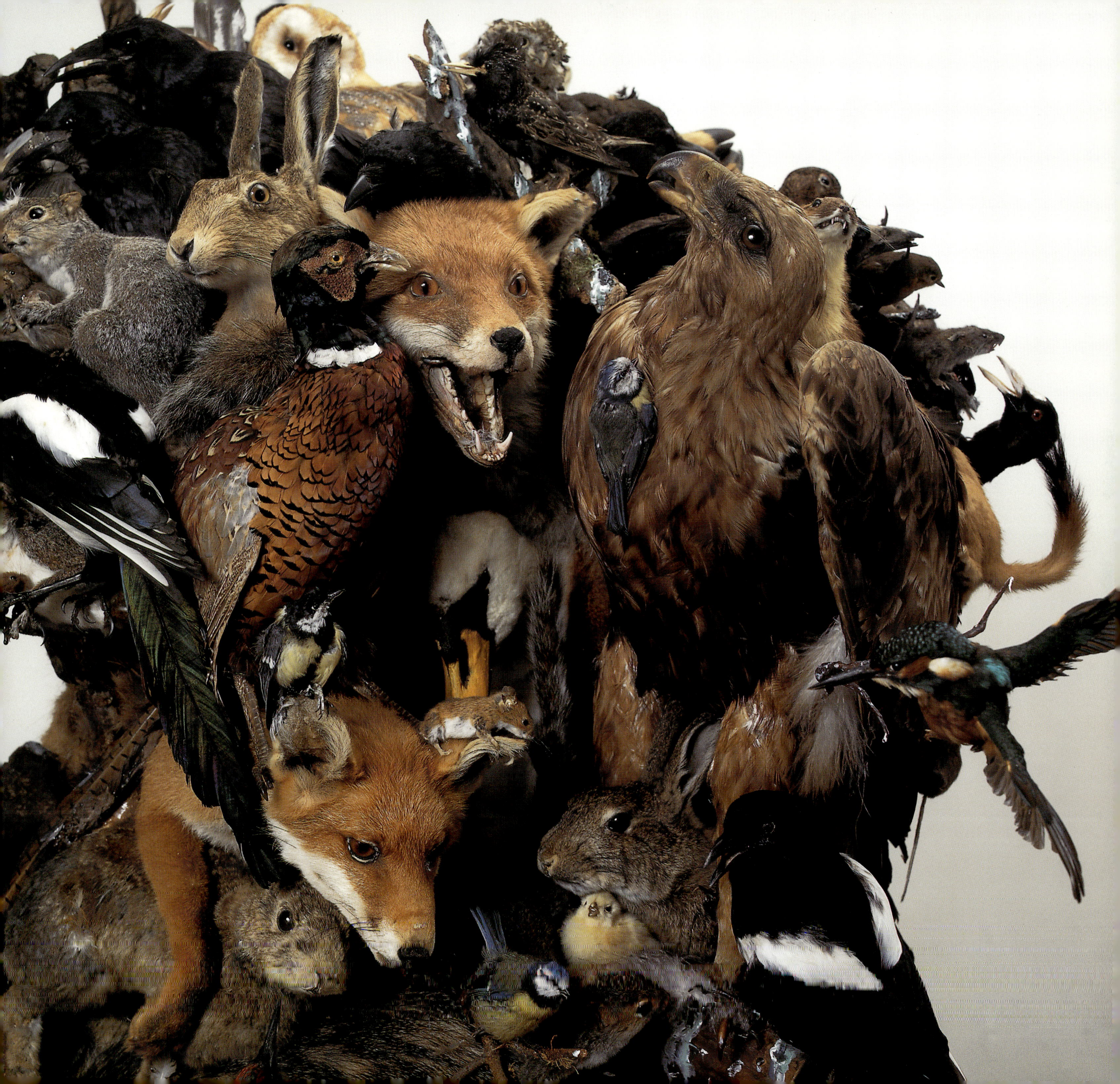

British Wildlife, 2000

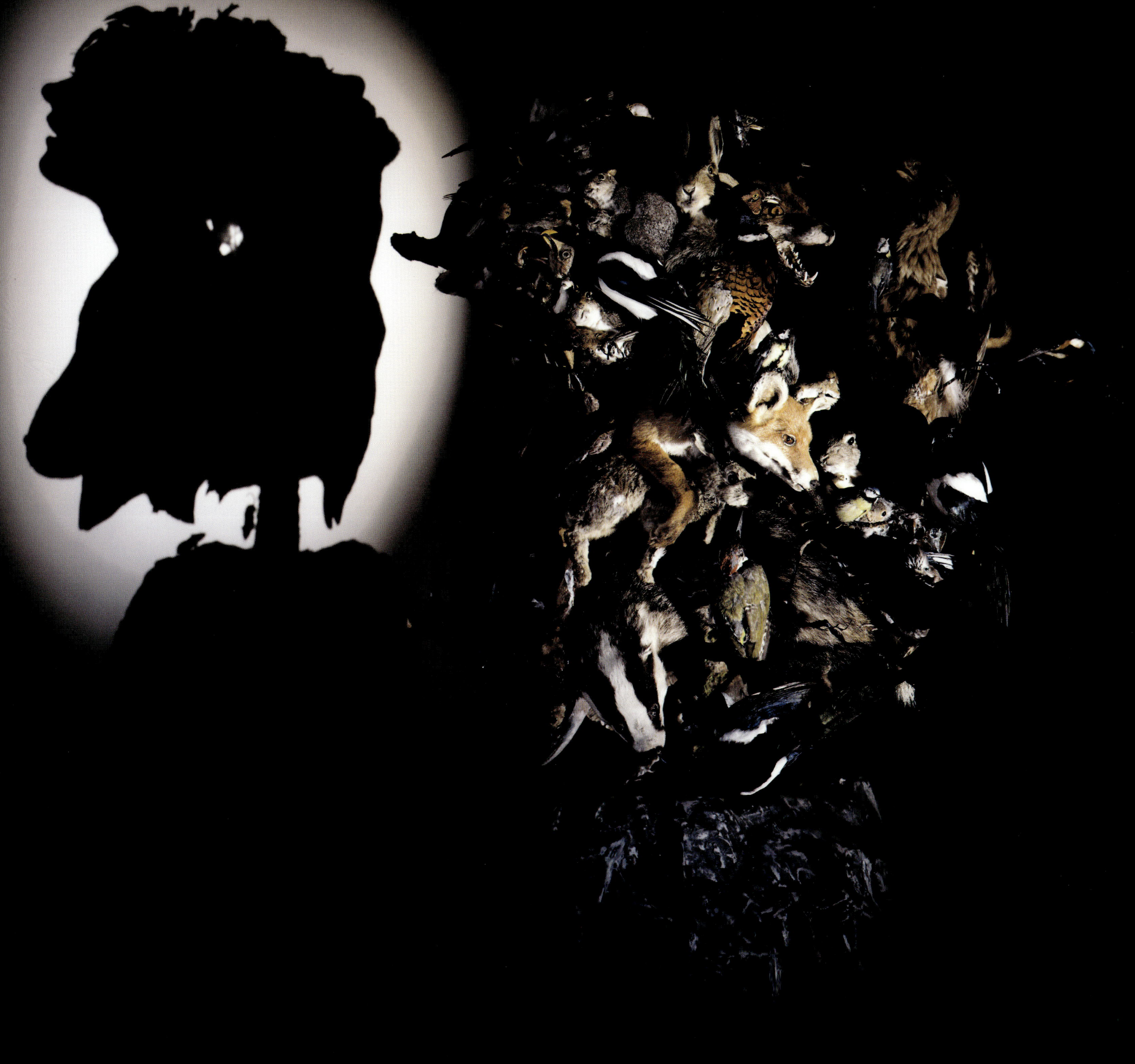

REAL
IS RU

LIFE
BBISH

Real Life Is Rubbish, 2002

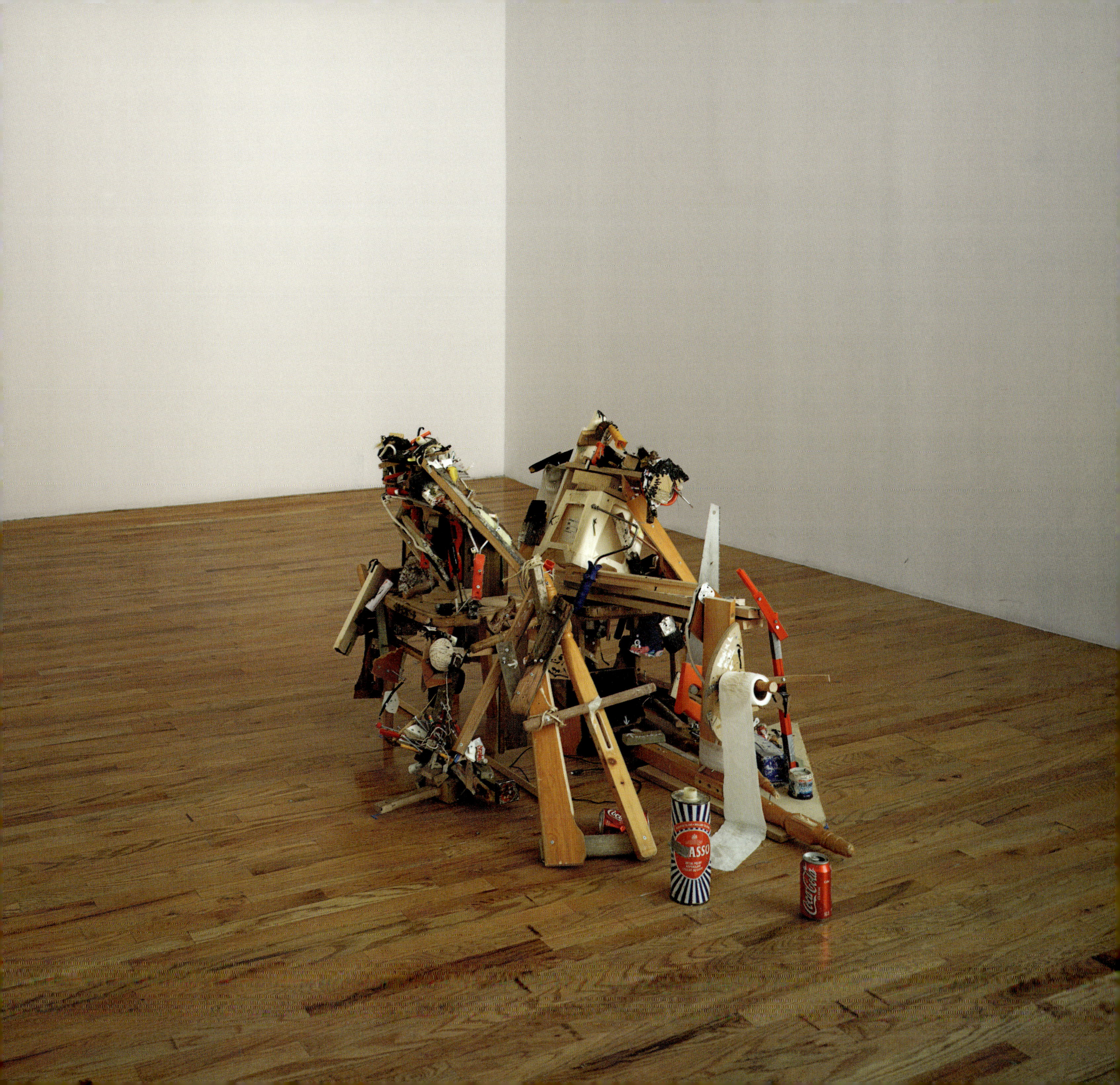

Real Life Is Rubbish, 2002

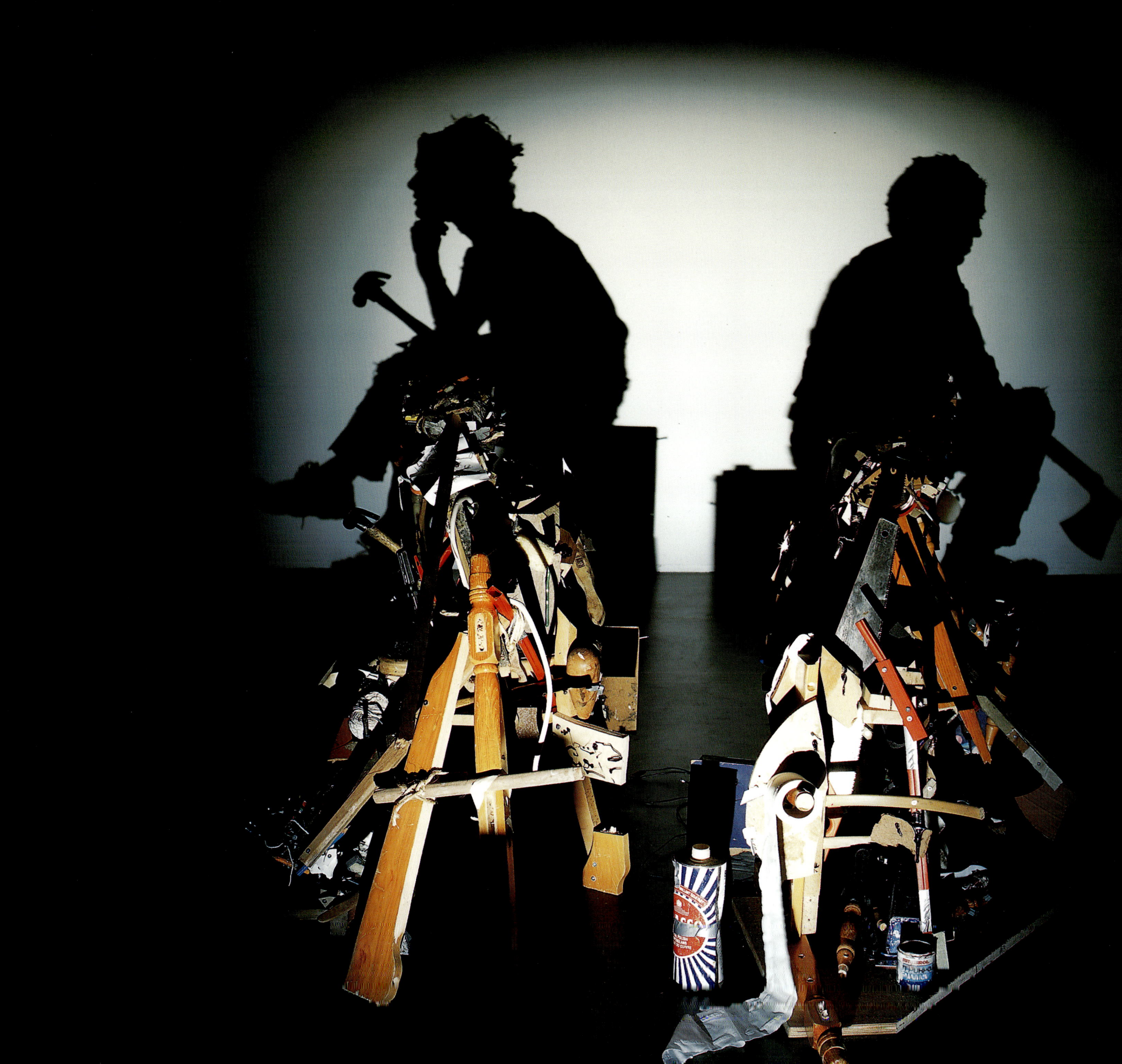

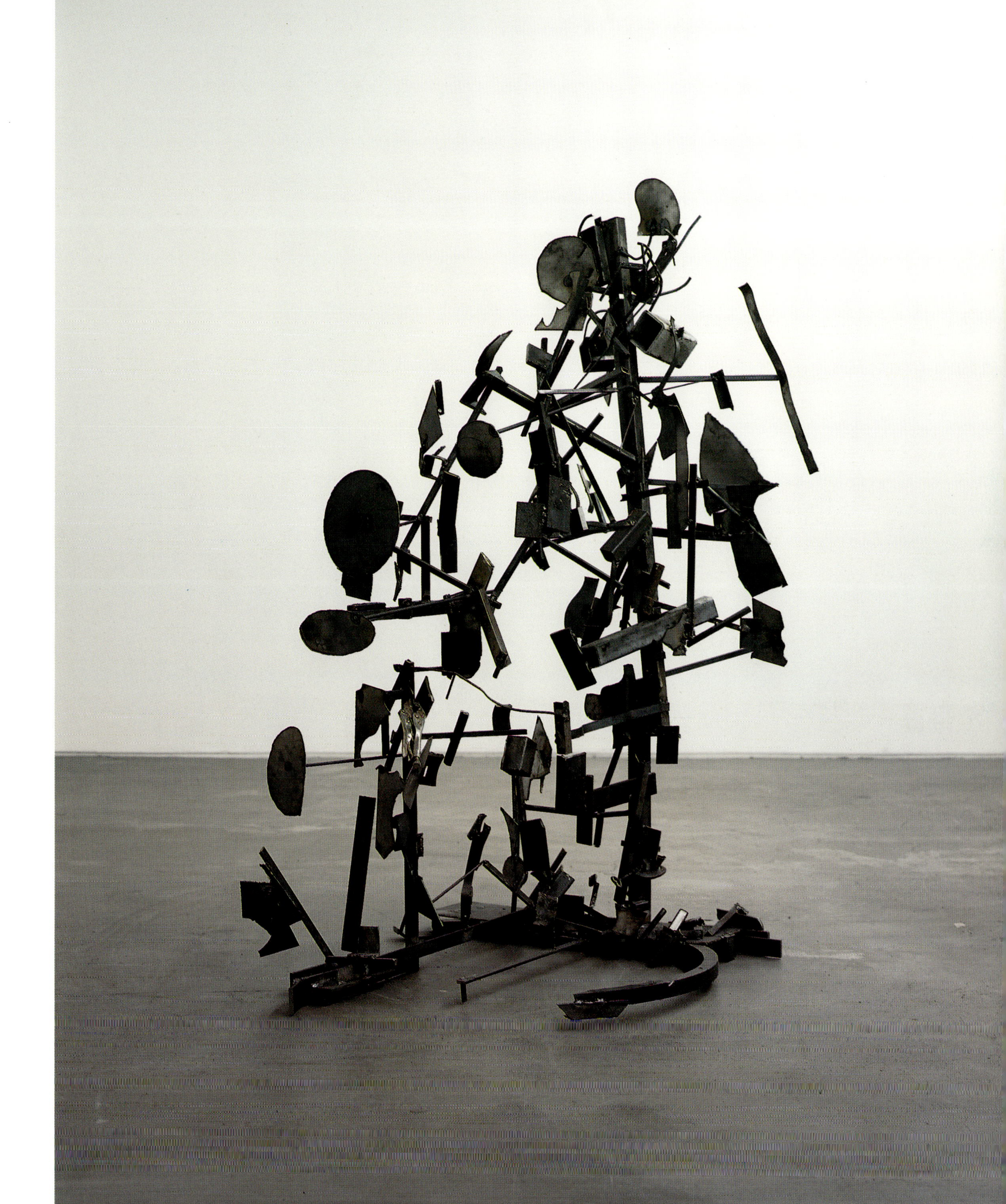

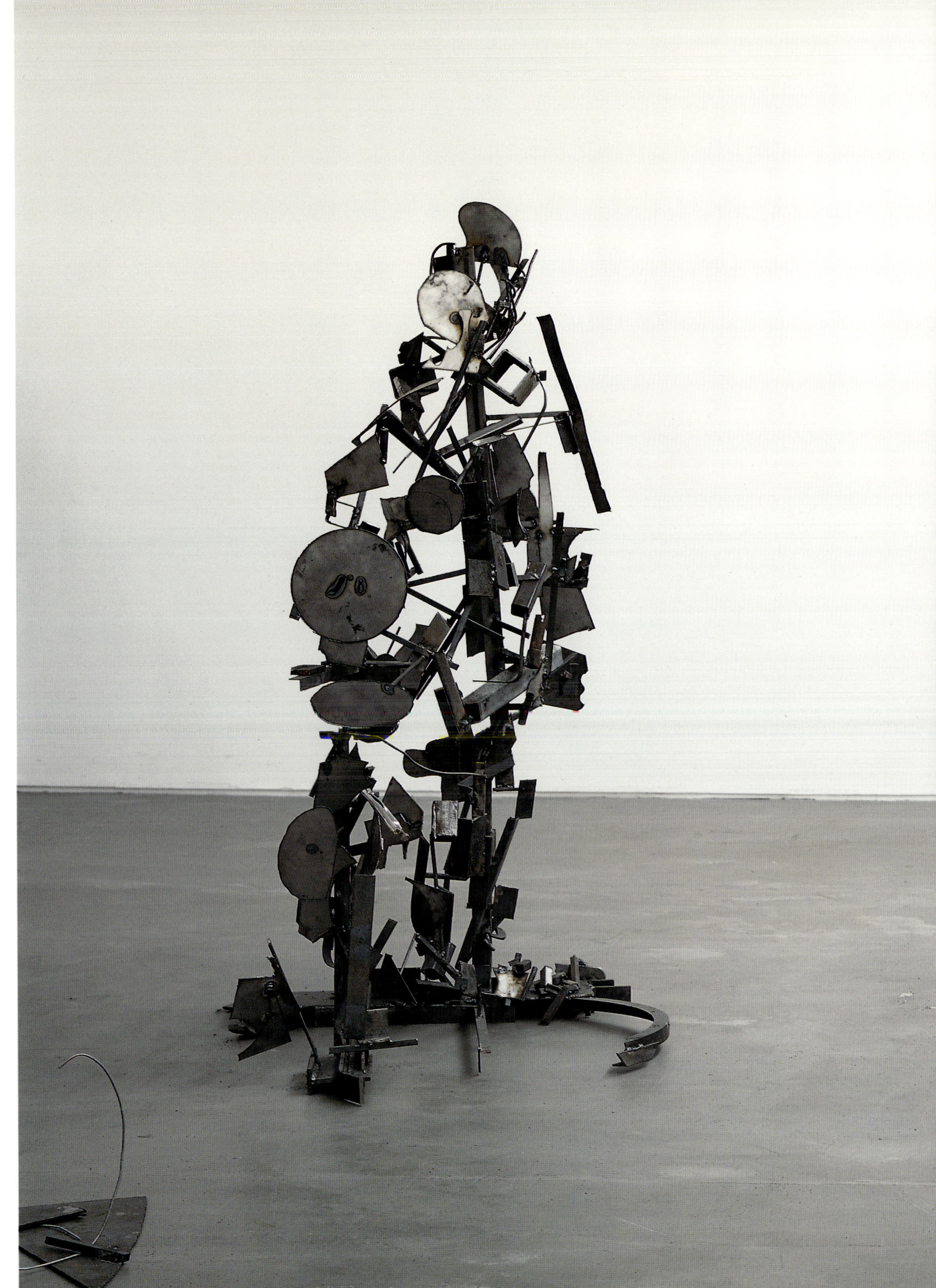

HE, 2004

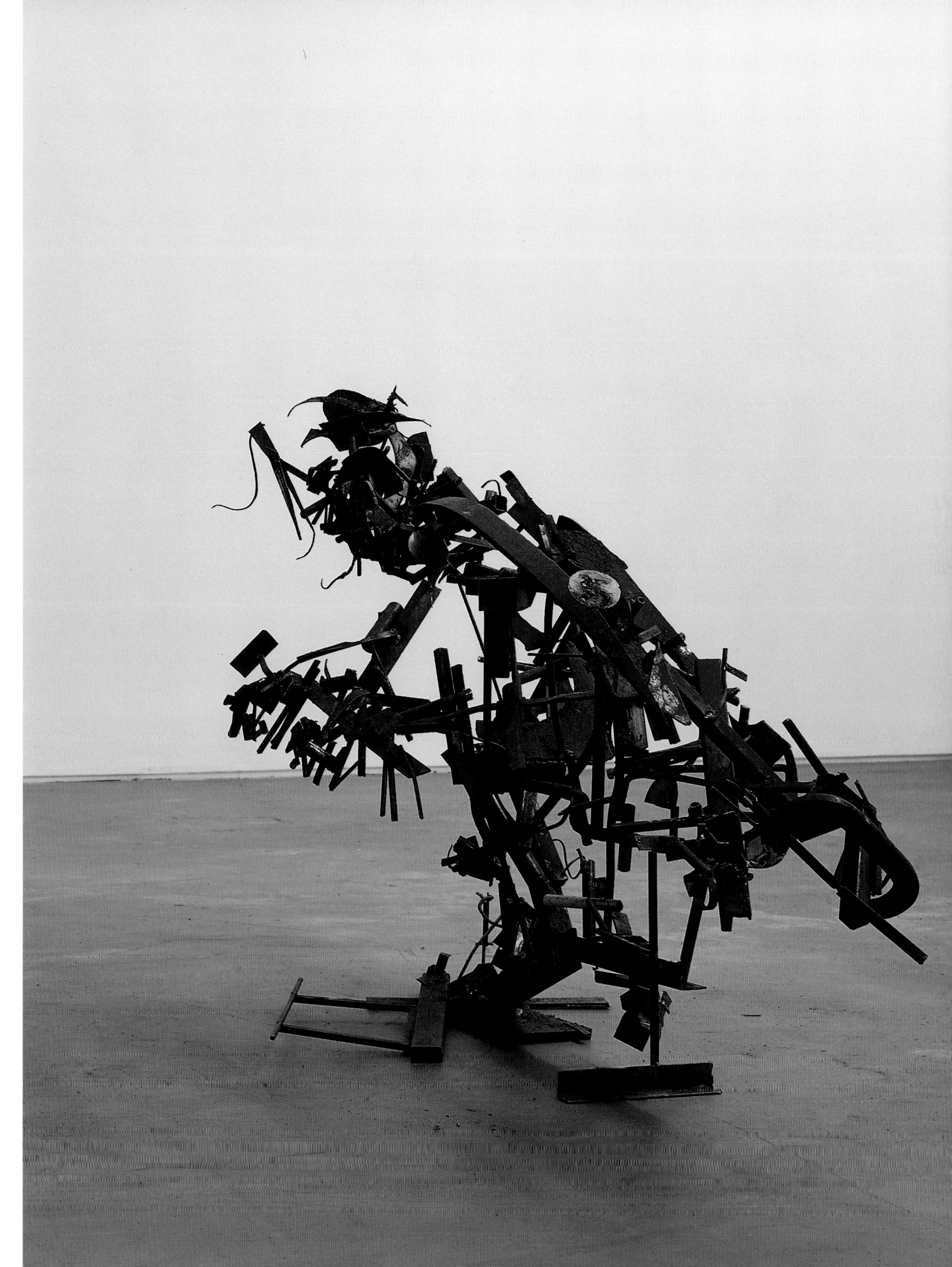

SHE, 2004

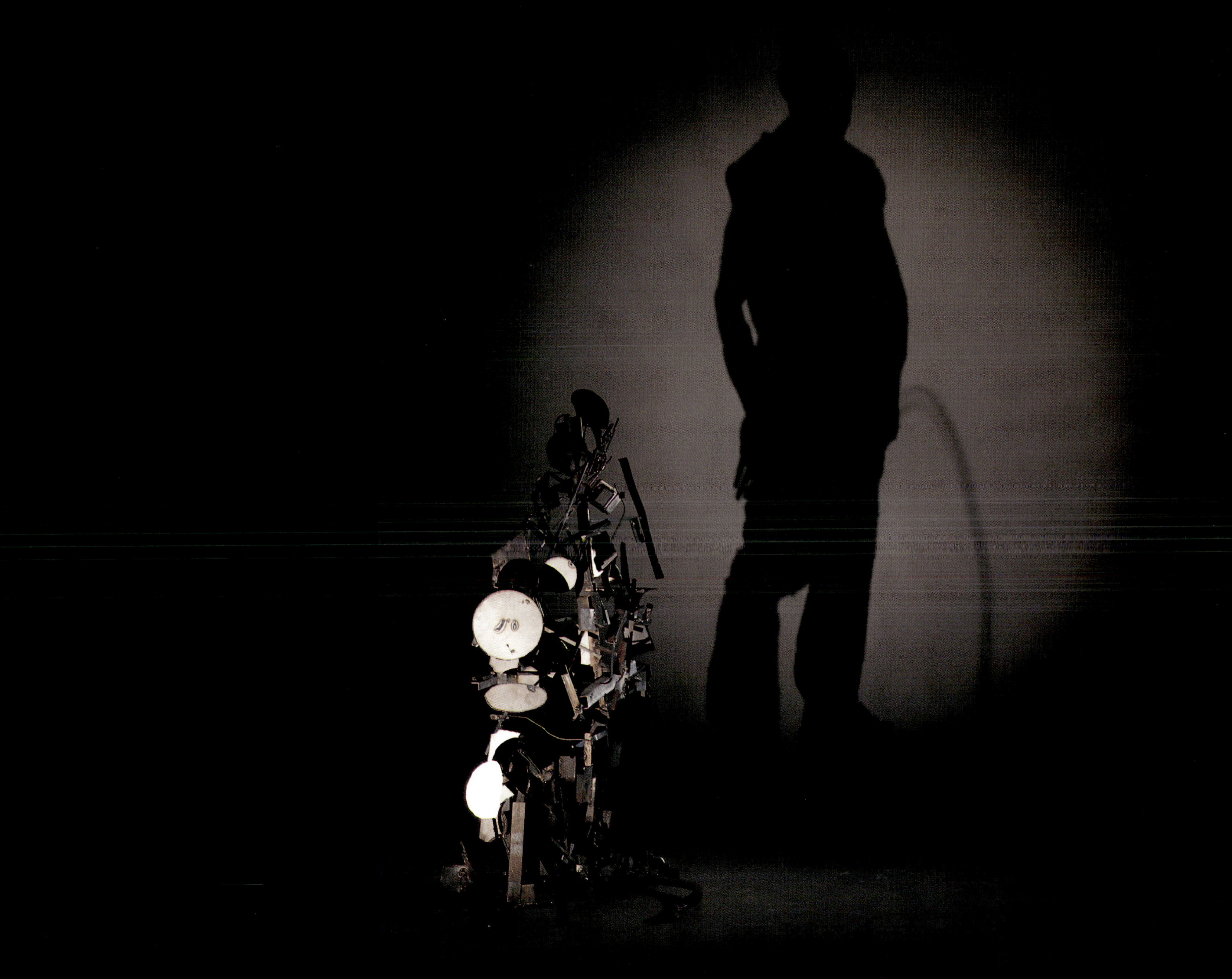

HE, 2004

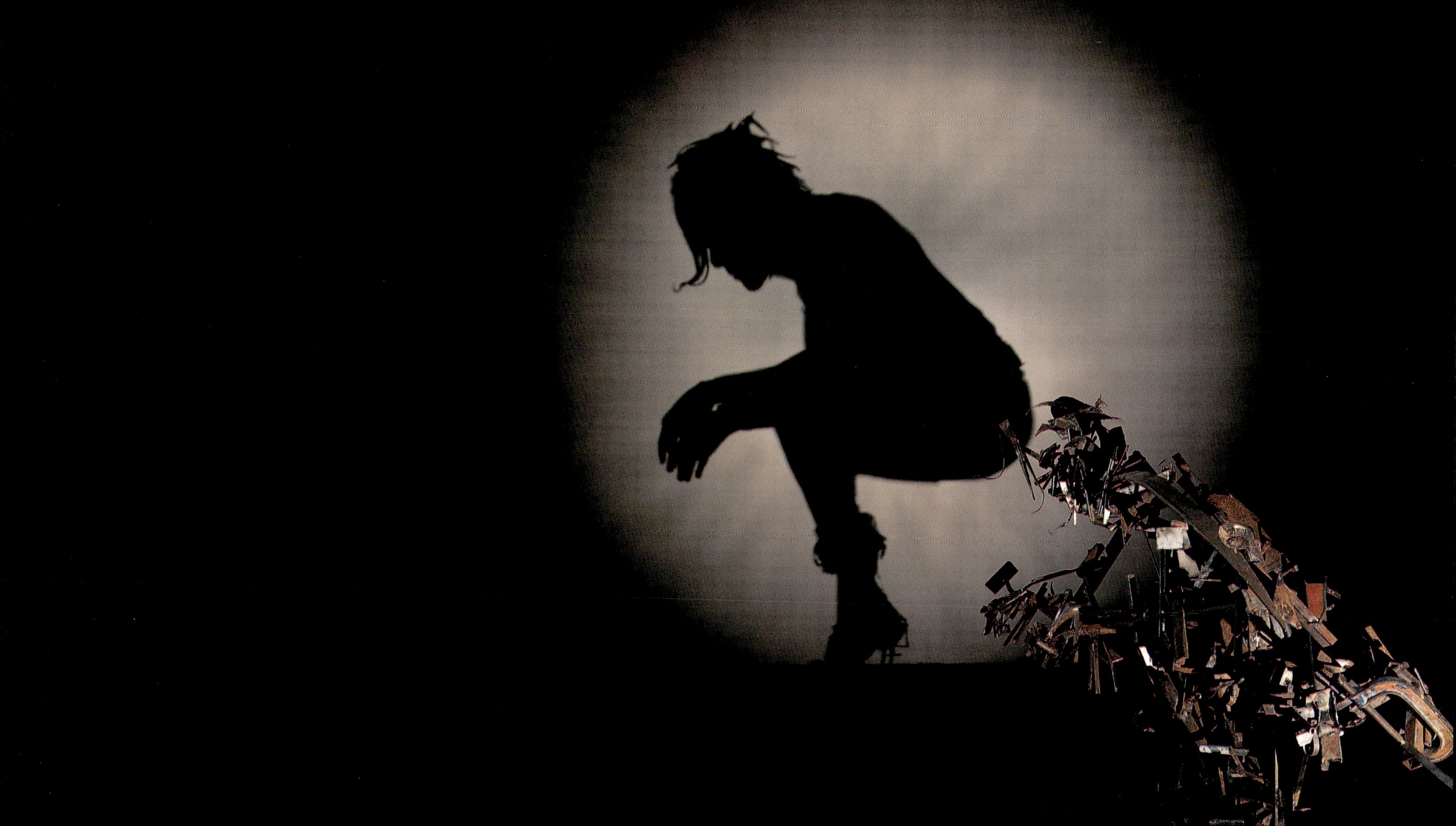

The Spikey Thing, 2005

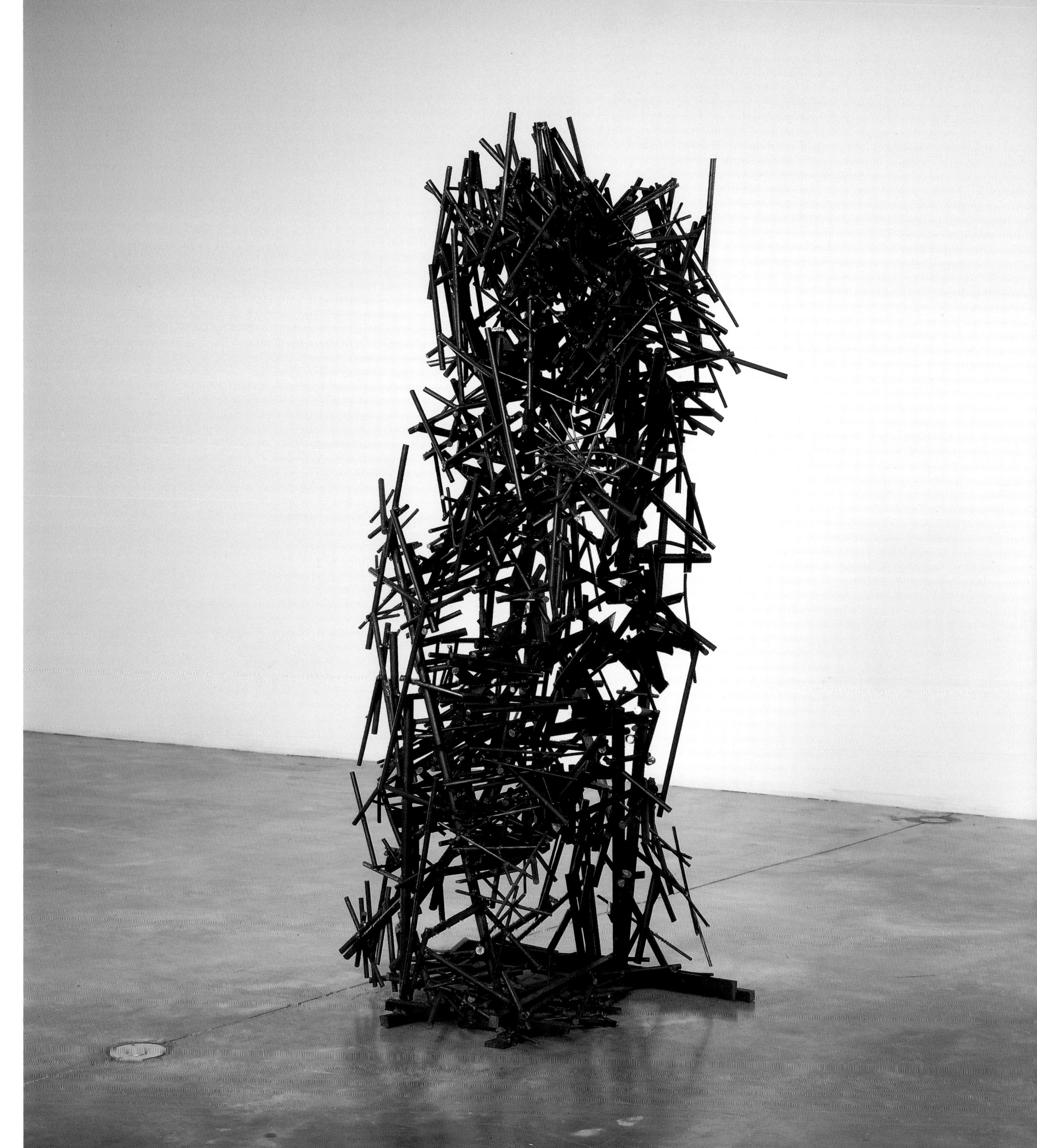

The Spikey Thing, 2005

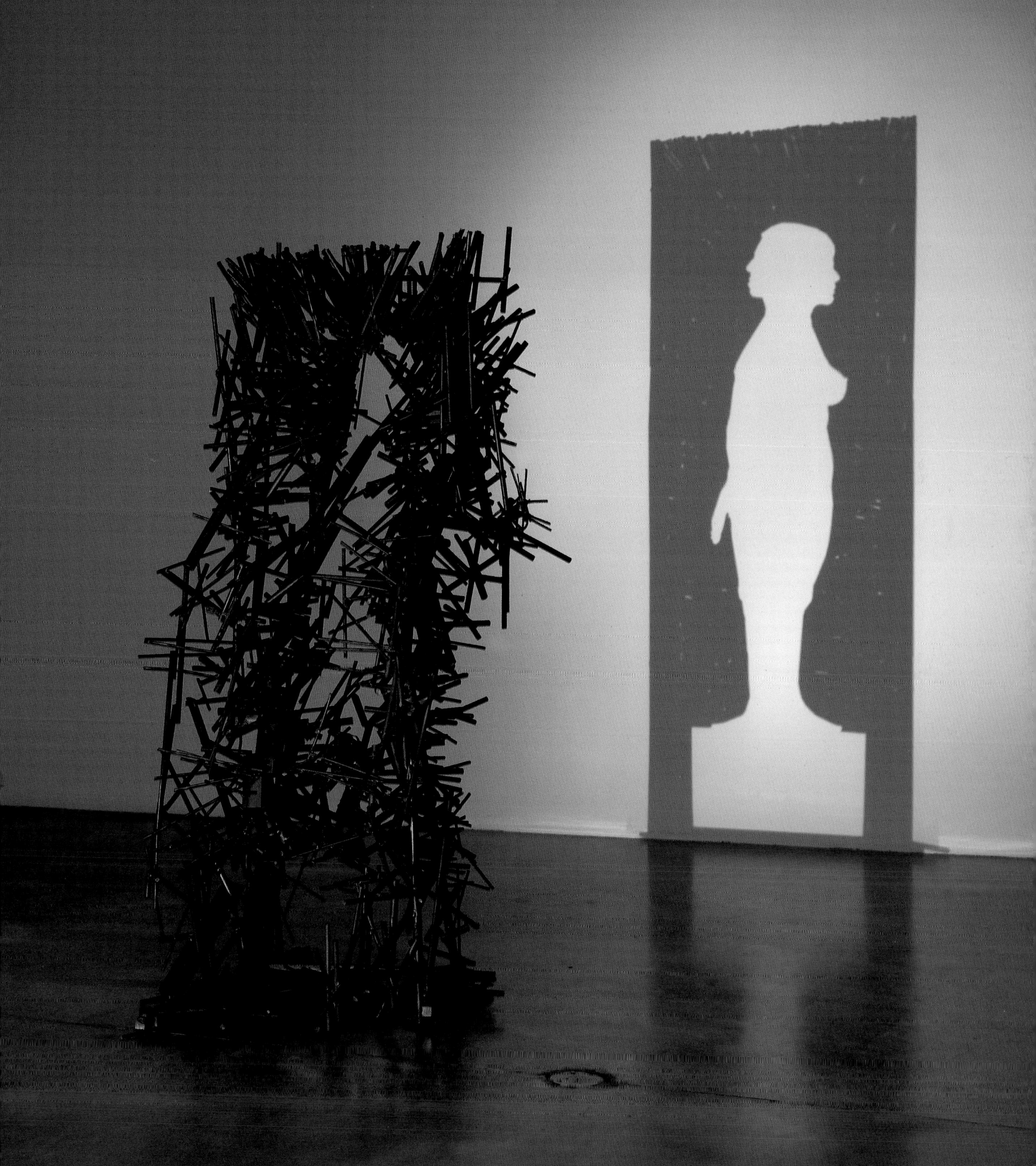

The Crack, 2004

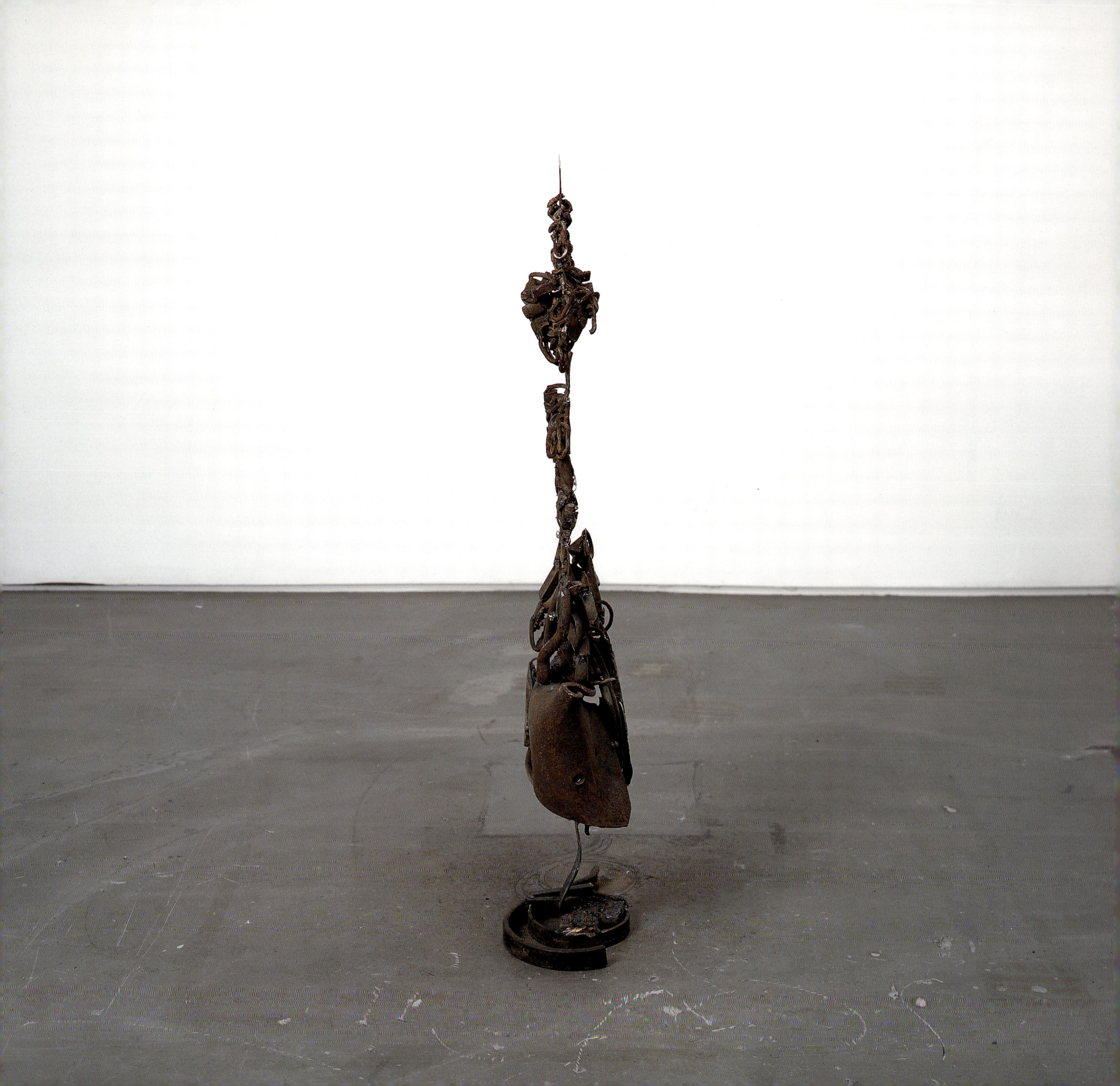

The Crack, 2004

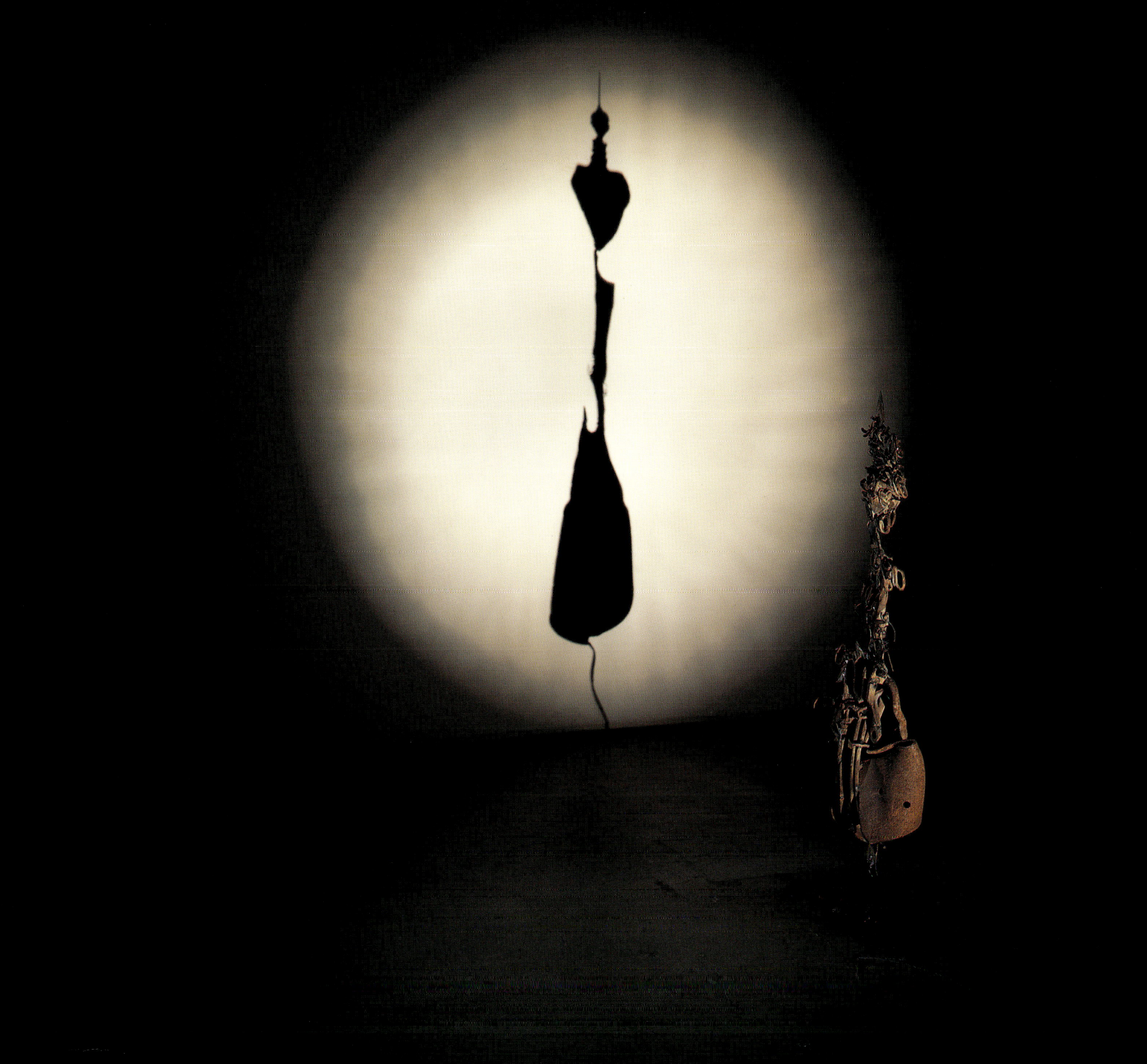

Twin Suicide, 2005

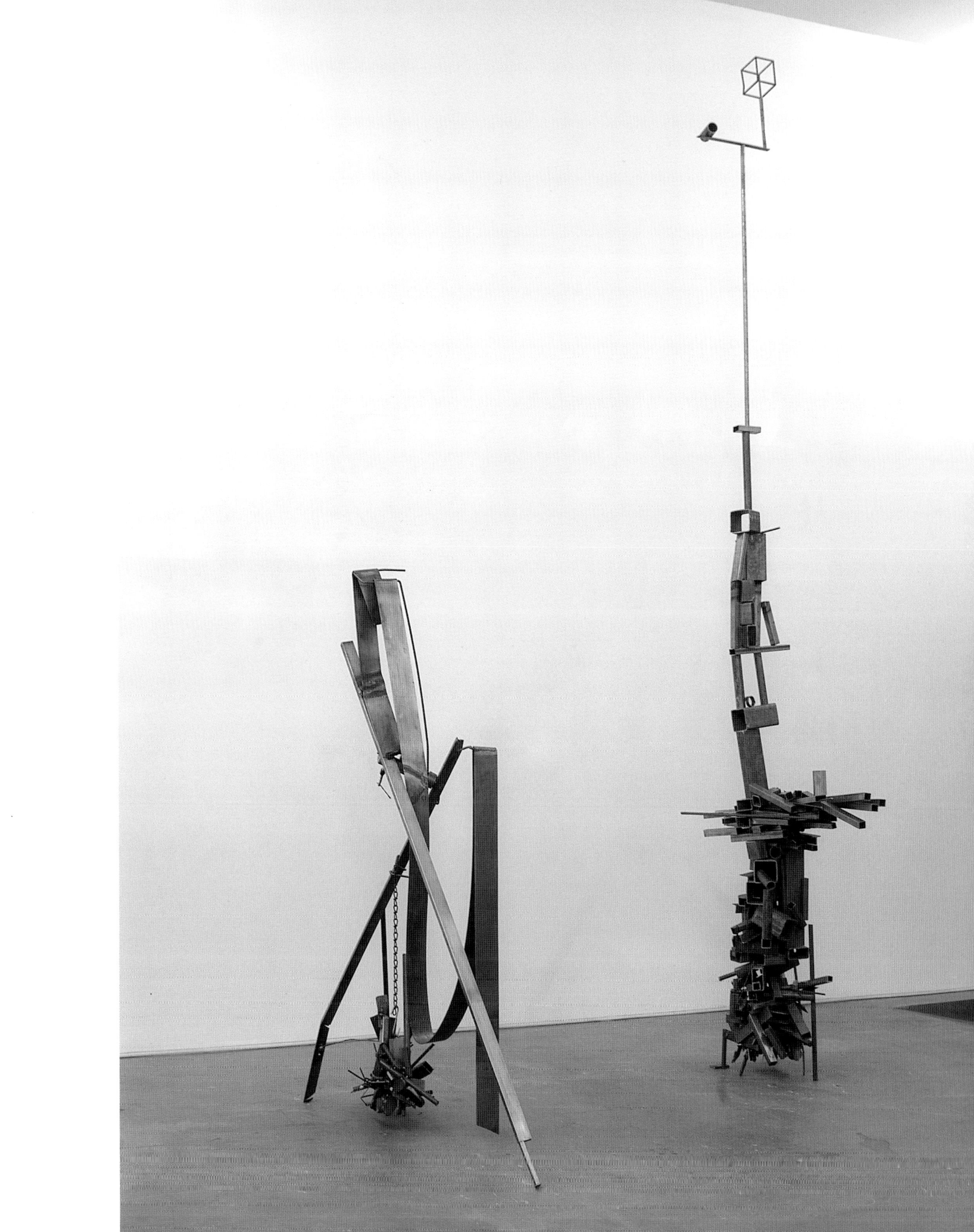

MAST
THE UN

ERS OF
IVERSE

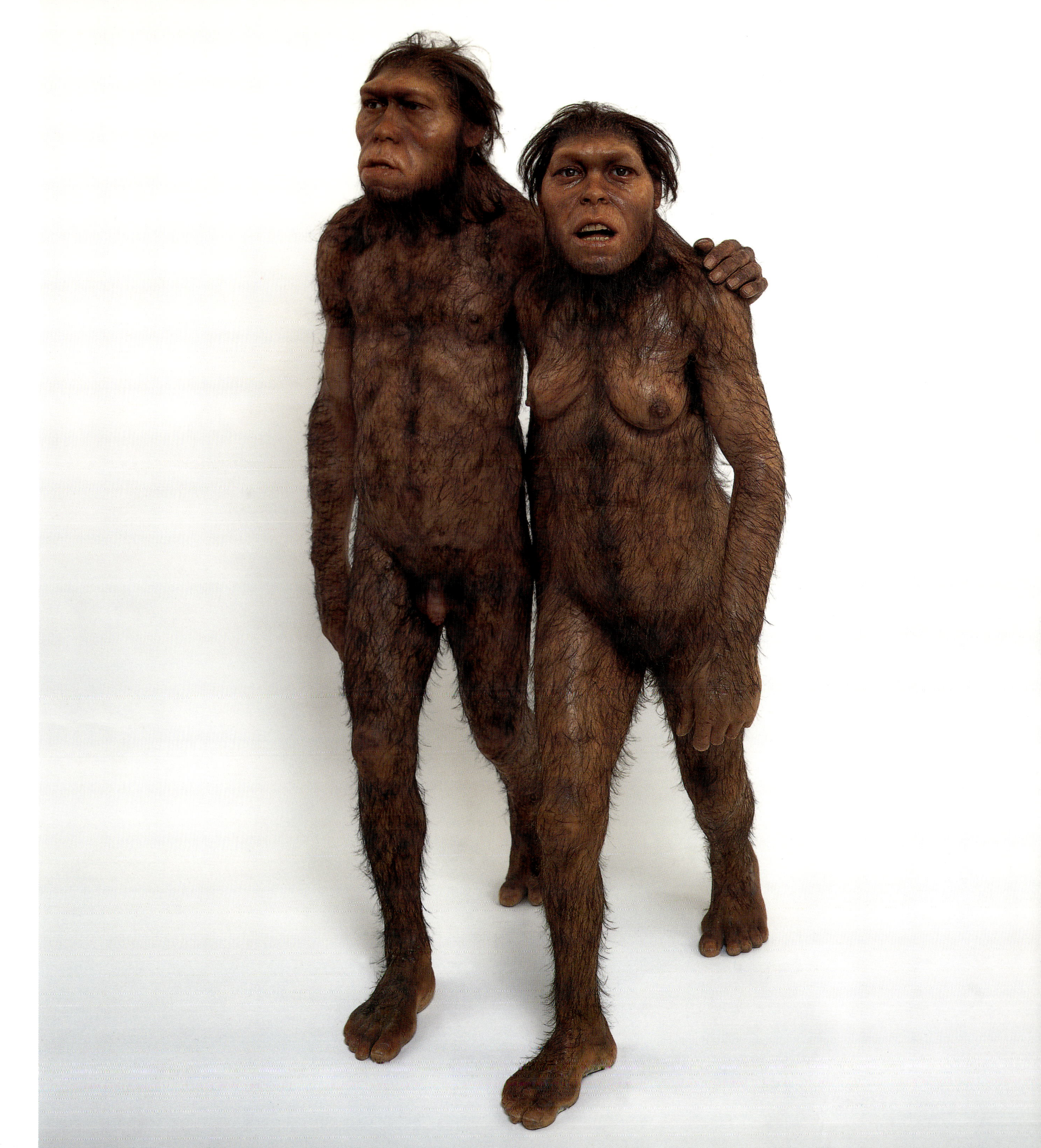

Masters of the Universe (detail), 2000

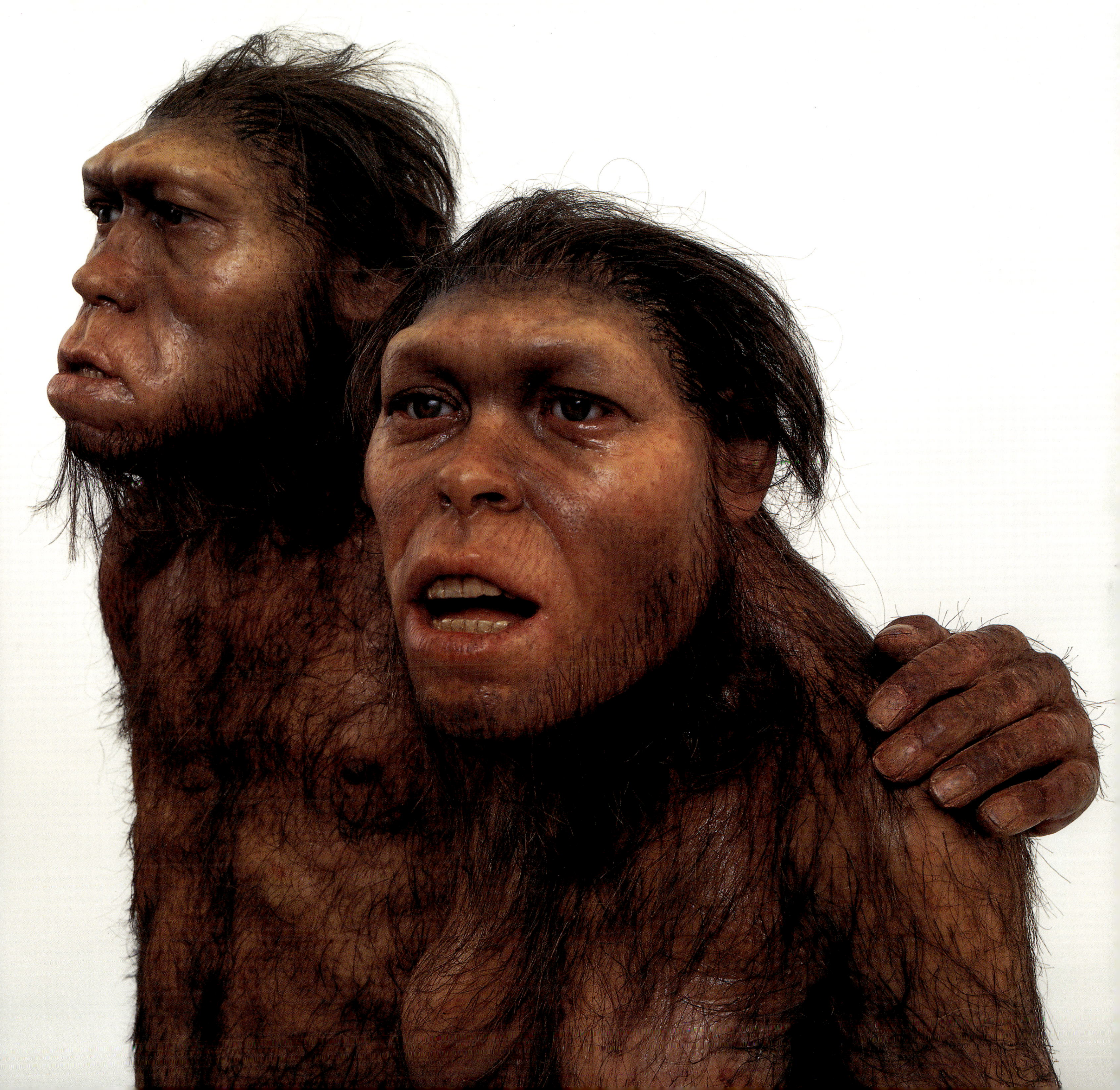

THE
BARBA

NEW

RIANS

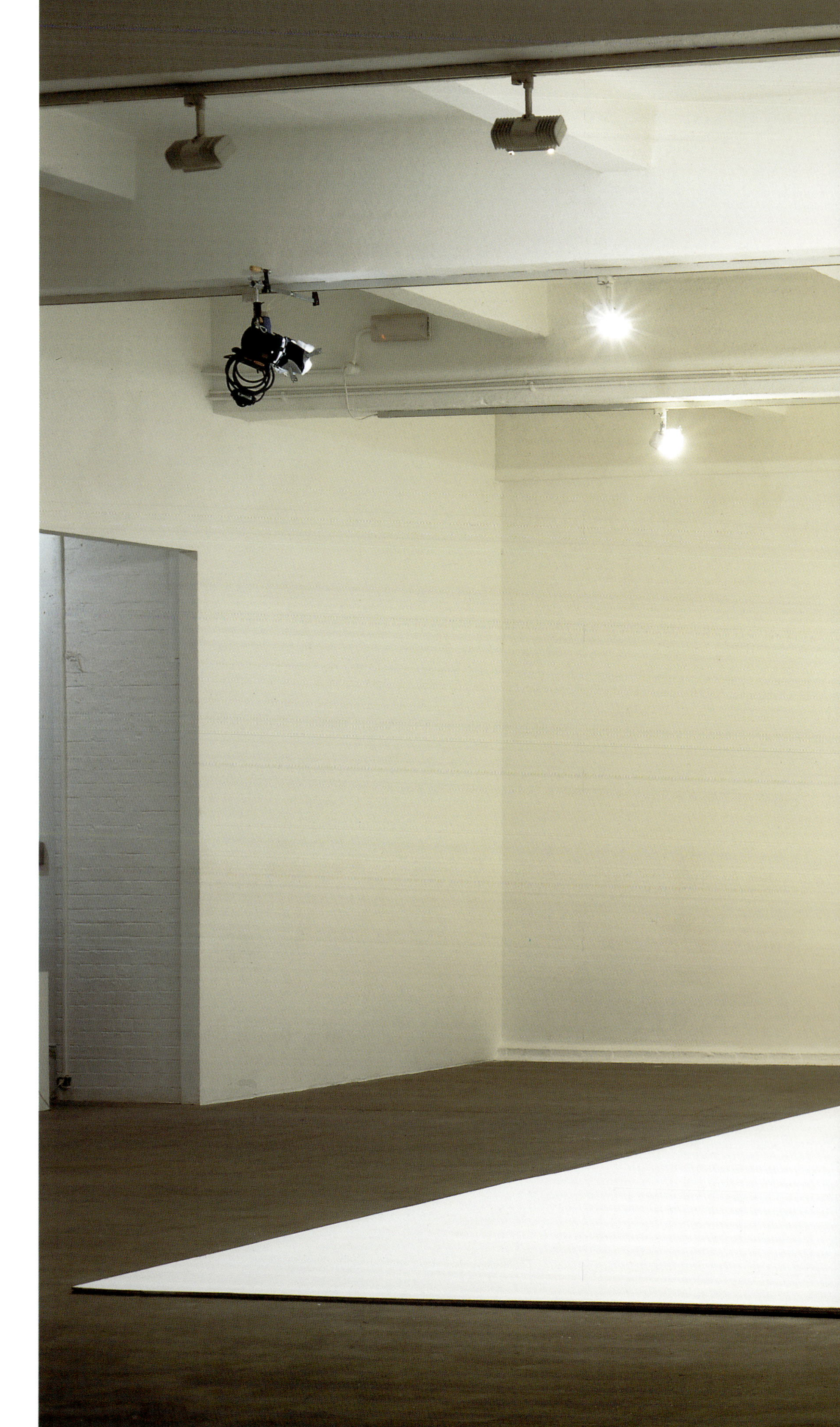

The New Barbarians (installation view), 1997–99

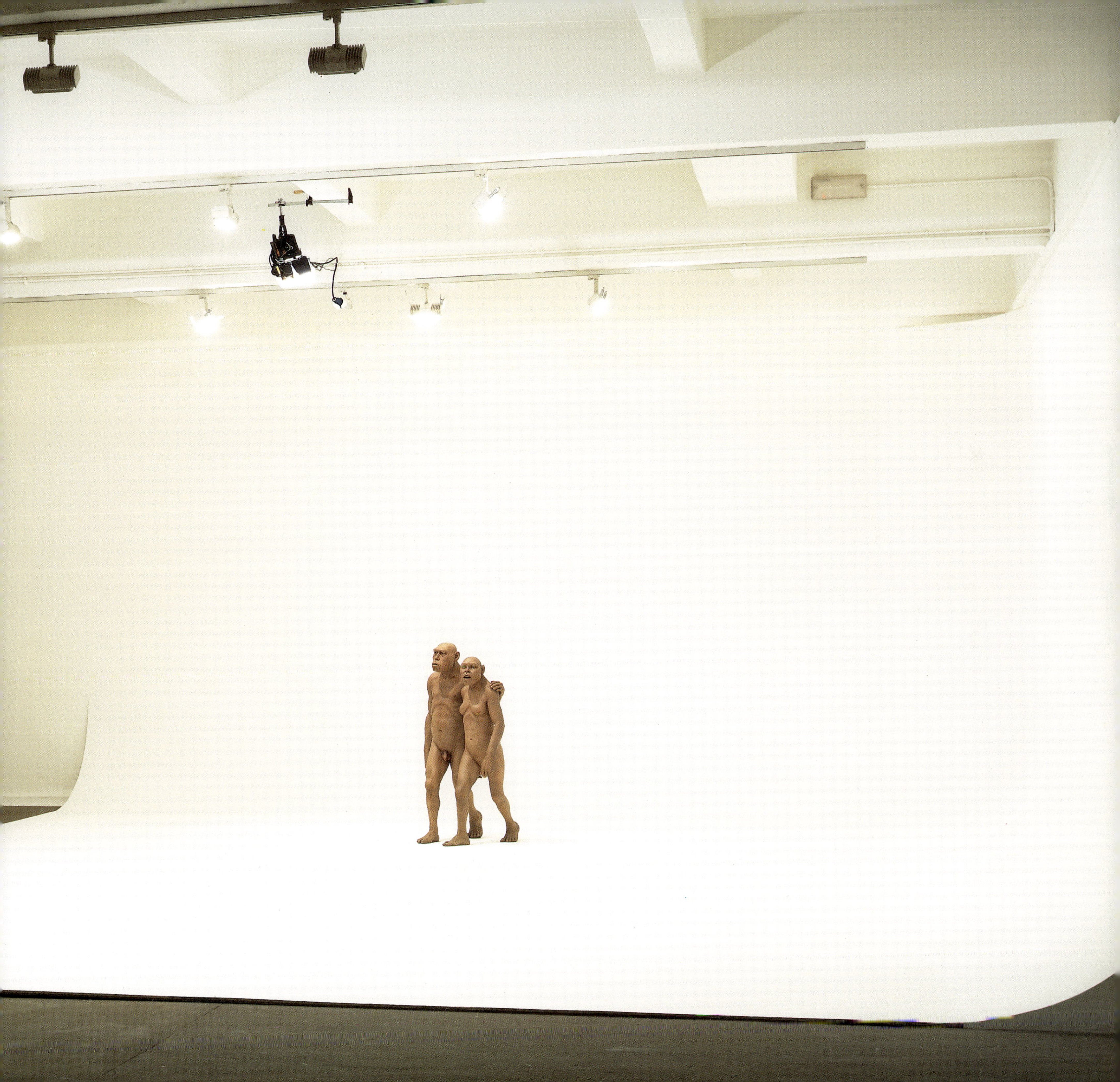

The New Barbarians, 1997–99

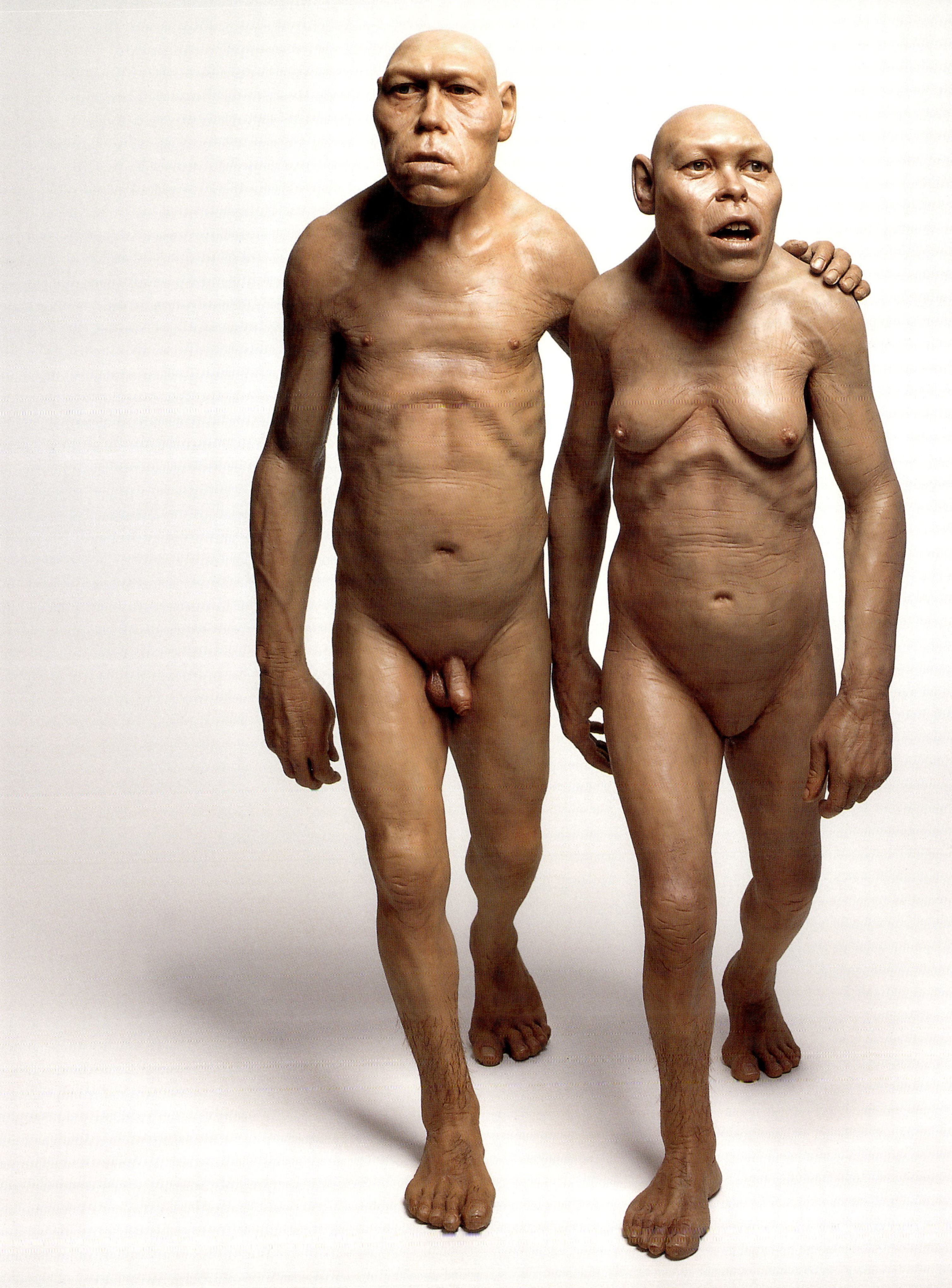

The New Barbarians (detail), 1997–99

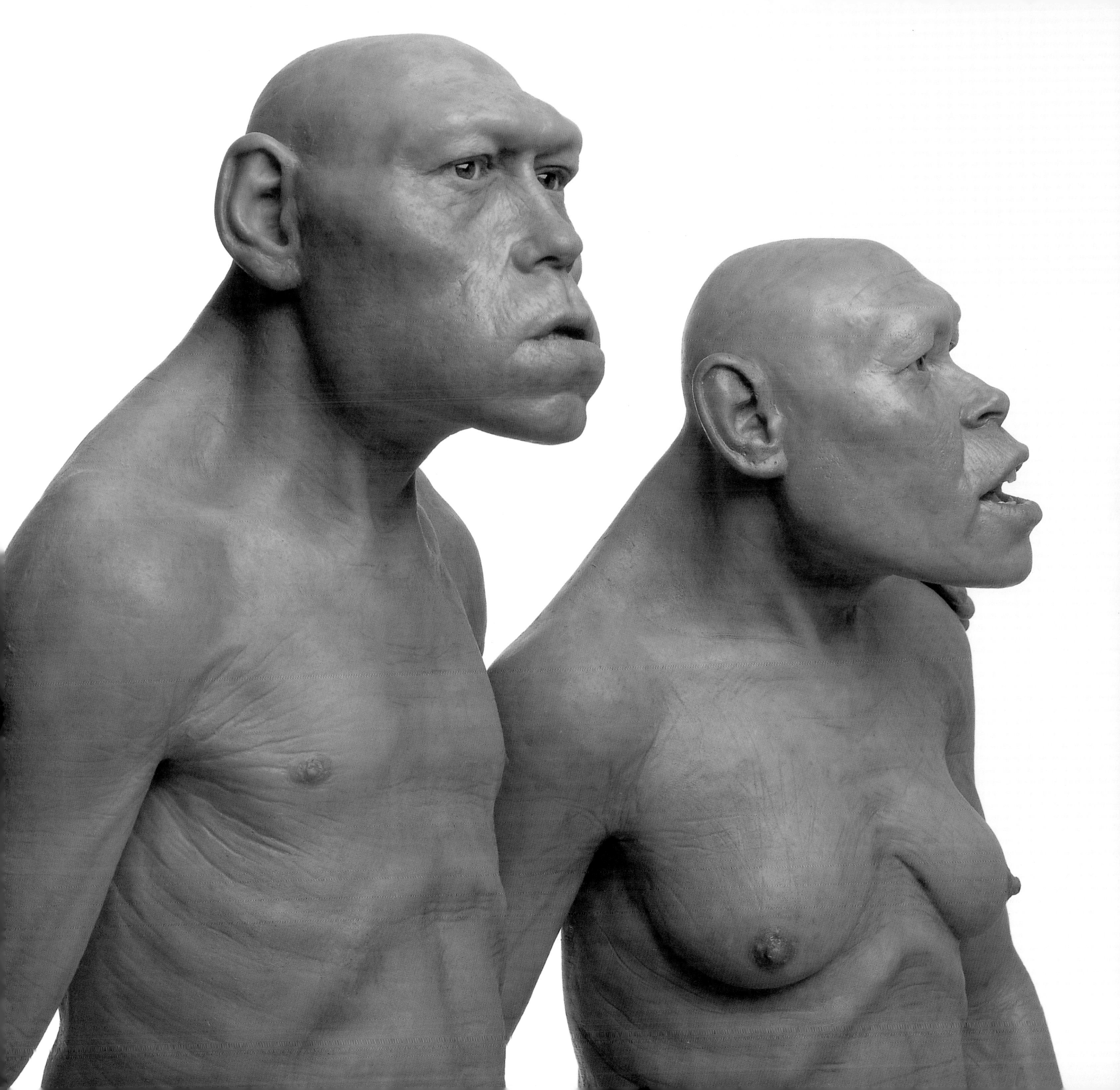

THE MAGIC ARTS OF NOBLE & WEBSTER—TIM AND SUE

Norman Rosenthal

We live equally in ordinary times and in extraordinary times. Tim and Sue, Noble & Webster, exemplify this idea. This is why they are among the archetypal artists of London at the end of the twentieth century and the beginning of the twenty-first. Of course, they have more or less made it into the art pantheon, even if, as yet, inexplicably none of their work has been acquired by a museum collection in the UK. How Tim and Sue met as impecunious art students in Nottingham, England, modeling themselves after the artists Gilbert & George, two "provincials" who metamorphosed in true Dickensian fashion into Londoners, is a story that has been told before. For those who have made it, the streets of Young British London have been paved with gold. On the surface it all seems so easily won. Invent a little trick or two and the world is your oyster. Forget the past, invent your own present. Success—which each and every art student, whether partnered or not, dreams of—that great gift from the gods, will be yours.

Nothing could be further from the truth, and the work of the art partnership of Noble & Webster always runs far deeper than first appearances. Initial appearances can often deceive, and their work, which gradually came to public attention in the second half of the 1990s, like all real art exists on so many levels. At the most immediate, and most important, level, their work symbolizes a pair of artists clearly besotted and totally in love with each other, artists who are only interested in picturing themselves: sometimes surrounded by detritus; other times by pastiches of contemporary neon advertising, as though they were circus clowns walking a tightrope, in order to draw the attention of an audience. "Look at us," they seem to be saying, "Aren't we beautiful? Isn't life beautiful? Wherever we find ourselves, atop a heap of rubbish, making sex and love as only we

British can, sometimes thinking deeply, sometimes just wasting time." An antiaesthetic of vulgarity rules on the surface of their work. Both art and the world are filled with dollar signs, cheap parodies of Las Vegas lights, or expensive sculptures by Bruce Nauman, with the great Londoners' expression applied to all, and everything "fucking beautiful!" The implication is that wherever you are, life and art are simple; success is easy to come by, on the streets, or *Underneath the Arches*, to recall the classic work of Gilbert & George.

But, as with Gilbert & George, real art is always hard-won, through cultivated thought and more so through that most unfashionable commodity—skill—in an age when so much of it can even be ordered by mobile phone.

Let us first examine their skill. There is in the artwork of our artist-hero and -heroine an amazing skill and technique at work, aspects that are never—as is often the case nowadays, and historically—farmed out to studio assistants or even to craftsmen. Put quite straightforwardly, Tim and Sue do all their work themselves without any help, though it is hard to say which of them dominates in what aspect. But essential to their work is that shock, that sense of surprise as to how it is all done. How on earth is it possible to turn a huge pile of London trash, which seems to have been emptied from so many smelly black garbage bags into a Magic Mountain; on top of which sit our two romantic lovers as though in some innocent paradise imagined by, say, Wordsworth or maybe Blake, who in his poem *For the Sexes: The Gates of Paradise* writes with simple but not simplistic innocence (a quality that seems also to reside in Tim and Sue): "Mutual forgiveness for each vice/Such are the gates of Paradise"?

As with Blake's work, there is an extraordinary sense of craft and technical virtuosity that is both hard-won and has a self-taught and improvisational quality, achieved largely through arduous trial and error. The trash is collected, apparently arbitrarily, but then, with the aid of the projected spotlight, is transformed into an illusion like that of a Victorian theatrical magician who pulls an image out of thin air. One might recall Pepper's ghost, first staged by Dr. John Henry Pepper in 1862 by projecting light from below the stage. There are those of us who can project puppet-like creatures onto a white wall or a screen merely by using our fingers. Tim and Sue do some of the same tricks, but in a highly and precisely calculated manner, using not only trash but also sometimes stuffed birds piled up; most recently, in a brilliant series of sculptures, they used iron detritus, some of which—with delightful irony— was scrounged from the studio of the great artist Sir Anthony Caro. For example, when the spotlight shines on a piece constructed from iron and titled *The Crack*, 2004, a double image appears, redolent of Sir Ernst Gombrich's legendary reference to the "rabbit and duck" optical illusion, which he describes in the opening pages of his famous 1960 book *Art and Illusion*.[1] *The Crack* displays at one moment an abstract shape that is perhaps reminiscent of a heroic mountain landscape by Clyfford Still, with its cracks and gullies; gradually we begin to perceive the full-length naked profiles of our friends approaching each other, nipples touching, as though they are about to make love again for the millionth time. It is impossible to see both images simultaneously— the reality and psychology of perception make this impossible. And then the spotlight shuts off, leaving us with a hanging, welded metal construction, evoking the cubist work of Julio Gonzalez, Spanish sculptor and friend of Picasso. Thus, Tim and Sue

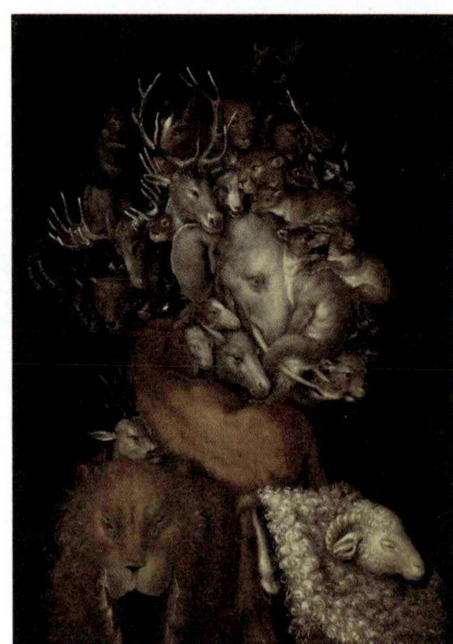

Earth, c.1570 (oil on panel)
Arcimboldo, Giuseppe (1527–93)
Private Collection, Vienna, Austria/The Bridgeman Art Library.

give us three works for the price of one, a conceit that also reflects the modern times with which they so clearly identify—their own personal history; their lifestyle and clothes; their public appearances; their binge drinking, to which they freely confess— all are part of the essential and incestuous world of modern artists living in London. Yet, maybe Tim and Sue are different; not only because of their fused artistic personalities, but because of their unity, which seems to run even deeper than that of Gilbert & George, if only because it is so obviously based on trust and also on that elusive thing called eternal love. In so many ways—whether face-to-face, adjacent to each other, or back-to-back; kissing, peeing, or defecating; in full view of each other, in shadow, or in front of us, the viewer—their trust and love for each other is touching, almost naive in its purity. This love justifies even the scary hideousness of their *Sensation*-like sculpture *The New Barbarians*, 1997–99, where Tim and Sue portray themselves as naked anthropoids at the very onset of human history, striding into some unknown future; or maybe as two unique, post-atomic, world-catastrophe survivors, despite their wildness able to resuscitate the human race. Are they like Adam and Eve, once again being expelled out of what Blake so beautifully referred to as the gates of Paradise? Countless artists over the centuries have depicted themselves as the Original Man and Woman, the Adam and Eve of the Judeo-Christian tradition. They are nearly always figures of beauty. We might recall from the Renaissance Albrecht Dürer and his figures of divine and perfect proportion. Tim and Sue's barbarian couple could be identified as Adam and Eve, but they leave us in no doubt as to their democratic ordinariness and ugly presence as they stride forward with apparently ruthless determination.

But this sense of naive and even primitive self-depiction is in fact only part of the artists' story. Another part is their highly sophisticated feeling for cultural history, either all-knowing or only partially sensed— there is no point in asking which, it is undoubtedly there. All art comes from art. Nothing is totally original. The interest lies in the transformation and metamorphosis of motifs and ideas that, in the case of Tim and Sue, stem not only from surrealist ideas developed in the twentieth century, but also the sophisticated ideas of art entertainment and pleasure developed and expressed during ancient times, through the Renaissance, and beyond. This is not to make ridiculously transcendent claims for Tim and Sue; that would stretch the point to absurdity. No generation is the same as any other, and one of the mysteries of art is that in many ways technical progress counts for little, if anything. An enigma of cultural history suggests that earliest is best: the finest artifacts of ancient Egypt produce in us more of a "shiver" factor than ancient Greece, which in turn scores over Rome. So, in another recent piece titled *The Negative*, 2004, when we see shadows projected in black and white as though atop a plinth, of Sue (whose shadow we perceive in black) and Tim (in white), we can also imagine Egyptian heads, maybe of both male and female pharaonic figures. This is not to give banal equivalence to both moments in the history of art—one from maybe three or four thousand years ago, the other from the present day— but to illustrate the concept that cultural memory is brought into play here. It is an important aspect of all culture that, however slowly or quickly, transformations occur. On the surface, the transformations in ancient Egypt were slow, even nearly immutable. Today, the exigencies of fashion seem to demand endless novelties of expression, while discarding, like so much waste, the culture of yesterday, with only

a sentimental nod toward anything "retro" having validity as the culture runs out of new ideas. But "the culture," as some journalists insist on describing it, is one thing and art is another. In art, *memory* is everything, and the art of Tim and Sue is a receptacle of cultural memory. In 1970, the endlessly quoted French cultural philosopher Roland Barthes wrote an essay on the extraordinary and mysterious Italian mannerist artist Giuseppe Arcimboldo, who was born in Milan in 1527 and who after many strange adventures in central Europe—particularly in Vienna and Prague—died in his hometown in 1593. Arcimboldo is famous, of course, for his portraits constructed of animals, birds, fruits, flowers, vegetables, and so on. For Barthes,

> Arcimboldo's art is an art of fabrication— that is to say a message to be delivered. When Arcimboldo intends to signify the head of a cook, a peasant, a reformer, he ciphers the message. Ciphering means to hide and not to hide simultaneously. The message is hidden because the eye is distracted from the sense of the whole by the sense of the detail . . . . Arcimboldo imposes a substitution system (an apple substitutes a cheek, just as in a coded message a letter or syllable stands for another letter or syllable), and also a transposition system (the whole picture is in a sense shifted back toward the detail).[2]

Tim and Sue work in a similar way. Arcimboldo's name was virtually forgotten until well into the twentieth century, when Alfred Barr showed his work in his legendary 1936 exhibition *Fantastic Art, Dada, and Surrealism* at the Museum of Modern Art, New York. In fact, the first two objects in the exhibition were works by Arcimboldo, including *Summer*, 1573, an allegorical head constructed entirely of fruit, with a suit of armor made of ripe wheat. As has been pointed out by art historians, notably Thomas Da Costa Kaufman, the meaning of *fantasia* and the fantastic—concepts that also play significant roles in the works of Tim and Sue—has changed since, say, the seventeenth century, when such paintings, conceits, and entertainments were symbolic of power structures (in this case the power of the Habsburg emperors of Vienna and Prague). But there are also, as in all echoes of art through time, constant elements that link the past with the present; Arcimboldo's paintings and transformations of the human face of the sixteenth century were compared to the products of dreams in a neo-Platonic sense. Indeed, as we learn from Horace, paintings of such fantastic creatures as the centaur (a hybrid animal with a human torso and a horse's body) or the chimera (a fire-breathing monster with a lion's head, a goat's body, and a serpent's tail) were common-place in ancient times. He compared them to the dreams of the sick. Later, during the Renaissance, the use of the imagination to create form was much admired. It was the imagination that gave rise to conceits and moments of magic, which made the skilled practitioners of such arts—like Arcimboldo—valued personages. Arcimboldo was not merely a painter. Like many other artists of that period—now considered far greater than Arcimboldo, whether we speak of Leonardo, Bernini, or Rubens—all were "magicians" on a grand scale, flattering rulers with fantastical entertainments created to surprise, delight, and maybe to stimulate dreams.

There is in the work of Tim and Sue a dream-like quality; even the absence of light, apart from the spotlight in some cases, helps create a magic shadow effect that the viewer hardly believes can be possible. The concept of the dream—even the nightmare—is a recurrent theme in their imagery, as it is in that of, say, Henry Fuseli or René Magritte, to mention only two examples. Sitting on a pile of trash, atop the detritus of contemporary society, is a veritable nightmare, even if just through the imagination that "love conquers all." What could be more nightmarish than the idea of a carrion crow perched atop Tim's head, as in the sculpture *Kiss of Death*, 2003, the bird brutally pecking at the eyes and eyebrows of the artist, with his partner-in-crime looking on in total horror. Tim and Sue only depict themselves, refusing all requests from those who might want to have their own portraits made out of rubbish, stuffed birds, or the like. It should be emphasized to those who have not met Tim and Sue how precisely recognizable their self-portraits are, whether they are only of their heads, their complete figures, or a radical transforma-tion as in *The New Barbarians*. There are also rats, the archetypal animals of human fear, which they are prepared to represent alongside the carrion crow. There is a sinister, even deliberately creepy aspect as well as a happy side to the work of Tim and Sue. A dagger stuck through the heart, as found in an early work like *Toxic Schizophrenia*, 1997—its Piccadilly Circus-like lights flashing on and off full-tilt, a depiction of the classic Christian emblem, the bleed-ing heart—also indicates the levels of ambiguity and human feeling that permeate their work. The concept of the emblem is central to art: An emblem that can represent faith and fidelity, love as well as hate, fear as well as resolution, understanding and igno-rance, sophistication and vulgarity, waste and value, friendship and alienation, male and female, negative and positive. In other words, an endless string of opposites that can tear the world apart or hold it together, either from the perspective of society in general or of two individuals who are joined as one. We can come to understand all this and more through the work of Noble & Webster, Tim and Sue.

1. Ernst Gombrich, *Art and Illusion: A Study in the Psychology of Pictorial Representation*, (New York: Pantheon, 1960).

2. Roland Barthes, *The Arcimboldo Effect: Transformations of the Face from the 16th Century to the 20th Century*, ed. Karl Gunnar Pontus Hulten, (New York: Abbeville Press, 1987).

3. Thomas Da Costa Kaufman, *The Arcimboldo Effect: Transform-ations of the Face from the 16th Century to the 20th Century*, ed. Karl Gunnar Pontus Hulten, (New York: Abbeville Press, 1987).

BLACK MAGIC

Jeffrey Deitch

The artistic career of Tim Noble and Sue Webster almost ended the day it began. Tim had a concept to make a video work with his head inside a fish tank as if it were a live sculptural ornament, with Sue filming and directing. They hoped to create the illusion of a disembodied head placed inside the tank, with fish swimming around it and other decorative elements in the background. Their goal was to make their own disconcerting version of a relaxing fish tank video, the kind that people buy to play in an endless loop on their TVs.

A homemade aquarium was set up in the studio with a hole at the bottom, and made watertight with a rubber seal, into which Tim inserted his head, along with a thin plastic breathing tube. Pebbles were spread around and the tank was filled with water. Using a little net, Sue dropped in the live fish that had been held in cooking pots. There was no provision for an emptying plug at the bottom of the tank.

The video begins with the perfectly realized illusion of Tim's head placed in the fish tank as a live ornament with goldfish swimming around it and a mechanical clam opening and closing its shell beside him. Offscreen, Sue is creating a bubbly sound effect by blowing through a straw into a pot of water. The scenario does seem relaxing in a strange way until the viewer begins to notice some distress on Tim's face. Off-camera, Sue is oblivious, continuing to make her sound effect. Gradually, Tim's distress becomes alarming. He is starting to turn blue and it is clear that he is hardly able to breathe.

Sue finally recognizes that something is wrong, but unaware of the seriousness of the situation, she starts trying to save the fish before trying to rescue Tim. The viewer sees her reaching into the tank with her little net to pluck out the fish while Tim looks like he is about to expire. Finally, there is a climactic moment of panic when Sue realizes that Tim is about to drown inside his own artwork and reaches in with a siphon while Tim spits out his clogged breathing tube, his head bobbing helplessly in the water. Just in time, and as the video becomes too painful to watch, Tim musters some superhuman strength to force his head down through the hole, with the water pouring through behind him. The video ends in chaos and Tim is heard gasping for breath. The work, which was originally to be titled *Ornament*, was given the new title *Ornament (in crisis)*, 1995. From that point on, after understanding that everything about their art relied on their mutual trust, Tim and Sue decided that all of their work would be made in collaboration. On June 19, 1995, a day when Sue's diary entry reads, "Tim almost drowned," Tim Noble and Sue Webster became Noble & Webster.

The relationship between Noble & Webster had actually begun nine years earlier, in 1986, when they met in the Fine Art Department office at Nottingham Trent University where they both arrived a day late for the start of classes. Sue was late because she had gone to Amsterdam to attend a Siouxsie and the Banshees concert. She was also uncertain about whether or not to proceed with her enrollment in art school. She was one of six people short-listed from over three thousand applicants to become a television host for the cult music program, *The Tube*, and the first few weeks of school were interrupted by her TV interviews in London. Tim had already become intrigued by this brash young woman who he was afraid would be gone before he got to know her.

The judges for *The Tube* probably made a big mistake in not choosing Sue for the job, as she would have likely become a wildly popular television celebrity, but the painting department of Nottingham Trent University gained a student with extraordinary drive who already had her own way of defining fine art. The qualities that would have made Sue a successful television host were eventually channeled into Noble & Webster's innovative approach to art.

It is extraordinary that Sue Webster actually arrived at a college art department, given her upbringing. She was the first person in her family to attend college, and a few years earlier had not even been aware that art colleges existed. Tim, in contrast, was almost raised to be an artist. Every person in his immediate family was an artist and his father was a senior lecturer at Cheltenham Art College. Upon meeting Tim and Sue today, one is struck by their similarities and their seamless artistic collaboration. When they met, however, they had come from almost opposite backgrounds.

This fusion of opposite approaches is central to the dynamic of Noble & Webster's work and to their relationship. Their work is structured around the opposition of light and dark, object and shadow, trash and romance, high art and low, form and anti-form, and other usually incompatible concepts. The tension between these contrary strategies creates an artistic version of nuclear fusion.

The fusion at the foundation of their work is not only one of opposite forces, but also a merging of performance, sculpture, painting, photography, film, and art as event. Elements of advertising and graphic communication have been incorporated as well. These multiple approaches are often combined in a single work. Noble & Webster's art can be watched like a performance, contemplated like a painting,

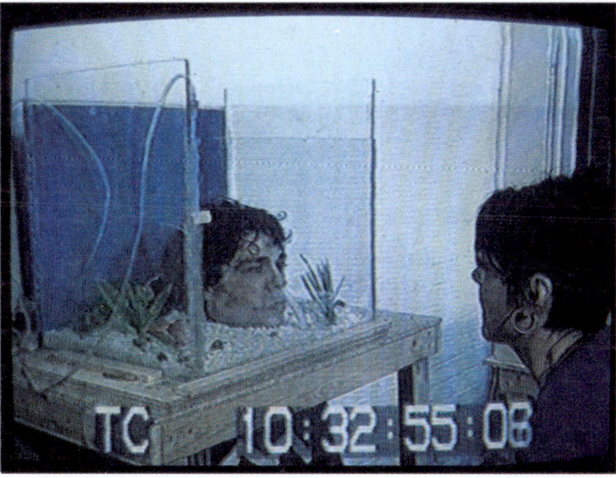

Ornament (in crisis), 1995. Video still.

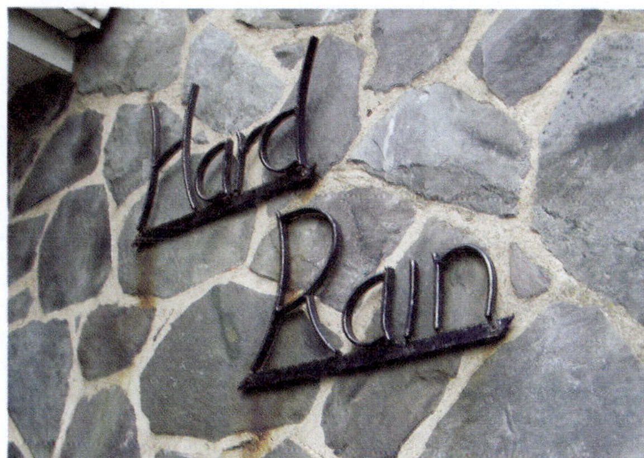

The iron sign of Sue's childhood home in Leicester.

engaged spatially like a sculpture, participated in like a happening, or absorbed in the way a person encounters an instant visual assault from a garish nightclub sign.

A punk attitude also infuses Noble & Webster's work. They identify with the dispossessed and with cultural outlaws like bikers, strippers, and criminals. Their work addresses high culture but celebrates anti-culture. Like a punk rock performance, the work sometimes threatens to dissolve into chaos before unexpectedly ending with a knockout punch. Tim has said "a good band has one foot in destruction and one foot in the real world." Their work is confrontational and can provoke outrage before ultimately seducing the viewer with its visual excess.

Noble & Webster are like a rock band, orchestrating their aesthetic mix into a high-energy, high-volume performance. They have adapted a musician's approach to artistic composition and presentation. As an artistic team, their model is as much John Lennon and Paul McCartney as it is Gilbert & George. This fusion of a musician's attitude into artistic attitude is one of Noble & Webster's most interesting innovations. They are among the first to refine the concept of artist as band. Watching the sequencing of their large light sculpture *Forever*, 2001, with its crescendo and climax, or the rotation of *Cheap 'n' Nasty*, 2000, culminating in the kiss of Tim and Sue's shadows, is like attending a live performance.

Like rock musicians, the persona of the artists is central to the content of the work. The art and the artistic characters of "Tim 'n' Sue" are inseparable. They are building on the "artist as art" tradition of Marcel Duchamp, Salvador Dalí, Andy Warhol, and Yves Klein. They are also helping to define a more contem-

porary tradition of artist as punk provocateur in the mold of Martin Kippenberger, with references to John Lydon, Suicide, and Siouxsie Sioux. With their matching black hair dye, their shrunken vintage American T-shirts, and their provocative behavior at art-world events, and through their interventions into the mainstream media, Noble & Webster's carefully constructed image is part of their artistic message.

Since no model existed of the type of artists who Noble & Webster aspired to be, they had to create their own. It involved escaping from their backgrounds and what was expected of them, but also embracing the essential Englishness of their roots. The daughter of an electrician and a part-time worker in a hosiery factory, Sue jokes that she was "born in the wrong place," a suburban neighborhood of Leicester. Her upbringing was, on the surface, as conventional as Tim's was unconventional, but some unusual circumstances contributed to her artistic formation. Sue's father Ray was an electrician who specialized in wiring electrical control panels. He was always striving to better his family's situation, constantly moving them into new homes in nicer neighborhoods as he tried to pull himself into the middle class. Incongruously for an electrician in Leicester, he was, and remains, an enthusiastic fan of Bob Dylan and Leonard Cohen. He now spends much of his leisure time corresponding with fellow members of Dylan and Cohen fan clubs and traveling to attend their concerts. The American-style ranch house that he was finally able to build to satisfy his aspirations for his family was named Hard Rain in homage to one of his favorite Dylan songs. The wrought-iron letters spelling out "Hard Rain" on a plaque beside the front door are echoed by the wrought-iron sign reading "Black Magic" at the entrance to Tim and Sue's London home and studio.

As a teenager, Sue spent some of her spare time helping her father wire cigarette vending machines, eliminating any sense of intimidation she might have felt for working with electrical and mechanical devices and giving her a skill that was to become part of the foundation of her later artwork. Her father took the family on a trip abroad each year, giving Sue an unusual worldliness for a girl from the suburbs of Leicester. It was rock music, however, that gave Sue the inspiration to lead a larger and more creative life. She remembers precisely buying her first record at age eleven, "Wuthering Heights" by Kate Bush; and at age twelve her first album, by The Specials. Sue recalls that she "spent much of her teenage years making sense of reality through music." At the age of sixteen, she went to London to see Siouxsie and the Banshees live for the first time and then spent the next few years touring England and Europe to "support the band." She began dyeing her hair black and dressing in black leather, and connecting with the local music scene that emerged in Leicester in the mid-1980s. Without any conventional female role models and without an awareness of any female artists, Siouxsie became Sue's role model. She especially appreciated that Siouxsie had no musical training and could not play an instrument when she was first asked to perform in a band. It was her attitude and her vision that was more important than training or technique. An image of Siouxsie is still tacked to the wall over Sue's desk in Noble & Webster's London studio.

The lack of creative guidance from her schoolteachers and from her family, and her lack of a sense of belonging began to have a dramatic impact on Sue. It led to severe bouts of depression and a complete sense of alienation from her school friends. Sue remembers withdrawing into her totally black

Ornament (in crisis), 1995. Single screen video, approx 19 minutes.

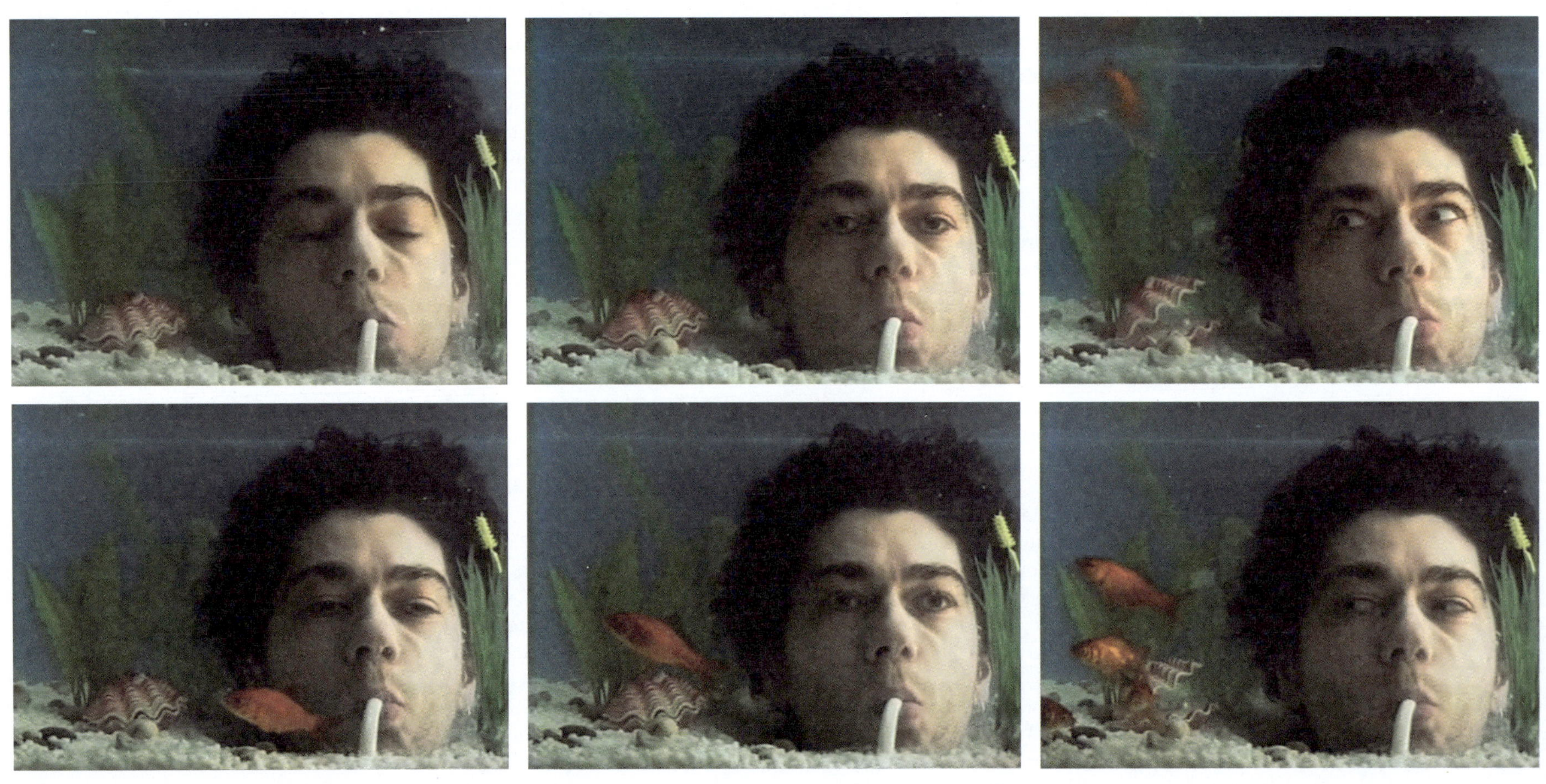

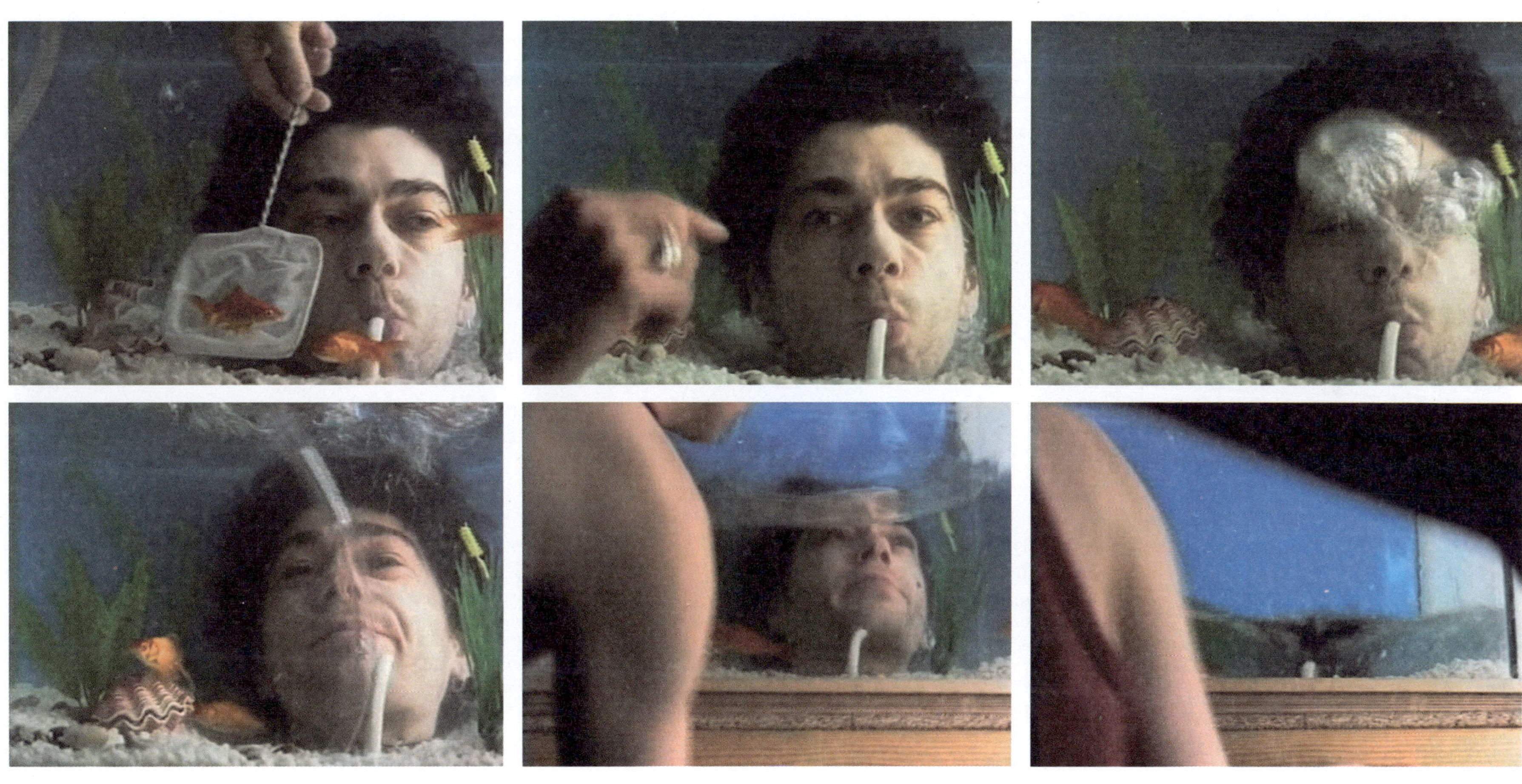

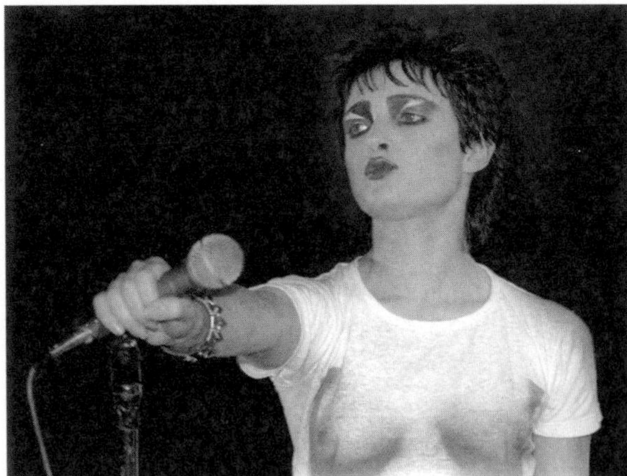
Siouxsie Sioux, 1976. Photograph by Ray Stevenson.

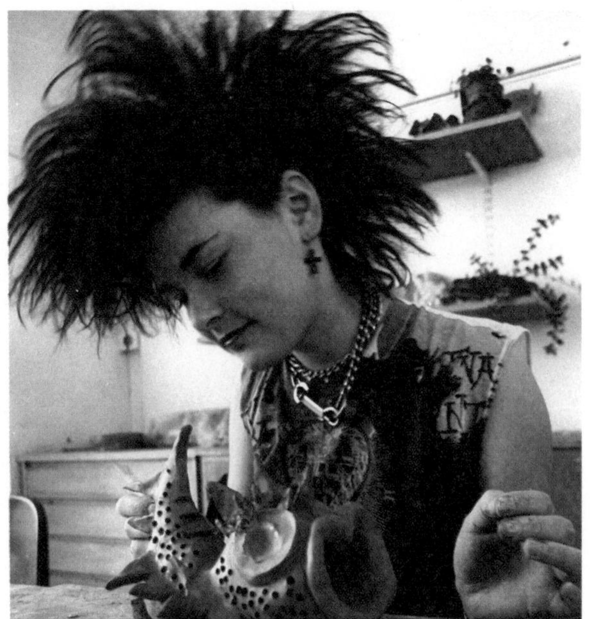
Sue during high school A-Level art class, 1984.

painted bedroom for long periods repeatedly listening to the Joy Division album "Unknown Pleasures." This withdrawal and subsequent depression drastically affected her mental and physical state, resulting in a series of psychiatric treatments that disrupted her schooling. Sue was eventually admitted into psychiatric care for two six-month periods during the early 1980s. During her spells in the hospital, Sue may have missed out on crucial academic work, but she always continued to draw. She would make caricature portraits of the nurses on the ward, which became quite in demand during her "residency."

Sue relates her struggle and her recovery from this period in her life to a quotation from W. H. Auden:

> The so-called traumatic experience is
> not an accident, but the opportunity
> for which the child has been patiently
> waiting—had it not occurred, it would
> have found another—in order that its
> life become a serious matter.

Although Sue was good at drawing and showed an aptitude for art, she was never taken to art museums or galleries and initially had no notion of fine art as a possible profession. Her interest in visual communication was channeled into a fascination with advertising. Sue would write away to advertising agencies to get copies of advertising posters, which she would hang in her room. At the age of sixteen, when she was ready to leave school and get a job like her elder sister, an art teacher encouraged her to stay in school, telling her that it was possible to take a degree course in fine art. After passing her A-level high school exams, Sue took an art foundation course at Leicester Polytechnic, where she first learned about the work of Warhol and Dalí. *My Life with Dalí* by Amanda Lear, was the first book she ever read outside of the school curriculum. At the age of nineteen, she traveled by herself to Barcelona via Paris to visit Dalí's birthplace and the Salvador Dalí Museum, giving an early indication of her approach to art.

Tim Noble grew up in a bohemian paradise, in a run-down, three-hundred-year-old cottage in a small village in Gloucestershire, where until his family and the family of another artist arrived, no outsider had lived for generations. The cottage was situated inside a large unkempt garden and surrounded by expansive fields and streams. Growing up, Tim had little contact with pop culture and spent most of his time playing in the woods, climbing trees, building hidden dens and damming streams. Encouraged by his parents and by the example of his older brother, he was often drawing and making things out of scrap materials. An astonishingly accomplished gouache drawing, made in the open air during a thunderstorm when Tim was in his mid-teens, still hangs in the cottage. It shows a figure and a dog walking through a violent landscape, preceded by their shadows.

For much of the winter, the cottage and garden were submerged in shadow. Tim became fascinated by the extreme contrast between the gray winter and the seductive colors of spring, when flowers overwhelmed the garden. This childhood experience recalls that of another sculptor obsessed by figure and shadow, Alberto Giacometti, whose home village in a Swiss mountain valley was also blanketed in shadow during the winter.

Tim's father, David, made meticulously rendered figurative sculptures that Tim describes as looking like "sad toys." David was disdainful of the art market, and believed that rather than selling art, teaching was the ethical way to make a living. It may be that his wariness of the art market had something to do with the sexually provocative and explicit quality of his work, which was criticized by feminists. He was also extremely painstaking in his modeling, taking years to make a single sculpture. An unfinished sculpture of cartoon-like animals remains hidden in the woods beside his garage studio. It looks like something that Jeff Koons might have made, only more extreme.

Contrasting with Tim's father's anti–art-market attitude and his painfully slow production was the example of their friend and neighbor, the sculptor Lynn Chadwick. Chadwick lived like a lord in an enormous mansion on acres of parkland where his sculptures were displayed. He had a son Tim's age whose electric go-kart and other extravagant toys contrasted with Tim's homemade go-kart fashioned from old baby carriage wheels. Chadwick's career was an example of how successful an artist could become by embracing the art market, and provided an alternative model to the Noble family's disregard for material reward.

Andy Warhol was never mentioned in the Noble home. Tim's early experience with art was connected to his immersion in nature. Tim would spend hours watching a bird or a wasp build a nest and was constantly constructing imaginary machines, developing his own intuitive sculptural language. He also observed his father in the studio, studying the human figure. When he was a teenager, his mother would take him to London where they visited the Tate Gallery. Two exhibitions stand out in his memory, the Francis Bacon and Jean Tinguely retrospectives. This unlikely combination of Bacon and Tinguely

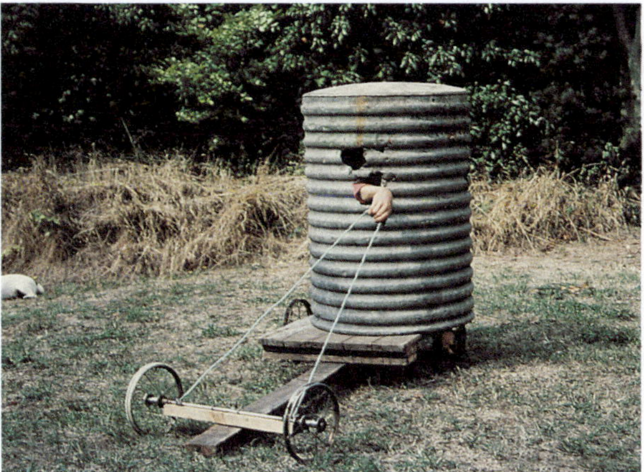

Tim's go-kart, Gloucestershire, early 1970s.

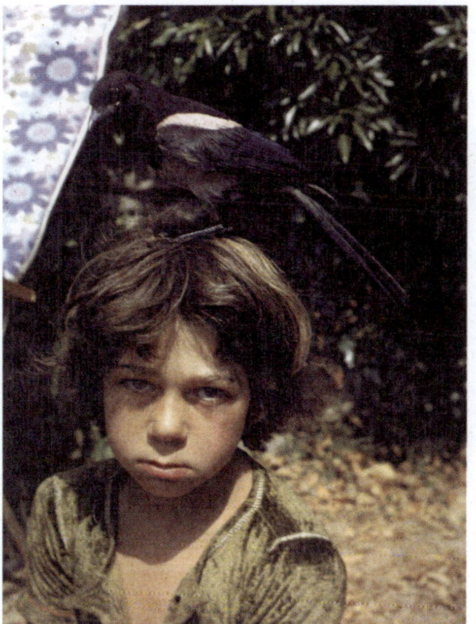

Tim with his pet magpie, Mortimer, Gloucestershire, early 1970s.

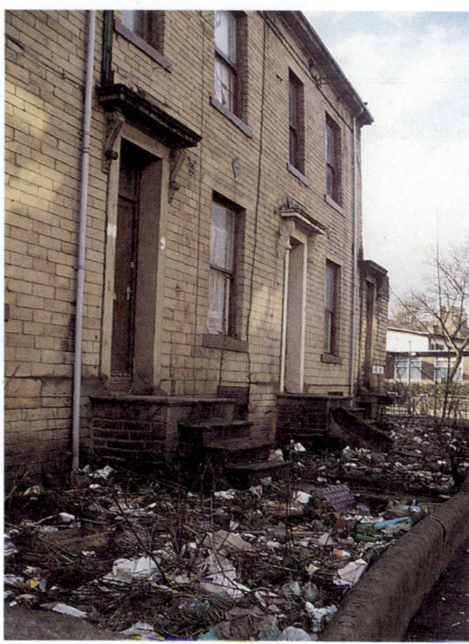

9 Claremont Terrace, Bradford. Tim and Sue's house, 1990–92.

expresses a lot about Tim's vision of sculpture, in which transgressive and expressive figuration is fused with exuberant junk assemblage. Chaos breeds gripping images.

Tim and Sue experienced two different sides of British culture in their childhood and teenage years, but their common interests brought them to the Fine Art Department at Nottingham Trent University in 1986. For Sue, Nottingham was only thirty miles from Leicester, and the largest nearby city along with Birmingham. She had only looked at art schools in the north of England and chose Nottingham because of its multidisciplinary course where, like Goldsmith's College in London, students were free to move through different media. Tim chose Nottingham because he did not want to go to art college in London like his mother, father, and elder brother had, and because a family friend who taught there encouraged him. Though their backgrounds diverged, Tim and Sue found that they had a lot in common when they met, particularly their tastes in music. They had similar record collections, and a mutual enthusiasm for ska and 2 Tone music. A performance by The Specials was the first live concert that either of them had attended.

Extracurricular activities quickly became more stimulating for Tim and Sue than the academic program. Nottingham was a great venue for bands, and Sue perfected a method of attending the afternoon sound check, making friends with the band's roadies, and getting into the concert for free. The local carnival with its tacky displays and flashing lights was another strong influence. Tim and Sue would spend time foraging for strange pieces of junk and scrap metal which they would then assemble into sculpture. Their basic approach to art and their artistic collaboration

were formed during their Nottingham years. A large part of their artistic direction was channeled through their experience of music. Both Tim and Sue had tried to form bands when they were in high school, and the attitude of rock performance continued to permeate their art aesthetic. The performances of Tim's band, The Skillers, seemed to predict his later-art-making process: he would pour junk and scrap metal onto the stage and beat on it.

During the summer breaks between the school years at Nottingham, Sue induced Tim to accompany her on two adventurous roadtrips, the first summer to Turkey, and the second to the United States. Rather than trooping through the usual Turkish tourist sites, Tim and Sue became fascinated by the scrapped American cars and trucks left behind by the U.S. military. Instead of visiting mosques and archaeological sites, they toured junkyards, foraging for discarded auto parts that they would be able to use in their sculpture, and eventually dragging sacks of this lovingly selected junk back to England.

The following summer they flew to New York, bought Greyhound bus tickets to Los Angeles, and began a cross-country tour of junkyards and shopping malls that stoked their continuing fascination for the residue of American popular culture. Almost all of their money was spent on the bus tickets so they slept in cardboard boxes in parking lots and ate from the copious quantities of leftover pizza and other fast food that they scavenged from the tables at shopping mall food courts. All the way across America, they continuously filled their duffel bags with choice pieces of scrap metal to lug back home.

One would have thought that after graduating from their degree course in 1989, Noble & Webster

would have moved to London like most enterprising young British artists. Instead, Tim and Sue decided to move to one of the bleakest and most depressed cities in England—Bradford, in West Yorkshire—where they spent three years immersing themselves in English vernacular culture. In a way it was a self-exile, like when Lenin retreated to Switzerland to gather his strength before returning to Russia to lead the revolution. The move to Bradford may also have been a result of Tim's reluctance to join the London art world that his parents had come out of, but disdained.

Bradford was once the world's wool capital, but had fallen into decline as the mills closed, throwing out of work the thousands of Pakistanis and Bangladeshis who had come to work in the mills. Much of the city's population was on the dole and the entire city seemed to have sunk into a psychological and economic depression. Most of the original English inhabitants had left and the city now had one of the largest Asian populations in Britain. In a city with row after row of deteriorating housing, Tim and Sue somehow chose to live on the most decrepit block in Bradford. They began making mechanical stage sets for the rave scene that was developing in the nearby city of Leeds, an interesting precedent for a work like *Toxic Schizophrenia* made eight years later in 1997, that has the presence to be installed on a stage behind a rock band. A number of these early commissions were inspired by car customization.

In 1990, Noble & Webster were offered a studio by the Henry Moore Foundation in Dean Clough in the nearby mill town of Halifax. They began making welded metal assemblage sculptures in addition to their commissioned work for clubs and local bands. A fascinating early sculpture remains on view in the

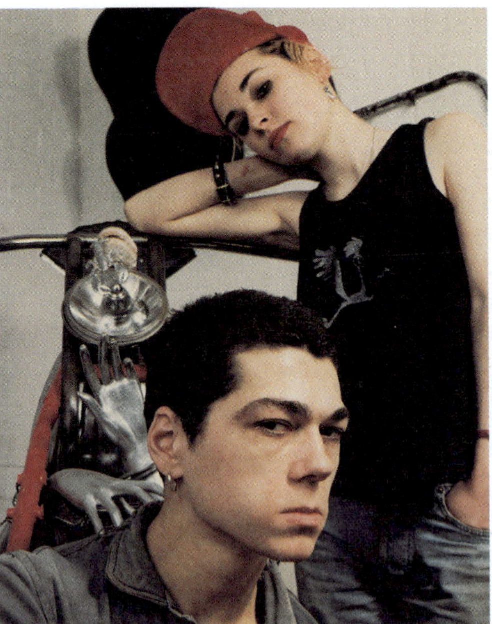

Tim and Sue at Nottingham Trent University, 1989.
Photograph by Tony Medley.

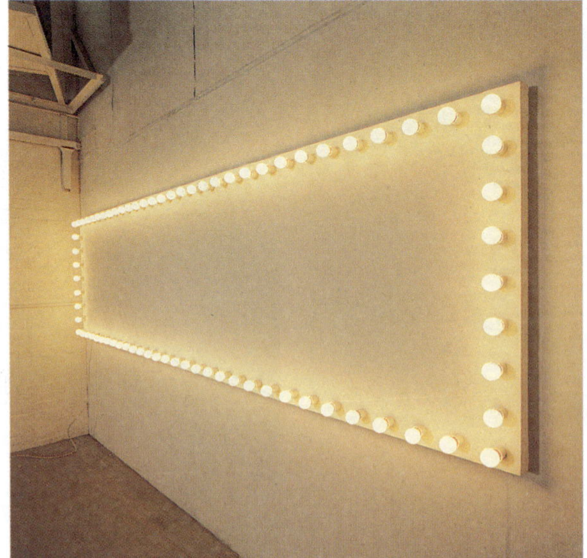

Flash Painting, 1993. 15 x 3 ft, 76 golf ball lights, canvas,
wooden frame, electronic light sequencer (chase effect).

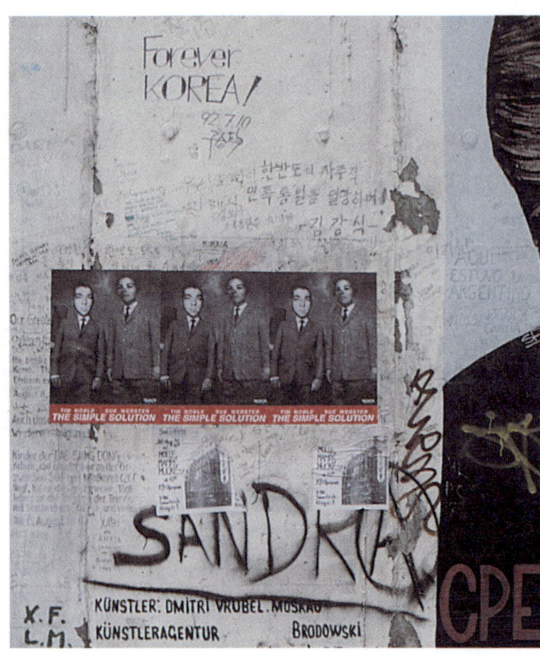

The Simple Solution, 1994. Poster montage, Berlin Wall.

Dean Clough galleries: a three-foot-high welded metal assemblage reminiscent of the late 1950s work of the American Richard Stankiewicz and an astonishing prediction of *The Crack, The Negative*, and other works in their 2004 *Modern Art Is Dead* series. The work is installed on a small pedestal inscribed with the name of the artists, "The Junkies." Luckily, it was not a name that stuck, although it was a good reflection of the artists' outlaw attitude and their obsession with junk and scrap metal.

Bradford was the home of Peter Sutcliffe, the Yorkshire Ripper, and Tim and Sue's neighborhood was infused with the creepiness of his murderous prowling. A particularly frightening looking lane near their flat was fenced off, perhaps in deference to a victim, or to deter imitators. Deliberately keeping themselves apart from the pretentiousness of art establishment, Tim and Sue absorbed what Tim described as the "rubbish landscape" of Bradford. They understood that the inspiration for the work that they wanted to make was more likely to come from the seedy slums of Bradford and the gritty rock clubs in Leeds than from the London galleries.

After three years in Bradford, Noble & Webster had already established many aspects of their art strategy and their collaborative process. There was their rock-band-like embrace of theatricality and spectacle and their effort to push chaos into virtuosity; their fascination with junk and their ability to transform it into art through assemblage; their delight in light effects; their inspiration in advertising and vernacular culture; and their genderless approach to making art. Like a good band with male and female leaders, the music, and in their case, the art, was neither masculine nor feminine. What was still not fully conceived was their insight about how to make their personas central to their art. That would come later.

By 1992, Noble & Webster had become aware of a new group of London artists with an entrepreneurial attitude to presenting their work. Damien Hirst and other members of this generation did not wait for established galleries and curators to endorse their work but produced their own exhibitions and opened their own spaces. Tim and Sue decided that it was time to move to London and both applied for the master's degree program in sculpture at the Royal College of Art, which would give them a structure to concentrate on their work. Tim was accepted into the program, but Sue was not. They turned Sue's rejection into an advantage, conceiving Tim's enrollment as a two-for-one special. Tim gave Sue his security code and she was able to take advantage of the facilities, learning how to make computer graphics and collaborating with Tim on his work. Most fellow students assumed that Sue was also enrolled.

Noble & Webster's career as London artists began with a blaze of publicity and scandal around Tim's first-year interim exhibition in 1993. Reacting to a friend's comment about Tim's prospects at the Royal College of Art—"the shit and the cream always rise to the top"—he constructed a sculpture to demonstrate the phenomenon. A capsule of his excrement, combined with Sue's, was floated in a vitrine filled with water, and a capsule of cream floated in another. The vitrines were cordoned off by an electric fence. The piece was intended to be shown alongside a gigantic fabricated metal sculpture of the word "HYPE!" rotating on a circular base, but the *HYPE!*, 1993, sculpture was not completed in time for the show. Sue drew on her brief experience in the music business and her flair for advertising to organize a

publicity campaign, conceiving of the hype as part of the art. She tipped off the newspapers and "the shit hit the fan." A major story appeared in *The Independent*, complete with a large photograph of Tim pissing on the main entrance door to the Royal College of Art and a headline reading "STUDENT TO DEFECATE IN THE NAME OF ART." The reporter, Dalya Alberge, commented, "critics will feel that art has once again reached the bowels of degeneracy."

Tim was almost thrown out of the Royal College. The faculty was upset because Tim had upstaged the graduating second-year students, in addition to provoking critics of the liberal art-school curriculum. But by publicly pissing on the door to the Royal College, Tim had marked his territory. Noble & Webster had made their presence known in the London art world. The piece itself was juvenile, reflecting the influence of Hirst's floating shark, Jeff Koons's *Total Equilibrium Tank* and the work of Piero Manzoni. It remains an important milestone for Noble & Webster, however, as the first time that they achieved public recognition as artists.

HYPE! was shown later in 1993 with a simple but brilliant work called *Flash Painting* in a warehouse exhibition on Brick Lane that Tim and Sue organized with other students, including Chris Ofili. *Flash Painting* is a 3 x 15 ft. white canvas with a border of white sequenced lights with a chase effect. It placed minimalism within the pop art vernacular, a union that Noble & Webster would eventually develop and it was a step towards their mature light sculptures, which appeared three years later. Tim and Sue created another artwork in the form of a publicity campaign with *The Simple Solution*, 1994, a Dadaistic poster with their heads pasted onto the bodies of Gilbert & George. The posters were

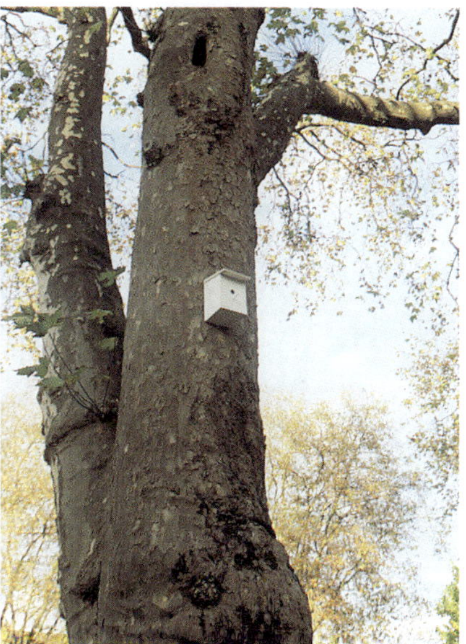

Abusive Crow, 1995. Birdbox, looped audio tape.

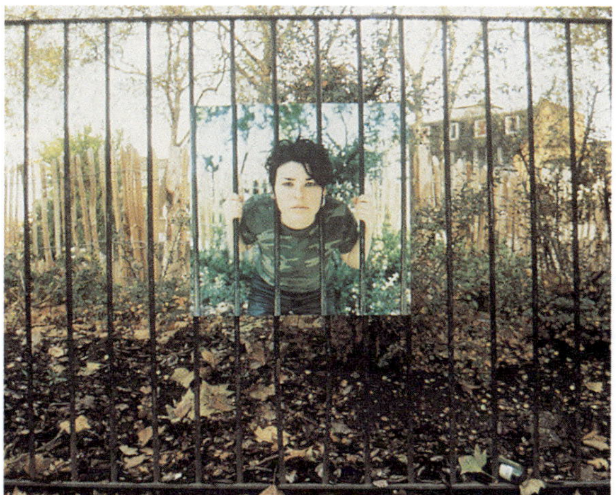

(Untitled) Head In Bars, 1995. Photographic installation.

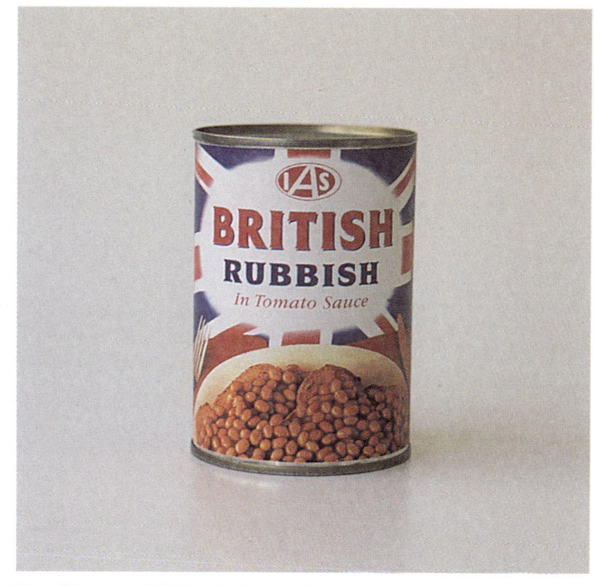

Tin of beans, exhibition invitation for *British Rubbish*, 1996.

fly-posted across London in 1994 and later that year in New York during a school trip. It is unclear what "the simple solution" was. Perhaps it was a solution to the question of how Noble & Webster, who had already been working together as students and independent artists for eight years, could model their continuing collaboration.

The previous months before his final year show, Tim became increasingly frustrated with the idea of having to present a "ground hugging" sculpture and needed to find a new angle on the situation. As the sculpture department then was a huge warehouse space, Tim did what he had done as a child to gain a new perspective on things, only this time instead of climbing to the top of the nearest tree he climbed into the warehouse rafters to discover a huge undiluted space he could call his own.

This revelation resulted in Tim's Royal College graduation exhibition in 1994, which included an accomplished video performance work, *Knocking*, 1995, and which was both provocative and poignant. A video of Tim with his face in the monitor, knocking insistently on the glass, was installed in a skylight above the exhibition gallery. An audio track filled the gallery with the knocking sound. The work affirmed Tim's image as an outsider and a provocateur, trying to get inside the art dialogue, but still keeping his distance. The artist is central to the art, is a theme that would continue to be developed. As in many of the subsequent works, the image was developed out of conceptual performance. The gallerist Nicholas Logsdail showed an interest in Tim's early conceptual video works and in 1995 exhibited *Knocking* in one of his summer group shows and *Ornament (in crisis)* in another.

London in the early 1990s was one of those rare situations when a surge of artistic energy occurs in a city where cheap live/work spaces are available in a concentrated neighborhood. A vibrant artistic community was developing in the East End of London. Tim and Sue met the young art impresario Joshua Compston and participated in his *The Fête Worse Than Death* event in Hoxton Square in 1994, a mock village fair in which artists set up stalls. During the *Fête*, they met a number of other young artists who were finding inexpensive live/work spaces in the abandoned factories and storefronts of Shoreditch. They decided to look for a place in the neighborhood themselves, and the following Monday they found an empty, small three-story commercial building on 20 Rivington Street in the heart of the burgeoning Hoxton Square artist district. It took them a while to negotiate the lease but six months later, in early 1995, they were installed in the space that would become not only their first London studio, but also their first exhibition space. Shortly after moving in, Tim decided to make the video performance piece *Ornament*, later *Ornament (in crisis)*, which after the traumatic experience of its realization, became the first official Noble & Webster work.

Noble & Webster continued developing performance sculpture and both contributed works to another Joshua Compston project, *The Hanging Picnic*, in Hoxton Square in 1995. Tim showed *Abusive Crow*, a sound sculpture in which the artist identifies with the abusive pet crow he kept as a child. Tim asked a musician to help him to distort his voice so that he sounded like a crow squawking obscenities. A twenty-four-hour tape loop of Tim's squawking emanated from speakers in bird boxes placed in the trees. The sound was subliminal, like a drunk muttering to himself on a park bench, but not surprisingly,

someone was so annoyed by the noise that they ripped the wires out. Sue also showed a work with the "outsider trying to get in" message of *Knocking*. *(Untitled) Head in Bars*, 1995, was a photograph of her pushing her head through a pair of iron bars in a fence. The bars of the iron fence that Sue pried apart to create the illusion are still visible in front of White Cube. During *The Hanging Picnic*, Tim and Sue met the curator and future gallerist Max Wigram who asked them curate a show for his Independent Art Space in 1996.

The program of the Independent Art Space was to ask artists and curators to organize exhibitions and Wigram invited Noble & Webster to curate an exhibition of other artists' work. Noble & Webster developed a thematic show called *British Rubbish* and asked a number of fellow artists to participate. While organizing the show, their frustration over not yet having a show of their own work prompted them to change direction and make *British Rubbish* a show of their own art. They telephoned all of the invited artists to disinvite them. Sue recalled that, not surprisingly, the uninvited artists were "quite upset."

Tim was thinking about making more complex flashing light sculptures and Sue was beginning to conceptualize a sculpture of themselves as a pair of apes. These concepts needed more time to develop, so for the show they instead exhibited a group of fascinating transitional works, four small animatronic figures inspired by a mechanical figure they had seen in the window of a cobbler's shop, depicting a miniature cobbler hammering the heel of a shoe. Tim and Sue were inspired to make a set of animatronic figures that, rather than making shoes, were making art. They tracked down the manufacturer of the miniature cobbler and commissioned him to make

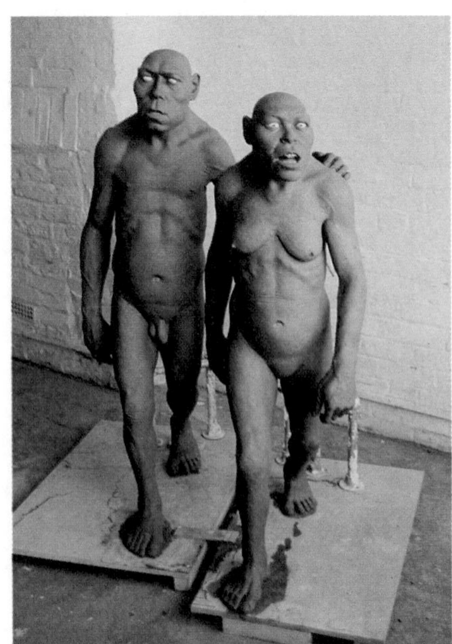

The New Barbarians (work in progress), 1997–99
Rivington Street Studio, London.

the bodies, while they made the mechanisms and sculpted the faces to resemble unsettling combinations of their own. One figure was constantly banging a nail with a hammer, another was sawing, another was painting, and another was defecating. The figures looked like a miniature gang of prison inmates. The show did not register in a big way with the art public, but it was a crucial experience in the development of Noble & Webster's work.

One result of *British Rubbish* was that Wigram invited Noble & Webster to participate in *Fool's Rain*, an exhibition he curated for the ICA in 1996. In *Fool's Rain*, Noble & Webster showed their first mature work, *Excessive Sensual Indulgence*, 1996. It was an astonishing debut. It is the work they consider their first light sculpture, a pop fountain with the impression of flowing water made from carnival lights flashing in a chasing effect. The work confronts the viewer with a logo-like directness, yet it is in constant motion. It draws the eye in like a bonfire. It is a sculpture with its own built-in aura. It recalls the kind of tacky fountain that one might find installed at the entrance to former mob wife Victoria Gotti's mansion, but it also has an iconic symmetry like an elegant minimal sculpture. It is excessive and minimal at the same time, over-the-top and rigorously systemic. It is also enormously seductive, brimming with an implication of sexual excitement. The flow of the streams of light is like a nonstop ejaculation.

Later that year, Noble & Webster were among ten artists commissioned by a public art organization to make works to be placed outdoors above bus-stop shelters in central London. For this project, they created *Forever*, 1996, their second iconic light sculpture. The word "Forever" is spelled out in a nostalgic cursive script reminiscent of the souvenir T-shirts

that one used to be able to buy at dilapidated American tourist attractions. The letters are animated with flashing white fairground lights. The work dazzles with cheap effects, but is also a meditation on the abstraction of the word, building on the tradition of the word paintings of Jasper Johns and Ed Ruscha. It is a study of both the emotional connotations of a word and of how its meaning can be emptied into an abstract form. The work plays on the romantic notion that love is forever and art is forever, even though it is constructed from tacky carnival lights. *Forever* is so seductive that it induced a collector who had never heard of Noble & Webster to bid $150,000 for the work at a New York auction in 2002. The sculpture had originally sold for £3,000.

The following year, 1997, was a period of remarkable progress and innovation in Noble & Webster's work. It was the year of their first major solo exhibition and the development of their signature imagery, a year in which they would establish some of the major relationships that would shape their career, as well as a year of great frustration. Despite the development and increasing public recognition of their work, they had no gallery representation and were unable to sell. They still had to survive through odd jobs and occasional window display work for HYPER HYPER, a clothing store on Kensington High Street. They took a job with Gilbert & George, making the frames for their *Fundamental Pictures*, which were to be shown in New York. This enabled them to begin work on the sculpture of themselves as a pair of apes that they had been developing for several years.

Tim and Sue flew to New York to study the dioramas of apes and other human predecessors at the Museum of Natural History. They were fascinated by the famous sculptural tableau of two australopithecines,

representing the first indication of prehumans forming social relations, and they were inspired to make a reconstruction using their own facial features. While in New York they visited the galleries and took a particular interest in the program and atmosphere of Deitch Projects. At a post-opening party, they met Stuart Shave, a young curator also visiting from London, who was equally frustrated by the difficulty of financing the realization of his dreams.

Back in London, they commissioned a sculptor from Madame Tussauds to help them model their life-size sculpture of themselves as australopithecines. Each morning they experienced the irony of admitting the sculptor from Tussauds into their studio as they left for their job at Gilbert & George's on Fournier Street. The fabrication of *The New Barbarians*, required additional resources, and they had to sell their beloved VW camper van to help finance the work. It was a challenging project and it would be an additional two years until the work was ready to be shown.

Meanwhile, other projects were being developed in the studio. Before leaving for New York, they had finished their most elaborate early light sculpture, *Toxic Schizophrenia*, 1997. The title is taken from a passage in Tom Wolfe's *The Kandy-Kolored Tangerine-Flake Streamline Baby* in which the author describes "the marvelous impact Las Vegas has on the senses." The work is a monument to trash romance and to the artists' enthusiasm for anti-culture. It is like a giant biker tattoo, a knife through the heart, pulsating and bleeding with its candy-colored carnival lights. Romance and pain are experienced simultaneously. It is built to be an icon, easily seen from a distance and large enough to be installed behind the stage in a rock arena. It *has* become an

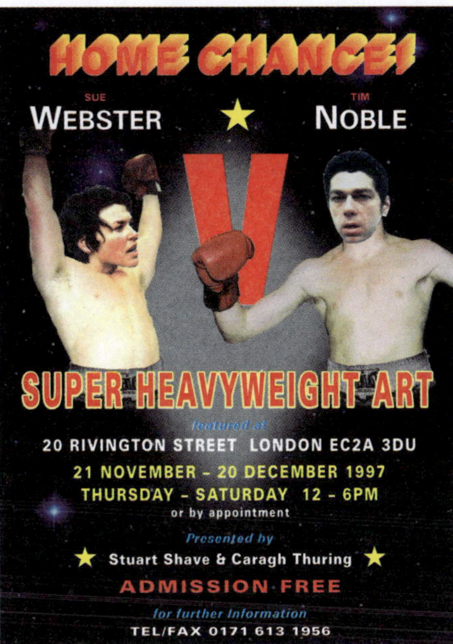

Home Chance, 1997. Exhibition poster.

icon, in fact, through the hundreds of T-shirts with its image emblazoned on the front, sold at the Saatchi Gallery. It can be displayed in an intimate space, but it is more of a public than a private work. It does not need a white cube gallery to function as art. It is also able to function as mass communication. The construction of the work drew on Sue's experience helping her father wire up the control panels of cigarette vending machines. The imagery reflects Tim and Sue's fascination with the visual language of rock and biker culture. The sequencing of the lights makes an exciting show, an example of how Tim and Sue have appropriated the spectacle of the rock show into sculpture.

The other work being developed in the studio involved a return to the junk assemblage sculpture that they made in Dean Clough, outside of Bradford, several years before. This time, instead of using the classic 1950s sculptor's materials of scrap metal and machine parts, they were experimenting with the assemblage of personal items and household rubbish. While shining a spotlight onto one of their gestating forms, they got an insight that would lead to the development of their best-known work. They were fascinated by the shadow formed on the wall by the light shined at their sculptural assemblage. With the kind of conceptual leap that can only be achieved through the trial and error of studio practice, they began sculpting the mounds of trash so that their own silhouettes could be read in the shadows. The result was their first shadow sculpture, *Miss Understood & Mr Meanor*, 1997.

Miss Understood & Mr Meanor is an example of how one can become strangely fascinated with something horrible. The silhouettes formed by lights shining on the oddly shaped clumps of trash are exact likenesses of Tim and Sue, astonishing, but chilling, as they are portrayed dead, rather than alive. Their heads have been severed, and impaled on stakes like trophies displayed on the battlefield after a brutal massacre. The severe black silhouettes of the death heads contrast with the cacophonous sculptural assemblage of discarded personal effects. The assembled objects range from broken sunglasses and overused toothbrushes to old badges for rock bands like Gay Bikers on Acid, items that had been kept in drawers and boxes around the studio because they embodied too much personal history to be thrown away. A magical, almost alchemical transformation has taken place. One would like to say that waste has been turned into life. Actually it has been transformed into death. Noble & Webster's first shadow sculpture depicts them committing sculptural suicide.

The violent end portrayed by *Miss Understood & Mr Meanor* was strangely prophetic as the sculpture was destroyed in the 2004 Momart art warehouse fire along with a number of other well-known works from the Saatchi Collection. It now exists only as a memory or as a photographic reproduction. The work brought together all the directions that Noble & Webster had been pursuing and fused them into a single structure: light sculpture, assemblage, mining the detritus of pop outlaw culture, and making the artist central to the art. *Miss Understood & Mr Meanor* also took the artists toward the realization of one of the most avidly pursued artistic goals in modern and contemporary art, the fusion of representation and abstraction. This is a pursuit that had consumed Jackson Pollock, Willem de Kooning, and Bacon. Through their shadow sculpture, Noble & Webster had found a new way to achieve this combination of the abstract and the representational. Frustrated by their lack of gallery representation,

but excited by the new work that they had developed, Noble & Webster decided to take the presentation of their art into their own hands. They had reconnected in London with Shave, the visionary young gallerist who did not yet have a gallery, and with him they decided to mount an exhibition in their own Rivington Street studio. Titled *Home Chance*, the exhibition was promoted like a boxing match with a poster featuring Tim and Sue's heads grafted onto the bodies of opposing pugilists. It was inspired by the famous Basquiat vs. Warhol poster for gallerist Tony Shafrazi's 1985 exhibition of their collaborative paintings. It was another example of Sue incorporating her fascination with the communicative power of advertising into the structure of their art.

Home Chance opened on November 21, 1997, and took up all three floors of the Rivington Street building. Three works were presented, one on each floor: *Toxic Schizophrenia*, *Excessive Sensual Indulgence*, and *Miss Understood & Mr Meanor*. The almost completed sculpture of Tim and Sue as prehuman australopithecines was covered up and hidden in the bedroom. *The New Barbarians*, 1997–99, would be kept under wraps until the right situation materialized two years later.

The exhibition drew a large audience and critical acclaim. A memorable moment for Noble & Webster was when Charles Saatchi came to visit and left a taxi waiting outside, something that astonished the frugal artists. They peeked through a hole in the wall as Saatchi viewed the works. After leaving, he telephoned Sue from the taxi to buy *Toxic Schizophrenia* and *Miss Understood & Mr Meanor*. It was Tim and Sue's first sale to a well-known collector.

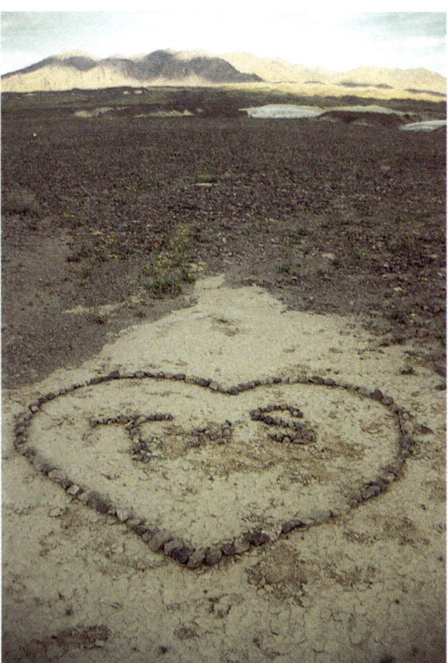

(Untitled) Stone Formation, Death Valley, Nevada, 1998.
Dimensions variable.

Noble & Webster celebrated their first important solo exhibition and their first important sales by making a pilgrimage to Las Vegas, the source of much of their artistic inspiration. They were ecstatic to have the opportunity to study the city's vulgar illuminated signs the way other artists might study paintings in a museum. They also took a side trip to Death Valley where they were inspired to create a site-specific stone sculpture that sends up the ponderousness of some of the artists of the Earthworks generation. They outlined a stone heart on the desert floor with the initials "T 'n' S" in the center, like a Richard Long work interpreted in the way teenagers carve their initials in a tree.

On their return to London, in early 1998, Noble & Webster began a remarkable sculpture that expanded on the innovations of *Miss Understood & Mr Meanor.* For six months, the empty packaging of everything that the artists ate, drank, smoked, or otherwise consumed was dumped into a pile on the studio floor. The artists' concept was to construct a work out of the remains of all the products that they needed to survive during the work's creation. They began sculpting a new kind of self-portrait out of this mound of discarded packages of fish fingers, tins of baked beans, tubs of peanut butter, boxes of black hair dye, and everything else they used for grooming, nourishment, entertainment, and the fabrication of the work. Appropriately, the work was titled *Dirty White Trash (with Gulls)*, 1998, reflecting both its actual composition and the artists' identification with the denizens of the English underclass.

For the artists' friends and art-world associates who were invited to see the finished work in the studio, it was at first a disconcerting and confounding experience. Noble & Webster were not yet identified with

shadow sculpture and viewers did not arrive expecting to see the silhouette that completed the experience of the work. It was so startling to see this ripe pile of trash on the studio floor that many visitors remained transfixed, neglecting to look at the wall behind. Some never even looked up to see the perfect silhouette of Tim and Sue in shadow, relaxing on the garbage pile, that was formed by the light shining onto the trash. They left confused, thinking that they had just been invited to view a mound of household and studio garbage.

For those who were able to transcend their initial shock and slowly begin to perceive the pile of trash in its spatial environment, the silhouette of the artists that finally popped into focus was an astonishing revelation. Hovering above the rubbish was a realistic shadow of Tim and Sue, leaning against each other back to back, in a pose of relaxation and satisfaction. This flawless image was created by meticulously sculpting the mound of garbage to create an imperceptible outline that resulted in the artists' silhouette when light was shined onto it. Looking at the disorderly pile, no one would have imagined that its outline would have formed this perfect likeness. The work has a formidable conceptual logic and a fascinating engagement with the dialogue of modern and postmodern art, but one's first response was not intellectual; it was an almost primitive sense of awe. *Dirty White Trash (with Gulls)* is one of the rare works of art that creates an aura of magic.

The silhouette of Tim and Sue has the neoclassical perfection of a Canova sculpture, as well as the slightly hackneyed quality of a Kappa clothing logo. Tim is portrayed smoking a cigarette, Sue savoring a glass of wine. It is the pose of artists who are

pleased with the successful completion of a challenging work, not the tortured images of *Miss Understood & Mr Meanor.* The work captures the artists in a moment of contentment. After more than ten years at the margins of the art world, they had finally emerged at the center and created an amazing work of art that is uniquely their own, encompassing the entire range of their artistic influences and experiences.

Dirty White Trash (with Gulls) is a confluence of beauty and filth, form and anti-form. It is a work of art made out of the process of its own conception, an embodiment of formalist logic. At the same time, it is a negation of everything that formalism stands for. In a send-up of the formalist ethos, the work emphasizes everything that formalism excises. The artist is at the center of the work. It is deliberately entertaining, and revels in its own theatricality.

Despite its formalist logic, *Dirty White Trash (with Gulls)* also recalls the radical anti-form attitude of the toughest scatter art and Alan Suicide's punk sculptures of random piles of electronic debris. It is resolutely urban, but it is also inspired by the experience of nature. The work is constructed like the bird's nests that Tim spent hours studying as a child in the Gloucestershire countryside.

Dirty White Trash (with Gulls) is also an example of artistic alchemy. As alchemists claimed to turn humble materials into gold, Tim and Sue have transformed rubbish into art. In an additional twist, they have transformed the pile of inanimate refuse into a representation of life with their "real" shadows hovering above it. The work has a theatrical magic, but it also has a conceptual magic in the tradition of Duchamp, who delighted in the mixture of art and alchemy.

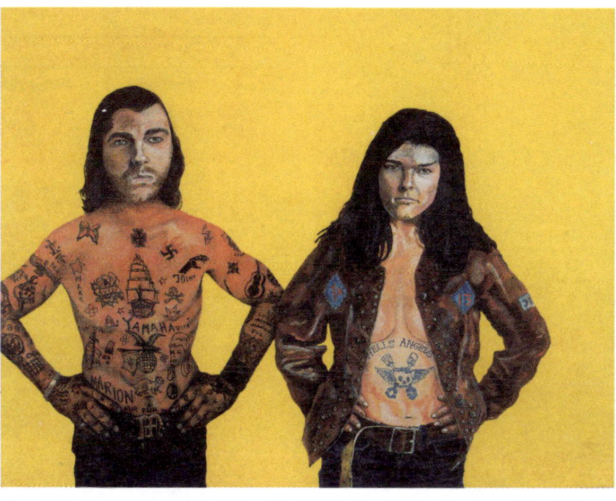

Don't Fuck with the Blackheads, 1998. Acrylic on canvas. 76 x 61 cm.

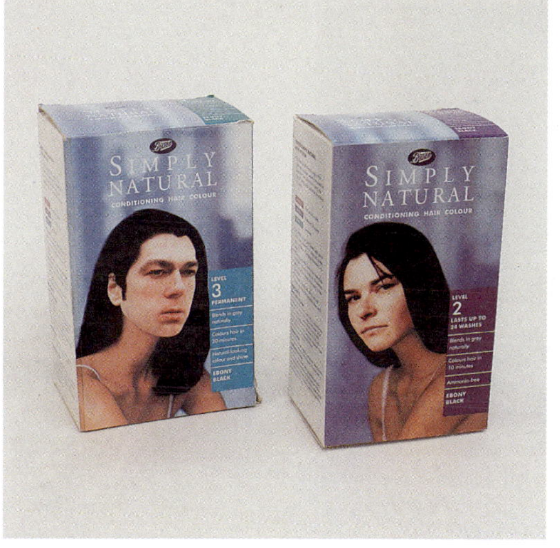

Simply Natural, 1999. Photographic montage on hair-dye boxes. Each box: 9 x 6 x 14.5 cm.

In 1913, when he supposedly abandoned oil painting and began working on his readymades, Duchamp made the following notes:

> after the bride . . .
> make a picture. of *shadows cast*
> —the *execution* of the picture by
> means of luminous sources.

Like Duchamp, Noble & Webster had embarked on an artistic project that combined performance, painting, sculpture, film, and photography. With works based on the shadow, they created "a double structure that belongs to two worlds at the same time: that of fiction and that of reality."

A friend had given Noble & Webster a copy of a fascinating book by Victor I. Stoichita, *A Short History of the Shadow*, published in 1997, the same year as the artists' first shadow sculptures. The quotation cited above comes from the book, which traces the shadow through art history from cave paintings through Warhol. Stoichita's book begins with a quotation from Pliny: "All agree that [painting] began with tracing an outline around a man's shadow." The book follows the history of representation of reality through the representation of the shadow in art. Without knowing about each other's work, Stoichita and Noble & Webster had in their own way been studying the metaphysics of the shadow in art, explaining how an artist can use the shadow to make "the absent become present."

Dirty White Trash (with Gulls) was shown at Shave and his partner Detmar Blow's new gallery Modern Art in November 1998, along with a three-dimensional flashing neon sign spelling out "WOW," for "walk on water." The neon work also must have reflected the artists' mood. With the exhibition of *Dirty White Trash (with Gulls)* they allowed themselves a rare moment of elation. Despite the work's impact on the visitors to the exhibition, it did not sell and was returned to the studio where it remained for the following year. The work began to acquire a mystique as Shave tirelessly brought a succession of interesting people to see it.

Another work that Noble & Webster created in 1998, *Don't Fuck with the Blackheads*, marked a further sharpening of the Tim 'n' Sue persona. They painted themselves as a biker and a biker chick, covered in tattoos. Tim is the cool one; Sue is the tough one. The work reflects their identification with this Anglo-American breed of biker/rocker outlaw but also references artists like Richard Prince and Ashley Bickerton who had found inspiration in trash culture. Bickerton had also painted a self-portrait as an outlaw biker. The work is an example of Noble & Webster's interest in "artist as art," the creation of an artistic persona that is a variation of living sculpture. The artists' presence becomes a continuous presentation of their art.

Their 1999 work *Simply Natural* also documents the refinement of their artistic persona. It is a recreation of the packaging for the Simply Natural black hair dye that the artists buy from Boots the Chemist, with their own faces substituted for those of the models. Tim and Sue had begun dyeing their hair the same shade of black in 1997, always using the same cheap Simply Natural hair dye from Boots. The double dose of dyed black hair was an essential step in the construction of the Tim 'n' Sue persona. Their tough East End punk rocker appearance is both a kind of homage and a send-up of Gilbert & George. Tim and Sue's approach is unpretentious and very different from Gilbert & George's studied historicism. Their creation of the Tim 'n' Sue identity is a very contemporary personality construct. It is anti-Freudian, not a product of self-discovery, but the adoption and perfection of an image.

Noble & Webster continued to create light sculptures along with the rubbish sculptures and the persona works and in 1998 they developed one of their most evocative flashing light sculptures, *The Sweet Smell of Excess*. The title reflects both their facility with words and their enchantment with the culture of Las Vegas and Hollywood. The work was inspired by the Lucozade factory sign that became a landmark on the M4 motorway from Heathrow to London. In the Noble & Webster version, the Lucozade has been stylishly transformed into a bottle of champagne. The movement of the lights combines the illusion of pleasure with the evanescence of champagne. The flow of liquid is rendered in sensuous light. The work combines the exuberance of Pop art with the impact of minimalist light sculpture. It also creates a sense of glamorous drunkenness, evoking the feeling of elation prior to inebriation.

During the late 1990s, Noble & Webster were still developing the public side of their artistic persona. Rather than choosing one artistic style and refining it, as is generally expected of artists who are serious about a career, they deliberately worked in several artistic modes simultaneously. They also challenged the conventional career path by working as a couple, a strategy that now seems more common, but was still very rare at the time, with only a few precedents. Their audience had to absorb a more complex definition of Noble & Webster as artists: they were at the same time light sculptors, trash sculptors, figurative sculptures, painters, advertising artists,

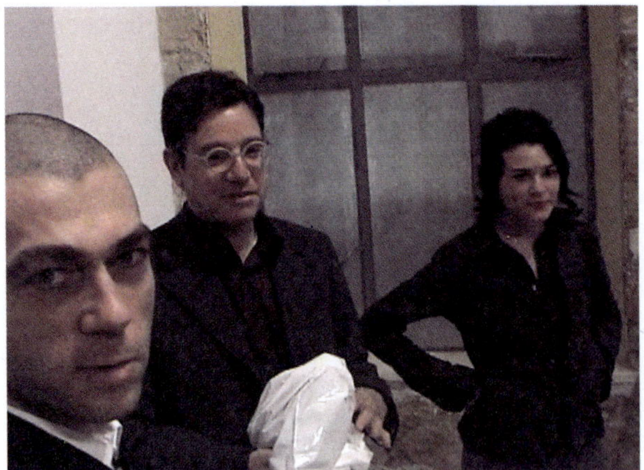

Tim Noble, Jeffrey Deitch, and Sue Webster, Cyprus, 2001. Attending the opening of *Shortcuts*, works from the Dakis Joannou collection, Nicosia Municipal Arts Centre, Cyprus. Photograph by Christian Scheidemann.

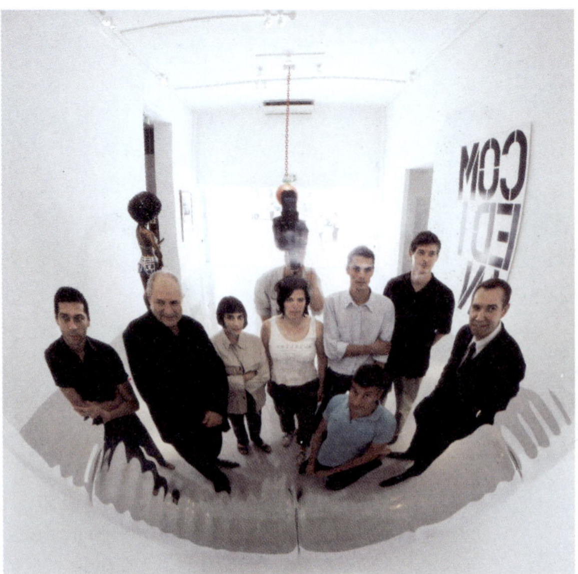

Artists and curators of *Monument to Now*, Athens, June 2004. Photographed in the reflection of Jeff Koons's *Moon*; (left to right): Tim Noble, Dakis Joannou, Nancy Spector, Sue Webster, Massimiliano Gioni, Dan Cameron, Jeff Koons, Maurizio Cattelan (sitting). Photograph by Todd Eberle.

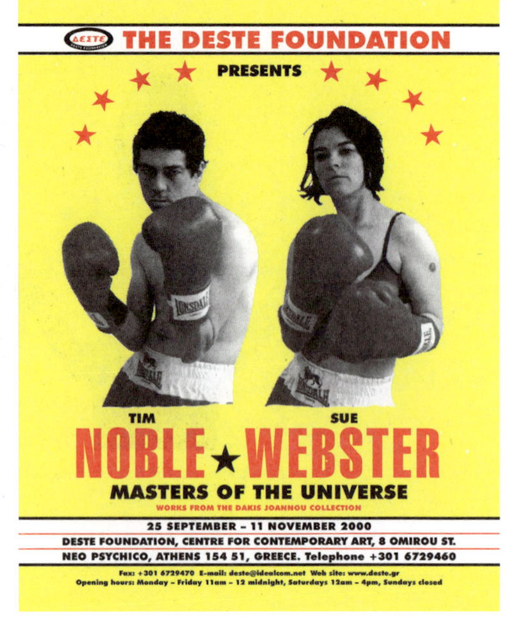

The DESTE Foundation presents *Masters of the Universe*, 2000. Poster invitation. 42 x 60 cm.

and performance artists. In addition they were life artists, living their art.

In February 1999, after three years in the making, Noble & Webster were finally able to show *The New Barbarians*, the astonishing sculpture of themselves as proto-human australopithecines inspired by the famous diorama in New York's Museum of Natural History. The work was shown in a solo exhibition at the Chisenhale Gallery in London, a publicly supported exhibition space. The slightly-smaller-than-life-size work was installed at the far end of the gallery inside a curved white cove, modeled on the rounded rooms found in high-end photo studios. The installation in this cornerless cove was remarkably dramatic, giving the illusion of the figures in the distance, walking the earth in isolation.

The figures in *The New Barbarians* could be either the first humans or the last, cave people or the survivors of a nuclear holocaust. They are hairless, either not yet fully human or radiation damaged. They are either pre-evolved, or devolved. The figures are together as a couple, but alone against the world. They are isolated, yet they are a social unit, perhaps a metaphor for the way Tim and Sue saw themselves as artists striving to put forward their vision in a world that was not yet prepared to accept them. The facial features and expressions of Tim and Sue are shockingly realistic, but faithful to the model in the Museum of Natural History. It is the anti-heroic image of the artist, especially notable for the figures' ape-like lope. The sculpture has a self-deprecating humor to it, but it is also remarkably poignant. Everyone can identify with the figures' essential human (or prehuman or posthuman) struggle.

The installation of *The New Barbarians* is a performance as well as a sculpture. It is sculpture as frozen theater. The placement of the two figures in the distance, at the end of the cove, is not just an installation; it is an inherent part of the structure of the work. The viewer's perception of the figures in their deep isolation is an essential part of the experience and the meaning of the work. The struggle to produce *The New Barbarians* was itself almost a conceptual performance piece. Tim and Sue had to finance the fabrication of the sculpture by making frames for Gilbert & George. As described above, a low point in their career was when they admitted their sculpture fabricator each morning to their Rivington Street studio as they left for their jobs with Gilbert & George.

A year later, Tim and Sue made another version of the work, *Masters of the Universe*, 1998–2000, that used the same sculptural model but this time covered with hair. This second version is more "first humans" than "last humans," more primitive in its attitude. The figures are like disaffected youth, outcasts roaming the earth. They stand for the artist as outsider, as a rebel against polite society. The figures' ape-like posture is actually frighteningly close to that of many of the people whom one might see shuffling down the street. They are prehuman, but only too human.

Shave helped Noble & Webster produce a small book documenting their work to date to accompany the Chisenhale exhibition. Armed with a stack of copies of the book, Stuart traveled to New York in the spring of 1999 to find a gallery ready to share his commitment to the artists. This is the point where the author of this text enters the story. Tim and Sue had felt a special connection with my gallery when they visited New York two years earlier, in 1997.

They had left a sheet of slides with the gallery receptionist and remembered her looking at the images and assuring them that "Jeffrey will like this!" I had in fact kept the sheet of slides on my desk for a while and was very receptive when Stuart visited and suggested traveling to London to view the Chisenhale exhibition and meet the artists.

I did not get to London in time to see the Chisenhale show, but my encounter with *Dirty White Trash (with Gulls)*, which was still unsold and back in the studio, remains one of my most memorable art experiences. We began planning our New York exhibition on the spot and set a date for February–March 2000. I telephoned my friend Dakis Joannou in Athens to express my excitement, and on his next visit to London, he acquired *Dirty White Trash (with gulls)* and went on to become Noble & Webster's most important collector and patron.

I was very lucky to connect with Noble & Webster at a propitious moment, when they were able to combine their unbridled youthful enthusiasm with their new artistic maturity to create their most ambitious exhibition to date. Their New York exhibition was conceived like a blockbuster Hollywood movie in exhibition form. All aspects of the production were carefully thought out in advance, from the advertising poster to the building facade to the sequence of works in the gallery space. Every element of the exhibition and its promotion was conceived to be part of the experience of the art.

The exhibition experience began with the poster design, featuring an over-the-top David LaChapelle photograph of naked supermodel Sophie Dahl lactating a stream of light in front of *Excessive Sensual Indulgence*, the first version of the Noble

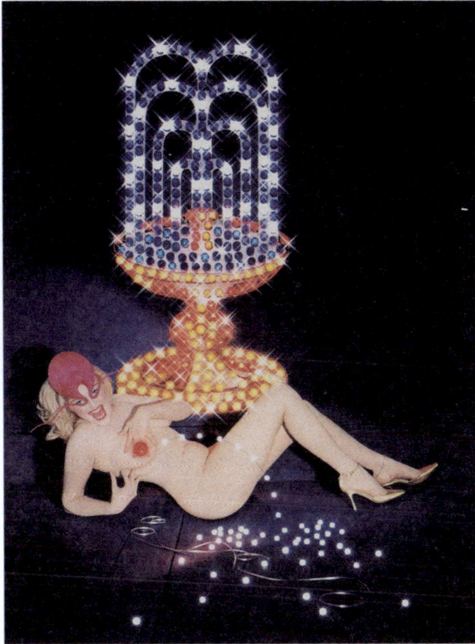

Sophie Dahl with *Excessive Sensual Indulgence*, 1996.
Photograph by David LaChapelle.

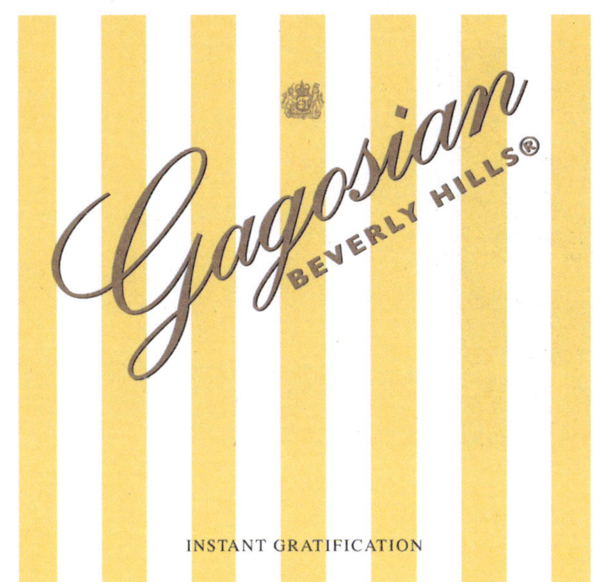

Instant Gratification invitation artwork, 2001.

& Webster light fountain that would be installed at the entrance to the show. The gallery obtained a sign permit to erect the exhibition's signature work, the light sculpture *I❤YOU*, 2000, on the building's facade. The work immediately became a draw for romantic New Yorkers and every evening during the course of the exhibition, couples could be seen embracing on the sidewalk across from the gallery. I suspect that several marriage proposals were made in front of the work. *I❤YOU* was also the artists' valentine to New York, its format adapted from the famous "I❤NY" logo. The work illustrated Noble & Webster's interest in the abstraction of simple word images and in the contrast between the instant communication of a logo and the gradual unfolding of the light sequence. The light sculpture on the facade was like a theater marquee, but it was also like a short theatrical film.

The entire exhibition was sequenced like a rock show, with a beginning that puts you in the mood, a second number that draws you in, several more works that wrap you into the experience, a full-volume climax, and then an unexpected denouement. Drawing the visitor in from the street was *Golden Showers*, 2000, the new version of the light fountain featured on the poster, with sequenced flashing lights mimicking the movement of water. The work is a sculptural spectacle, almost exploding with joyous visual excitement. The title of the work, however, cheekily refers to an act of sexual deviance. Pissing is an intermittent theme in Noble & Webster's work, a symbol of rebelliousness, outrageousness, and disrespect for authority. It is also a way of marking their territory. The confluence of streams of light with streams of piss connotes the confluence of beauty and filth, one of the artists' constant themes. The work also celebrates drinking to excess and its effects.

The pissing theme extends to the next work encountered in the exhibition, *The Original Sinners*, 2000, an oil-fountain shadow sculpture featuring silhouettes of Tim pissing and Sue squirting milk from her breast. Sculpted in the manner of Arcimboldo with the figurative shapes formed from an uncanny assemblage of fake plastic fruit, the work is both astonishing and horrifying. It is an extreme version of the gaudy plastic fountains that one encounters at the entrance to red sauce Italian-American restaurants and catering halls in Brooklyn, another example of the artists' infatuation with the aesthetic excesses of American popular culture.

The Original Sinners prepared the viewer for the exhibition's main attraction, *Cheap 'n' Nasty*, a rotating sculptural tour de force, the most complex work that the artists had created thus far. Two giant revolving globes of garbage dominated the space, with silhouettes of Tim and Sue looming above them. The work was assembled from piles of cheap and nasty toys and household junk bought from the "everything for £1" shops in the East End. The sculpture was cinematic in its conception, creating a movie in shadow form. As the globes of garbage slowly turned on their motors, rotating shadows of Tim and Sue were projected on the wall behind, gradually culminating in a kiss. When the shadow profiles meet in their embrace, the white space around them also creates the image of a vase, a double illusion that can be read either as a double portrait or as an object, depending upon one's perception. Watching the cycle of projections leading to the kiss was like being a voyeur, staring at the shadow of lovers through a window. Gallery viewers were drawn in to the spectacle, watching the convergence and dissolution of the lovers' profiles with fascination. The experience became a metaphor for the fragility

of relationships and aesthetic experience. *Cheap 'n' Nasty* is an example of a relatively new medium, the performance sculpture, a genre developed in part by Los Angeles artists like Paul McCarthy who had supported themselves by working on the fabrication of movie sets. The work is simultaneously a performance and a sculpture, providing both a theatrical and a phenomenological experience.

The exhibition culminated with *Wasted Youth*, 2000, which ultimately became the signature work of this book. *Wasted Youth* is the most punk of Noble & Webster's sculptures, a reflection of the reality of the fringe of London youth culture. It depicts a dissolute young couple, modeled on Tim and Sue themselves, lying in the gutter in their own garbage, or even worse, in someone else's trash. It is refuse of the most unappealing kind, with half-eaten junk food from McDonald's spilling out of torn plastic trash bags. Unlike the trashy romance of *Cheap 'n' Nasty*, the work has as much romance as the image of a junkie nodding out on the sidewalk. Installed by itself in the gallery storefront, it was a dark counterpoint to the exuberance of the rest of the exhibition.

I❤YOU turned out to be a blockbuster, just like the Hollywood movies that partially inspired it. The New York art world has a remarkable word of mouth network, and within days the show was drawing larger crowds than any exhibition ever presented by the gallery. By the second week, the word had spread beyond the circle of the art world, attracting luminaries from the film and literary communities, as well as parents with young children, some of whom came back day after day. The reception of the exhibition demonstrated the power of the direct experience of Noble & Webster's work. The work does not require a theoretical scaffold to be appreciated, and does

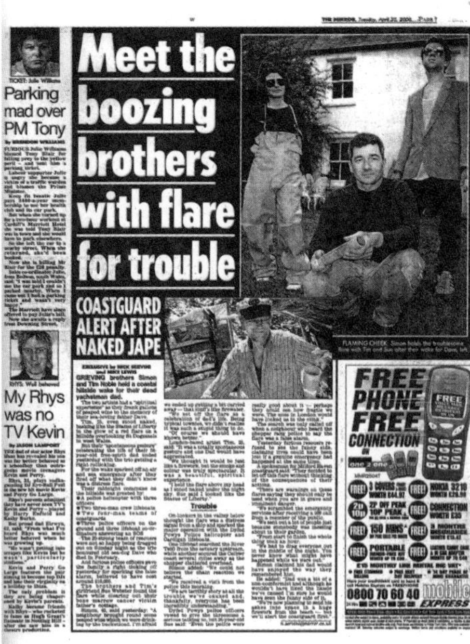

The Mirror, April 25, 2000.

not need the endorsement of art critics to connect with its public. The show attracted its large enthusiastic audience without having received a review in *The New York Times*.

The New York exhibition had opened, sadly, only three days after Tim's father was buried. After the exhibition opening, Tim and Sue returned to Tim's father's seaside home in Wales to stage a proper memorial. David Noble had moved to Wales after his retirement to live close to the sea, becoming an accomplished sailor and fisherman. Tim and his brother Simon created an impromptu memorial performance, dressing in their father's clothes, smoking their father's hash, and lighting up a distress flare that they had found among their father's fishing gear. The flare filled the garden with pink rays of light and made a spectacular tribute. The problem was that the flare also alerted the Welsh Constabulary who assumed that someone was in distress at sea. The detonation prompted the launching of a serious air/sea rescue operation that cost the authorities £10,000. The flare was finally traced to the Noble home where Tim and Simon were scrambling to hide their late father's drugs as the police arrived. The national press arrived the next day, resulting in headlines in the tabloids. If not a proper memorial, it was an appropriate one for their father.

In the division of their father's possessions, Simon wanted the furniture, but Tim wanted his father's collection of stuffed animals. David Noble had persuaded the local museum in Gloucestershire to lend him specimens from its collection of taxidermy animals for his art students to draw from, but the animals were never given back. David eventually amassed an extraordinary taxidermy collection of British wildlife—including birds, rodents, and wild

game—which was displayed in his home. Tim and Sue decided to create a shadow sculpture constructed from the taxidermy collection as their memorial to Tim's dad. *British Wildlife*, 2000, is one of the artists' most extraordinary works, an astonishing assemblage of forty-six birds, forty mammals, and two stuffed fish, mounted on a rock-like base. The sculpture features a kingfisher, a green woodpecker, blue tits, a badger, two foxes, a whole swan, and even Tim's pet crow from his childhood. Its crowning element is a golden eagle, a prized collector's item itself worth £6,000. Rather than selling off the valuable eagle, they incorporated it into the work, which ironically kept the work from entering the United States: even though the eagle is the symbol of American freedom, it is also an endangered species. The completed sculpture was sold to the Solomon R. Guggenheim Museum in New York, but after a three-year battle with U.S. Customs, the work was finally denied entry and the artists decided to make another work for the museum and keep the sculpture for themselves.

British Wildlife is a brilliant work in daylight as well as in shadow. Its sculptural form is as interesting as the shadow formed by its outline, "classical" busts of Tim and Sue in a pose of grief. In its formal sculptural quality, it is a prelude to the later welded metal works. The work is a tribute to Tim's father, but it is also a tribute to the tradition of wildlife as a subject in British art and an evocation of the special affection in British culture for the animals associated with bird-watching and hunting.

Tim and Sue's rising profile in the London art world led to an invitation to participate in *Apocalypse*, an exhibition of international contemporary art curated by Norman Rosenthal and Max Wigram that opened

at the Royal Academy in September 2000. Tim and Sue were given one of the largest rooms in Burlington House, which they transformed into a sculptural version of a New Age garbage dump. They presented a pair of sculptures, *The Undesirables* and *The Muthafucka*, 2000, which evoked the experience of stoned fans at a rock festival sitting on a hill to watch the sunset. The installation of *The Undesirables*, involved the transport of a mountain of actual garbage collected from the streets of the East End into one of the grandest galleries in the Royal Academy. The artists watched as the art shippers carefully crated the sections of trash like valuable artwork, which it subsequently became. The sculpture first appears to be nothing more than a giant mound of rubbish, like something one might see in the parking lot after a rock concert. Hovering above the trash pile, however, is the shadow image of the artists, contentedly enjoying the sunset. In this case, the sunset is not a sublime natural sunset but *The Muthafucka*, a dense circle of hundreds of flashing carnival lights forming the most intense Pop art sunset that one has ever seen.

The Undesirables and *The Muthafucka* are antimonuments to youth culture, evocations of the ritual of watching the sunset at a hippie beach, or at a music festival. The works were inspired, in fact, by Noble & Webster's visit to the Glastonbury Festival, where they broke through a fence, snuck in for free, and sat on a hill watching David Bowie perform. Together, the two works create a punk version of the English Romantic landscape, a contemporary rendering of Pre-Raphaelite lovers, sitting on a mound of garbage instead of a verdant hillside. The theatrical setting sun of *The Muthafucka* is maximal minimal art, an illumination of color field painting, or an animated Bridget Riley. The shadow images of Tim

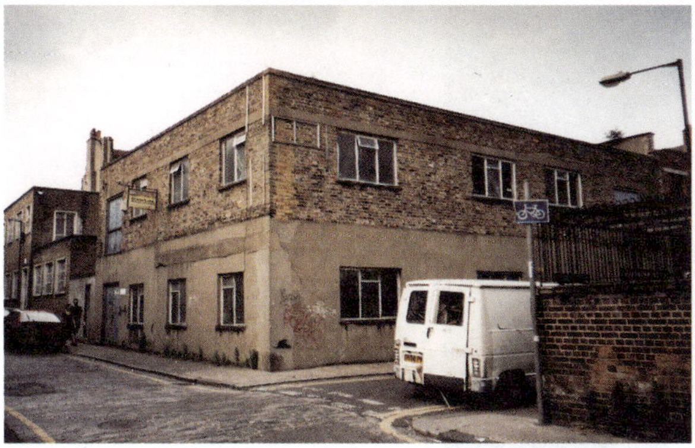

2–4 Chance Street, London, 2001. Photograph by Henry Bourne

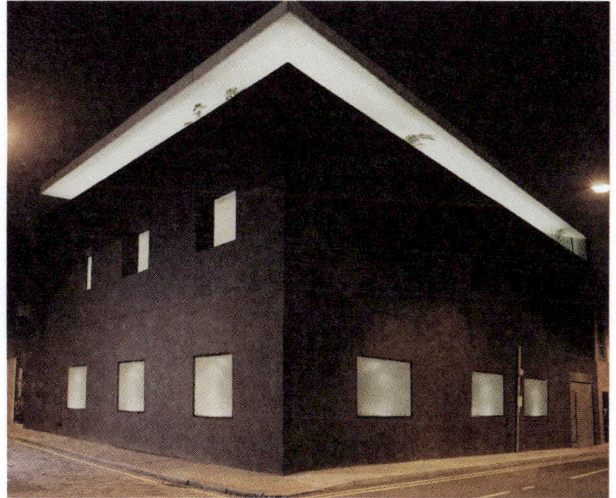

The Dirty House, 2–4 Chance Street, London, 2002. Photograph by Norbert Schoerner

and Sue sitting on the trash heap are worshipping an abstract image, a stylized artificial sun. The works represent the apotheosis of trash culture.

Early in 2001, Tim and Sue stretched their resources to purchase 2–4 Chance Street, a two-story, run-down factory building in the East End of London, taking advantage of one the last opportunities to buy an affordable studio space in their increasingly fashionable neighborhood. Consistent with their approach to art and life, 2–4 Chance Street was not envisioned as just an anonymous, practical studio building, but as part of their overall artistic state-ment. Even though they could scarcely afford it, they engaged their fellow Royal College of Art alum-nus David Adjaye to create a tough and radically beautiful design. In collaboration with Adjaye they proceeded to transform the nondescript factory into an astonishing but understated fusion of architecture and sculpture now known as The Dirty House. The pressure of scrounging for funds and applying for bank loans to support the project began to take its toll on Tim and Sue's relationship. There were frequent fights, including one in which Sue smashed a telephone into a mirror that Tim had inherited from his dad. Many other objects were thrown and broken, and then in the spirit of Noble & Webster's fusion of art and life, collected and transformed into a sculpture.

The resulting work, *Falling Apart*, 2001, is a horri-fying image, a sculptural fury. Tim and Sue recall that their relationship was in fact nearly falling apart. The sculpture is the most expressionist of their works, reminiscent of Bacon's portrait heads. The work conjures an image of Bacon's studio, strewn with debris and the alchemy of making art out of chaos. *Falling Apart* also follows his example of

pushing life to the extreme as a subject for art. While Tim was sculpting the exploding self-portrait heads with Sue, he was reminded of his mother's frightening stories of the London blitz. The heads looked like the sides of buildings half-demolished by bombs. *Falling Apart* foreshadows the deconstruc-tion that would later become central to Noble & Webster's work. It also illustrates the fragility of relationships and the creative process.

Following the New York and Royal Academy shows, Noble & Webster began receiving many enticing offers for projects and exhibitions, but they were determined to realize their fantasy of creating a sculpture made out of money for the gallery that best symbolized the confusion of art and commerce, Gagosian Beverly Hills. They asked Larry Gagosian for $10,000 in one-dollar bills and proceeded to sculpt a double self-portrait made entirely out of cash. The bills were retrieved in large wads from the bank and transported back to the studio by Sue on her bike. Halfway through the process of making the sculpture, they were advised by Gagosian's lawyers that it might be illegal to tamper with U.S. currency. With her usual determination, Sue rang up the F.B.I. and with her calls monitored by Treasury agents, tried to find out what was permitted. After their problems with *British Wildlife*, being refused entry into the United States, they did not want to spend months creating a work that would be confiscated. It turned out that it is illegal to take currency out of circulation and in the event of an inspection by U.S. Customs, it might be necessary to prove that every banknote in the sculpture could be unfolded, ironed, and put back into circulation. Piercing or gluing the banknotes was not permitted. The work had to be remade like a giant piece of origami. Anticipating that the sculpture would eventually be placed in a

vitrine, as it might prove too tempting to pilferers if put on public view, the artists also decided to construct a case around the work. They added a coin slot, which activated a fan that blew the dollars around the figures. A light mounted inside shined onto the sculpture, producing a silhouette of Tim and Sue showered with money on the wall behind. The work was titled *Instant Gratification*, 2001. Along with the light sculpture *A Pair of Dollars*, 2001, and the spectacular large version of *Forever*, it was shown at Gagosian Beverly Hills in 2001. A catalogue with graphics appropriated from luxury fragrance brand Giorgio Beverly Hills was produced to accompany the exhibition.

The large *Forever*, sculpture evoked the gaudy signs for Las Vegas hotels that were among Tim and Sue's primary artistic inspirations. Installed in a large gallery space, watching *Forever* run through its light sequence was like watching a Las Vegas chorus line in sculptural form. The work was stun-ning in its presence, as experiential as it was visual. Like David Hockney's British expatriate view of Los Angeles that captures the visual essence of the city better than most native artists, Noble & Webster demonstrated an uncanny ability to distill the aes-thetic of Las Vegas.

The fabrication of the large *Forever* was too com-plex to be handled by Tim and Sue themselves in their studio, and for the first time they contracted to have a work made by commercial fabricators. They had visited the Young Electric Sign Company in Las Vegas the year before, hoping to make a work inspired by the famous sign for the Flamingo Hotel, but ultimately determined that it was more practical to make the work in London and engaged the local art fabricators Mike Smith Studio to help them to

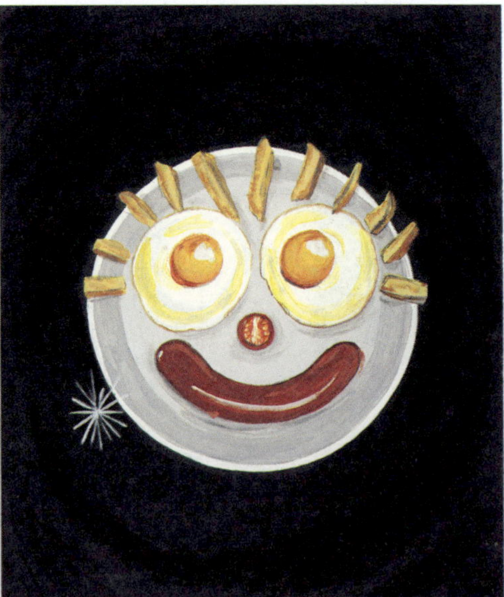

Happy Meal, 2002 (from the *Black Magic Paintings* series).
Acrylic on board. 30 x 37 cm.

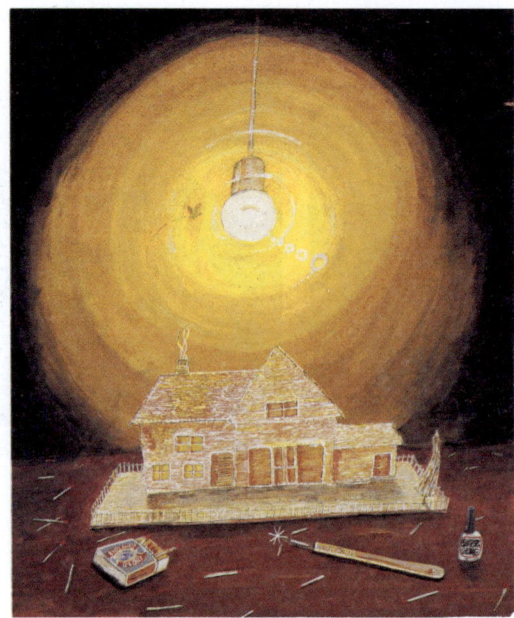

Matchstick House, 2002 (from the *Black Magic Paintings* series).
Acrylic on board. 34 x 41 cm.

construct the sculpture there instead. The Mike Smith Studio did an excellent job assembling the complex electrical and metal work for the large *Forever*, but Tim and Sue ultimately found the experience unsatisfying, feeling that commercial fabrication sterilized the work. It inhibited the creativity that emerges from the trial and error of the studio practice. They found that their most creative work comes out of the working process.

Disillusioned by the experience of using a commercial fabricator to produce expensive-looking work, Tim and Sue were eager to get back into the studio and return to their roots, making sculpture by hand from discarded and scavenged materials. But before embarking on a demanding new sculptural project, they took a detour in 2002 to create their spookiest and most uncommercial series of works, the *Black Magic Paintings*. This strange group of thirteen paintings was inspired by the depraved life of two of Britain's most notorious serial murderers, Fred and Rose West. The title of the series derives from the name of the bar that Fred installed in a bedroom of their modest house in Gloucester, close to where Tim spent his childhood. A wrought-iron sign reading "Black Magic" which Fred made during one of his stints in prison hung above the improvised bar. Perhaps the unusual detour into the twisted world of the Wests was also an attempt by Tim and Sue to reconnect with the outlaw and outcast roots of their aesthetic inspiration after the antiseptic environment of the Mike Smith Studio. Fred and Rose West are as outlaw and outcast as one can get, way beyond the bikers and punk rockers who inspired Tim and Sue in their formative years. Noble & Webster immersed themselves in the most anti-aesthetic source they could find for aesthetic inspiration. Perhaps their dark obsession with Fred and Rose had something to do with the whispered story that Fred used to do handyman work for one of Tim's mother's friends.

Like a number of depraved killers, including the American mass murderer John Wayne Gacy, Jr., Fred West made art. Tim and Sue were intrigued by the matchstick house that Fred made in prison, and even more fascinated by the "paintings" that he made on the plates of food that he served his children for breakfast. His favorite motif was a happy face made with two fried eggs for eyes and a sausage for the mouth. Fred's tool kit, in which he took great pride, contained tools that were used interchangeably for murder and craft. Tim and Sue installed their series of *Black Magic Paintings* in the entrance foyer of their new studio. Above the door they hung a wrought-iron sign reading "Black Magic."

The first sculpture made in the new studio on Chance Street, *Real Life is Rubbish*, 2002, was made entirely from the contents of Tim and Sue's old Rivington Street studio. Going back to the handcrafted, scavenger aesthetic of their earliest works, *Real Life is Rubbish* is one of the most raw and anti-form of all their works. It is brilliantly constructed, but appears deconstructed. The work is assembled from the tools that were used to fasten its parts together, the wooden chairs that the artists sat in while making it, as well as the cans of paint and Coke and the packaging for other substances that were consumed during the fabrication of the work. Many of Tim and Sue's best tools were lost in the process, becoming part of the armature of the sculpture. For instance, if Tim or Sue screwed an element into the sculpture, they might leave the screwdriver. If they had to fasten several parts together, they might leave the clamp. The work is perhaps the ultimate extension of the modernist ideal of making a work of art out of the process of its own construction.

In daylight, *Real Life is Rubbish* looks like a stack of studio debris waiting to be thrown into the dumpster. It is almost impossible that a figurative image could be connected with this seemingly random accumulation of the materials that one would find discarded on a studio floor. When the room is darkened and a light is shined onto the construction however, it is as if a contemporary Pygmalion has brought his inanimate sculpture to life. Full-figured shadows of Tim and Sue, seated on crates, separated and facing away from each other, are projected onto the wall behind. The figures appear to be preoccupied, lost in their own thoughts. The pose is very different from the look of self-satisfaction in the shadows behind *Dirty White Trash (with Gulls)*. The figures are perfectly rendered, with a convincing sense of weight. Even as shadows, they give the illusion of being able to get up from their seats and walk around the studio. The work captures the magic of creation in the studio, embodying the illusion of life emerging from inanimate studio materials. *Real Life is Rubbish* was a breakthrough, leading to the deconstructed constructivism that would be developed in the subsequent welded metal works. Tim and Sue had advanced their artistic process by going back to their roots.

The torment that the artists were experiencing as they struggled to push their art into a new place was evident in a searing new sculpture, *Kiss of Death*, made in 2003 from a tangle of dead birds and rodents. In its concentrated emotional fury, it is probably the artists' most disturbing image. It is a brutal look at themselves, conceivably one of the toughest self-portraits ever made. Like their earlier work *Falling Apart*, *Kiss of Death* draws on the inspiration of Bacon's portrait heads. Instead of paint, however, Noble & Webster used sculpted stuffed

Black

Magic

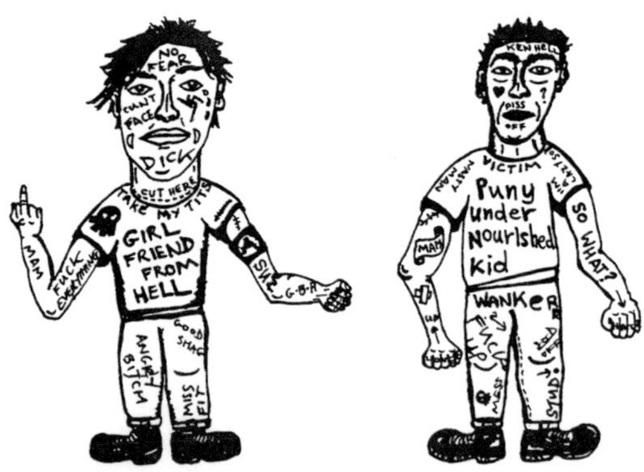

Puny Undernourished Kid & Girlfriend From Hell, 1995.
Pen on paper. 20 x 15 cm.

animals to achieve Bacon-like facial distortions. The artists deliberately chose to construct the work from taxidermy rats, crows, and other scavengers, the lowest form of animal life. The sculpture features a full mink with a rat emerging from its ass. The terrifying crowning touch is a crow pecking at Tim's eye. As in their first shadow sculpture, *Miss Understood & Mr Meanor*, the artists' self-portrait heads are impaled on stakes, like trophies of a brutal massacre. It is an example of how Noble & Webster can work on the edge, driving themselves to the brink of violence and chaos in order to realize their vision. After being shown at the Serpentine Gallery in London, *Kiss of Death* entered the collection of the Guggenheim Museum, a replacement for the embargoed sculpture *British Wildlife* that could not enter the United States.

Another effort to return to the ruggedness of their early work was the 2004 pair of sculptures *Puny Undernourished Kid & Girlfriend From Hell*, based on cartoon-like drawings that they had made of each other ten years before. Large neon figures covered with nasty neon tattoos, they are sculpture as punk rock, a visualization of punk attitude. The physical impact of the works is much stronger than is implied by their photographic reproductions. They are literally in-your-face embodiments of the aggressive characters that they portray. The Sue figure is in a pose of defiance, her middle finger sporting the fuck-you gesture. On her neck is a neon tattoo reading, "cut here." The Tim figure is sullen and threatening. The words "piss off" are tattooed in neon on his face. The works have the larger-than-life presence of performers on a stage. In their primitive impact, they draw on the example of Nauman's neon figurative sculpture. *Puny Undernourished Kid & Girlfriend From Hell* is an example of Tim and Sue's determination to keep

the edge in their work, to prevent their artistic statement from becoming too aestheticized.

Tim and Sue's ongoing project to stay in touch with their artistic roots led to a remarkable discovery in the spring of 2003. While visiting Tim's mother in Gloucestershire, Sue was engaged in one of her favorite activities, scavenging for potential sculpture materials, when she came across a pile of rusting scrap metal in a overgrown section of the garden. The cache was the forgotten material stockpile and the dumping ground for the unfinished sculpture of Tim's brother Simon, who in the 1980s had been the sculpture technician at Central Saint Martins College of Art and Design, where Sir Anthony Caro was teaching. Some of the heavier twisted metal forms turned out to be discarded elements from Caro's own studio. Sue loaded the metal parts into her car and brought them back to the London studio. This pile of scrap metal with its personal and art historical connections became the genesis of Noble & Webster's most sophisticated body of work.

In their ten-year career, Tim and Sue had already explored and exploited almost every innovation in modern and contemporary sculpture: the assisted readymade, accumulation, kineticism, performance sculpture, and even commercial fabrication. They were now ready to focus on the most influential and perhaps the most overused innovation in modern sculpture: the constructed sculpture. Picasso is credited with making the first constructed sculpture, his cardboard and string *Guitar* of 1912. Constructed sculpture was conceived from an opposite point of view from traditional modeled sculpture. The form of a constructed sculpture is built up from individual elements while modeled sculpture is carved from a mass. Picasso's constructivist innovation was further developed in *Glass of Absinthe* of 1914,

which includes found elements, and was most fully realized in his collaboration with Julio Gonzalez from 1928–31. These works form the foundation of the constructed welded metal tradition further developed by David Smith and Caro.

Formalist welded metal sculpture in the tradition of Smith and Caro would seem to be the unlikeliest sculptural approach to interest Noble & Webster. The genre had long been considered to be a dead end, so diluted by hundreds of academic sculptors of lesser talent that it had become a cliché. An ironic reinvention of constructed sculpture became one of the main themes of Noble & Webster's career, perhaps without their realizing it. Now the irony of taking discarded elements from Caro's studio to construct sculpture that philosophically and physically turns his work upside-down became the focus of their new body of work.

Noble & Webster's welded metal sculptures "look like art," but reverse the most revered premises of modern sculpture. They are like artifacts of high art, memorials to modernism. They are serious abstract works, but they mysteriously reverse the abstraction into figuration. The works delve into the existential issues associated with modern painting and sculpture in the 1940s and 1950s. They explore the tensions between abstraction and representation, materiality and illusion. They play with the juxtaposition of positive and negative space in the perception of sculptural form. Tim and Sue have revived a discredited technique, a medium consigned to the past, to explore essential issues in sculpture in a fresh, irreverent, but surprisingly serious way.

The first three works in the welded metal series were presented in an exhibition appropriately titled *Modern Art Is Dead* to inaugurate Shave's new

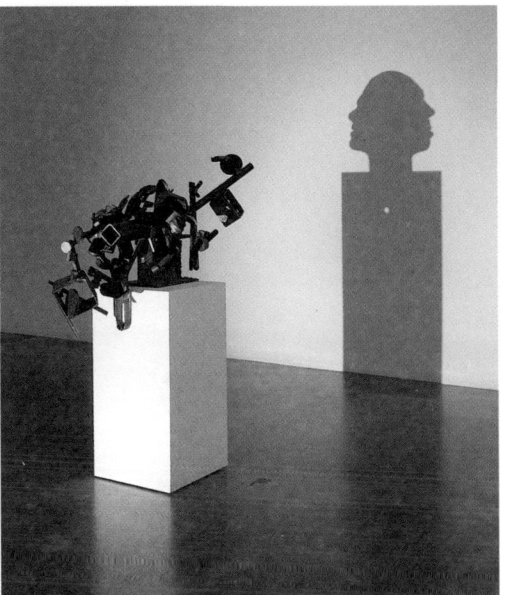

A Hole, 2005. Welded steel, light projector. 85 x 30.5 x 60 cm.

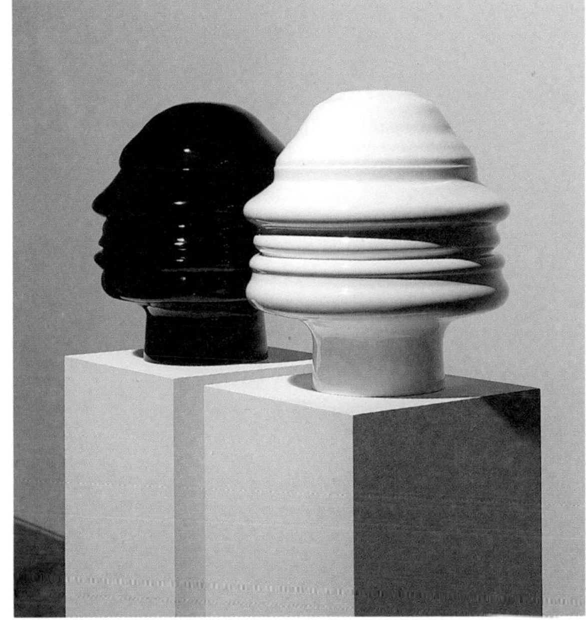

(Untitled) Spinning Heads, 2005. Painted bronze.
38 x 34 cm, 38 x 35 cm.

gallery space on Vyner Street, London in 2004. *HE/SHE*, was installed in the large gallery. The metal construction was so confounding and unexpected that it took some people time to perceive the shadows that the welded forms created on the wall. Gradually people looked up from the fascinating metal sculptures to see Tim and Sue matter-of-factly pissing, marking their art historical territory. More than any of their previous sculptural forms, the metal sculptures were amazing objects themselves, apart from their mysterious function in creating the figurative illusion of the shadow. They exhibited a mastery of sculptural craft, but their formalism was turned inside out by their hidden enabling of illusionism.

The most disconcerting work in the series was *The Crack*, installed in the smaller room of the gallery. A vertical welded metal stele-like form, somewhat reminiscent of a Giacometti woman, stood in the center of the room. The metal elements looked like they came from an earlier era and in fact much of the work was constructed from the discarded metal from Caro's studio. The form had an inscrutable, existential quality. It was the shadow behind it that was most inscrutable, however. A crowd of visitors stood staring at the wall trying to make out a figure, or a representational image, but most were stumped. The word finally got out that in order to decipher the form, one had to reverse one's normal perceptual pattern and focus on the white space around the shadow, rather than the black shadow itself. If you concentrated your vision and reversed your normal perceptual mode, you were able to make out the naked bodies of Tim and Sue facing each other. Some visitors found it impossible to see the image, unable to alter their modes of perception. Others were able to see the image only fleetingly until their perceptual mechanism jumped back to the default mode. The challenge of perceiving the shadow image brought

to mind the games of perception discussed in Ernst Gombrich's *Art and Illusion*, and especially the duck/hare reversible image that had fascinated Johns. Following Noble & Webster's subversive approach, *The Crack*, uses visual entertainment to explore challenging artistic issues. It is a meditation on the double meanings inherent in art and perception. The work's title, for instance, could refer to the body's posterior, the fissure between the two figures, or simply a crack in the wall.

An expanded version of the welded metal series was presented in *The Glory Hole*, an exhibition presented at the Bortolami Dayan Gallery in New York in November 2005. The title refers to holes punched through the walls of toilet stalls to facilitate dangerous anonymous sex. The sculptural experience was like entering a glory hole and exiting the other side. Except for a work titled *A Hole*, 2005, and the left side of *The Negative*, all of the shadows are negative images, with the figure visible in the white negative space around the black shadows. The works are like funerary monuments, particularly the largest work in the show, *Twin Suicide*, 2005. Like their first shadow sculpture, *Miss Understood & Mr Meanor*, it is a sculptural suicide, with death masks of the artists hovering behind guillotine-like forms. *A Hole*, the one piece where the image appears exclusively in black shadow, features a butt plug, a form seen recently in McCarthy's work. The profile of the butt plug takes the viewer on an uncanny creative leap to the perception of a human profile, leading toward one of Noble & Webster's most recent works, their self-portrait *(Untitled) Spinning Heads*, 2005.

The conceptual model for *(Untitled) Spinning Heads*—a connection between the profile of a butt plug and the profile of Benito Mussolini—is a good example of the unexpected synapses in Noble &

Webster's transgressive creative process. *(Untitled) Spinning Heads* is based on Renato Bertelli's disturbing but fascinating *Continuous Profile of Mussolini* from 1933, a patented sculptural portrait of the fascist dictator produced with Mussolini's approval. It is a profile of Mussolini rotated 360 degrees, more of a machine than a man's head. Tim keeps a photographic reproduction of Jacob Epstein's 1913–14 sculpture *Rock Drill* on his studio office wall, an indication of Noble & Webster's interest in sculpture as machine.

(Untitled) Spinning Heads also reveals the dark secret of the connection between modernism and fascism, a once untouchable subject in modern art history. The work addresses the conflation of utopian modern idealism and the totalitarian cult of personality, and raises questions about how the cult of personality pervades contemporary celebrity culture. The spinning heads are de-gendered, neither male nor female. They are formally pure, but morally impure, the ultimate extension of the shadow portraits. They are also the ultimate extension of "artist as art."

Noble & Webster have created a remarkable group of anti-monuments, using the strategies of modern sculpture to make art from anti-art. The work derives much of its power from its fusion of opposites: form and anti-form, high culture and anti-culture, male and female, craft and garbage, sex and violence. It is an art of magic and illusion, but it is also an art of direct experience. It combines sculpture, theater, advertising, and persona. The artists have succeeded in making their lives, and the experience of the viewer, part of the art. Noble & Webster works are not just objects, they are events.

Solo Exhibitions

2005
The Glory Hole, Bortolami Dayan, New York, U.S. 2005

The Joy of Sex, Kukje Gallery, Seoul, Korea. 2005

The New Barbarians, CAC Málaga, Centro de Arte Contemporaneo de Málaga, Spain. 2005

2004
Modern Art Is Dead, Modern Art, London, UK. 2004

Tim Noble & Sue Webster, Museum of Fine Arts, Boston, U.S. 2004

2003
Tim Noble & Sue Webster, P. S. 1 Contemporary Art Center, Long Island City, New York, U.S. 2003

2002
Black Magic, MW Projects, London, UK. 2002

Ghastly Arrangements, Milton Keynes Gallery, Milton Keynes, UK. 2002

Real Life Is Rubbish, Statements at Art Basel, Miami, U.S. 2002

2001
Instant Gratification, Gagosian Gallery, Beverly Hills, CA, U.S. 2001

2000
British Wildlife, Modern Art, London, UK. 2000

I ❤ YOU, Deitch Projects, New York, U.S. 2000

Masters of the Universe, Deste Foundation, Athens, Greece. 2000

1999
The New Barbarians, Chisenhale Gallery, London, UK. 1999

The New Barbarians, Spacex Gallery, Exeter, UK. 1999

1998
Vague Us, Habitat, Kings Road, London, UK. 1998

WOW, Modern Art, London, UK. 1998

1997
Home Chance, 20 Rivington Street, London, UK. 1997

1996
British Rubbish, Independent Art Space, London, UK. 1996

Group Exhibitions

2006
Masquerade–Representation and the Self in Contemporary Art, Museum of Contemporary Art, Sydney, Australia. 2006

2005
Les Grandes Spectacles, Museum der Moderne, Salzburg, Austria. 2005

Shadow Play: Shadow and Light in Contemporary Art—A Homage to Hans Christian Andersen, Kunsthallen Brandts Klædefabrik, Odense, Denmark; Kunsthalle zu Kiel, Kiel, Germany; Landesgalerie am Oberösterreichischen Landesmuseum, Linz, Austria. 2005–2006

2004
Beauty and the Beast, Museo d'Arte Moderna e Contemporanea di Trento e Rovereto, Italy. 2004

Jewellery by Contemporary Artists, Louisa Guinness Gallery, London, UK. 2004–2005

Monument To Now, The Dakis Joannou Collection, Athens, Greece. 2004

New Blood, Saatchi Gallery, London, UK. 2004

The Ten Commandments, Deutsches Hygiene-Museum, Dresden, Germany. Curated by Klaus Bisenbach. 2004

State of Play, The Serpentine Gallery, London, UK. 2004

2003
The Fourth Sex: Adolescent Extremes, Stazione Leopolda, Florence, Italy. Curated by Raf Simons and Francesco Bonami. 2003

Perpetual Bliss, Galerie Thaddeus Ropac, Paris, France. 2003

Skulptur 03, Galerie Thaddeus Ropac, Salzburg, Austria. 2003

2002
Art Crazy Nation Show, Milton Keynes Gallery, Milton Keynes, UK. Curated by Matthew Collings. 2002

Casino 2001: 1st Quadrennial, Stedelijk Museum voor Actuele Kunst, Ghent Belgium. Curated by Jeanie Greenberg Rohatyn. 2002

Form Follows Fiction, Castello di Rivoli—Museo d'Arte Contemporanea, Turin, Italy. Curated by Jeffrey Deitch. 2002

Melodrama, ARTIUM Vitoria-Gasteiz; Centro José Guerrero, Granada; MARCO, Vigo, Spain. 2002

Shortcuts–Works from the Dakis Joannou Collection, Nicosia Municipal Arts Centre, Cyprus. 2002

Summer Reading, Gagosian Gallery, Beverly Hills, U.S. 2002

When Philip Met Isabella, The Design Museum, London, UK. 2002

2001
The 1st Biennial de Valencia, Valencia, Spain. 2001

2001 A Space Oddity, The Colony Room Club, London, UK. 2001

Electrify Me!, Friedrich Petzel Gallery, New York, U.S. Curated by Mark Fletcher. 2001

London Orphan Asylum, University of Tasmania, Plimsoll Gallery, Tasmania, Australia. 2001

Tattoo Show, Modern Art, London, UK. 2001

2000
Apocalypse–Beauty and Horror in Contemporary Art, Royal Academy of Art, London, UK. Curated by Norman Rosenthal and Max Wigram. 2000

Exposure: Recent Acquisitions from the Doron Sebbag Art Collection, O.R.S. Ltd, Museum of Art, Tel Aviv, Israel. 2001

London Orphan Asylum, Open Space, Milan, Italy; Australian Centre for Contemporary Art, Melbourne, Australia. Curated by Gilda Williams. 2000

Man–Body in Art from 1950 to 2000, Arken Museum of Modern Art, Copenhagen, Denmark. 2001

Sex and the British, Galerie Thaddaeus Ropac, Salzburg, Austria; Paris, France. Curated by Norman Rosenthal and Max Wigram. 2000

1999
Shopping, FAT Bag Project, 15-21 Ganton Street, London, UK. 1999

1998
11th Rencontres Video Art Plastique, Herouville Saint-Clair, France. 1998

Impakt Festival for Audio-Visual Arts, Utrecht, The Netherlands. 1998

Internationales Videofenster, Basel, Switzerland, DOT Gallery, Barcelona, Spain. 1998

Let's Play Risk, Juice, London, UK. 1998

SupaStore Supastars, SupaStore at Tomato, London, UK. 1998

The Whole Year Inn, The Agency, London, UK. 1998

1997
John Kobal Portrait Award, National Portrait Gallery, London, UK. 1997

Livestock Market, Rivington Street and Charlotte Road, London, UK. 1997

Non Stop Body Rock, Transmission Gallery, Glasgow, UK. 1997

Turning the Tables, live DJ event, Chisenhale Gallery, London, UK. Curated by Tim Noble & Sue Webster. 1997

Unique!, Kunstpark Ost, Munich, Germany. 1997

1996
Bitter Twist, Unge Kunstneres Samfund, Oslo, Norway. 1996

Fools Rain, Institute of Contemporary Arts, London, UK. Curated by Max Wigram. 1996

Glass Shelf Show, artists' multiples, Institute of Contemporary Arts, London, UK. 1996

Mission Impossible, Bricks & Kicks, Vienna, Austria. 1996

New Contemporaries, Liverpool Tate, Liverpool and Camden Arts Centre, London, UK. 1996

Roadworks, site-specific bus shelter project, London, UK. Curated by FAT. 1996

Special Offer, Art Chain Store, Calvert Avenue, London, UK. 1996

Try, part of the VAA course, Royal College of Art, London, UK. 1996

Yerself Is Steam, 85 Charlotte Street, London, UK. 1996

1995
The Hanging Picnic, Hoxton Square, London, UK. 1995

Ideal Standard Summertime, Lisson Gallery, London, UK. 1995

Postscript, Lisson Gallery, London, UK. 1995

Self Storage, Wembley, London, UK. Curated by Artangel, Brian Eno, and Laurie Anderson. 1995

Young British Artists, EIGEN + ART at Independent Art Space, London, UK. 1995

1994
Absolut Art, Royal College of Art, London, UK. 1994

The Fete Worse Than Death, Hoxton Square, London, UK. 1994

Hijack, New York, U.S.; London, UK; Berlin, Germany. 1994

1993
Lift, Atlantis Basement, Brick Lane, London, UK. Curated by Tim Noble & Sue Webster. 1993

Selected Bibliography

Publications

2006

Kent, Rachel. *Masquerade—Representation and the Self in Contemporary Art*. Sydney: Museum of Contemporary Art, 2006

Nairne, Sandy, and Sarah Howgate. *The Portrait Now*. London: National Portrait Gallery Publications, 2006

2005

Grosenick, Uta, and Burkhard Riemschneider, eds. *ART NOW VOL. 2*. New York: Taschen, 2005

Noble, Tim, Sue Webster, and Alicia Murria, eds. *The New Barbarians*. Málaga: Centro de Arte Contemporáneo de Málaga, 2005

Noble, Tim, Sue Webster, and Mark Fletcher, eds. *The Joy of Sex*. Translated by Emma Son and Sabine Lee. Seoul: Kukje Gallery, 2005

Sadowsky, Thorsten, Roberto Casati, Jorgen Dines Johansen, and Anselm Wagner. *Shadow Play: Shadow and Light in Contemporary Art, A Homage to Hans Christian Andersen*. Heidelberg: Kehrer Verlag, 2005

Testino, Mario, et al, eds. *Visionaire 46: Uncensored*. New York: Visionaire Publishing, 2005

2004

Beauty and the Beast. Rovereto, Italy: Museo d'Arte Moderna e Contemporanea di Trento e Rovereto, 2004

Deitch, Jeffrey, et al, eds. *Monument to Now: The Dakis Joannou Collection*. Athens: DESTE Foundation, 2004

Maison Rouge, Isabelle de. *Mythologies personnelles—L'art contemporain et l'intime*. Paris: Éditions Scala, 2004

Steiner, Rochelle. *State of Play*. London: Serpentine Gallery, 2004

2003

Bonami, Francesco, and Raf Simon. *The Fourth Sex: Adolescent Extremes*. Stazione Leopolda, Florence, Italy. Milan: Edizioni Charta, 2003

Craig, Patsy, Gemano Cleant, and William Furlong. *Making Art Work: The Mike Smith Studio*. London: Trolley, 2003

Cruz, Gemma de, and Franca Sozzani. *British Artists at Work*. Photography by Amanda Eliasch. Paris: Assouline, 2003

Ellis, Patricia, and Charles Saatchi. *100: The Work that Changed British Art*. London: Jonathan Cape, 2003

2002

Collings, Matthew. *Art Crazy Nation: the Post-Blimey! Art World*. London: 21 Publishing Ltd, 2002

Dean, Cecilia, Stephen Gan, James Kaliardos, and Greg Foley, eds. *Visionaire 38: Love*. New York: Visionaire Publishing, 2002

LeVitte Harten, Doreet, et al. Melodrama. Spain: ARTIUM, Vitoria-Gasteiz; Centro José Guerrero, Granada; MARCO, Vigo, 2002

Ocampo, Brooke de, and Stuart Shave, eds. "Tim Noble and Sue Webster," *Bright Young Things, London*. Paris: Assouline, 2002

Sozzani, Franca, and Luca Stoppini. *KARTell: 150 Items 150 Artworks*. Milan: Skira Editore, 2002

2001

Buck, Louisa, and George Melly, eds. *2001 A Space Oddity*, The Colony Room Club. London: A22 Projects, 2001

Deitch, Jeffrey. *Form Follows Fiction*. Milan: Edizioni Charta, 2001

Ellis, Patricia. *New Labour*. London: Saatchi Gallery, 2001

Greenberg Rohatyn, Jeanne, et al. *Casino 2001: 1st Quadrennial of Contemporary Art*. Ghent: S.M.A.K. Stedelijk Museum voor Actuele Kunst, 2001

Gregos, Katerina. *Shortcuts: Works from the Dakis Joannou Collection*. Nicosia, Cyprus: Nicosia Municipal Arts Centre, 2001

Millard, Rosie. *The Tastemakers: U.K. Art Now*. London: Thames & Hudson, 2001

Noble, Tim, Sue Webster, and Larry Johnson, eds. *Instant Gratification*. Beverly Hills: Gagosian Gallery, 2001

Settembrini, Luigi. *The 1st Bienal de Valencia: Communication Between the Arts*. Milan: Edizioni Charta, 2001

Testino, Mario, et al, eds. *Visionaire 35: Man*. New York: Visionaire Publishing, 2001

2000

Buck, Louisa. *Moving Targets 2: A User's Guide to British Art Now*. London: Tate Publishing, 2000

Cooper, Jeremy. *no FuN without U: the Art of Factual Nonsense*. London: Ellipsis Arts, 2000

Gether, Christian, and Stine Høholt. *Mennesket: Et halvt århundrede set gennem kroppen (Man–Body in Art from 1950 to 2000)*. Copenhagen: ARKEN Museum of Modern Art, 2000

Hulten, Pontus. *Absolut Art*. Stockholm: V&S Vin Sprit AB/The Absolut Company, 2000

Joannou, Dakis, et al. *Masters of the Universe: Talking Rubbish*. Athens: DESTE Foundation, 2000

Mordechi, Omer. *Exposure, Recent Acquisitions of the Doron Sebbag Art Collection, O.R.S. Ltd*. Tel Aviv: Tel Aviv Museum of Art, 2000

Rosenthal, Norman, and Max Wigram, eds. *Sex and the British*. Paris, Salzburg: Galerie Thaddaeus Ropac, 2000

Rosenthal, Norman, et al. "Shadowplay," in *Apocalypse: Beauty and Horror in Contemporary Art*. London: Royal Academy of Arts, 2000

1999

Barrett, David. Richard Benson, and FAT. *Shopping*. 15–21 Ganton Street, London: FAT Bag Project, 1999

LaChapelle, David. *Hotel LaChapelle*. New York: Little, Brown and Co, 1999

Minogue, Kylie, et al, eds. *Kylie*. London: Booth-Clibborn Editions, 1999

Noble, Tim, Sue Webster, David Barrett, and Stuart Shave, eds. *The New Barbarians*. London: Modern Art Inc!, 1999

Price, Dick, Richard Cork, and Sarah Kent, eds. *Young British Art: The Saatchi Decade*. London: Booth-Clibborn Editions, 1999

1998

Dean, Cecilia, James Kaliardos, and Isabella Blow, eds. "Isabella Blow's Fantasy," in *Visionaire 26: Fantasy*. New York: Visionaire Publishing, 1998

Price, Dick. *The New Neurotic Realism*. London: Saatchi Gallery, 1998

1997

John Kobal Photographic Portrait Award. London: National Portrait Gallery Publications, 1997

1996

New Contemporaries. Tate Gallery Liverpool and Camden Arts Centre. Liverpool: New Contemporaries Ltd., 1996

Noble, Tim, Sue Webster, and Independent Art Space. *British Rubbish*. London: Independent Art Space, 1996

Periodicals

2006
"Arty London." *Code D'accès, Cultitude 1* (Printemps/Été 2006): 110–11.

Fortescue, Elizabeth. "To Be Young at Art." *Daily Telegraph* (27 March 2006).

"Frieze Frame." British *Vogue* (January 2006): 116.

"Valentine, July Heatwave." *Harper's Bazaar* (July 2006): 123.

2005
"All That Comes Up, Goes Down." *NEO2* (April 2005): 72–73.

"El CAC muestra por primera vez en España la obra de Noble y Webster *The New Barbarians.*" *El Mundo Málaga.* (8 April 2005): M7.

"El CAC inaugura la instalación *The New Barbarians.*" *La Opinión de Málaga* (8 April 2005): 64.

"El CAC Málaga muestra el arte de Sue Webster y Tim Noble." *El País* (8 April 2005): 8.

"Goings on About Town." *New Yorker* (5 December 2005).

Henry, Max. "Tim Noble and Sue Webster *The Glory Hole.*" *Time Out New York* (1–7 December 2005).

"Honestly Cheeky Drawings by a Couple." *Financial News* (12 October 2005).

The Joy of Sex. *W Korea* (November 2005): 206–09.

Kim, Areum. "Experiencing Heartbeat of the World's Contemporary Art Firsthand in Korea." *Korea Tatler* (November 2005).

Kyoung-tae, Ko. "Sex Life Laid Bare in Drawings." *Korea Herald* (10 October 2005): 16.

Lee, Inpyo. "Clear-cut Sexual Love Drawings: Rendezvous of Art and Pornography." *Munwha Daily* (8 October 2005).

Lee, Mu-kyung. "Daring and Realistically Shocking Drawings." *Kyunghyang Newspaper* (8 October 2005).

Lee, Young-ran. "Unconventional Erotic Drawings Exhibition Hits This Fall: Celebrated British Couple Artists Brings Sensational *Joy of Sex* Exhibition." *Herald Economic* (7 October 2005).

Myerson, Julie. "Close to My Heart." *Harpers & Queen* (April 2005).

"Narcissism Retrieved From a Stack of Trash . . ." *Wolganmisool* (November 2005): 74–75.

"Noble y Webster combinan provoación y reflexión en la instalación *New Barbarians.*" *Cultura y Sociedad 39* (8 April 2005): 40.

Sanders, Mark. "The Odd Couple." *Another Magazine* (Autumn/Winter 2005): 26.

Smith, Roberta. "Art Promoted Heavily (Even in Your Mailbox)." *New York Times* (12 November 2005).

Smith, Roberta. "Tim Noble and Sue Webster, *The Glory Hole.*" *New York Times* (9 December 2005).

"Tim Noble and Sue Webster." *Misoolsidae* (November 2005): 62–63.

"Una invitación para reflexionar–*The New Barbarians*" *Cultura Málaga hoy* (8 April 2005): 44.

2004
"Art Punk." *Boston Phoenix* (22 January 2004).

Buck, Louisa . "Tim and Sue Go Pole Dancing." *Art Newspaper* (May 2004).

Finel Honigman, Ana. "Tim Noble and Sue Webster." *Sculpture* (March 2004): 22–23.

Freidson, Michael. "Trash Talking." *Boston Metro* (16–18 April 2004): 11.

Gayford, Martin. "Artful Play for Today." *Daily Telegraph* (18 February 2004): 19.

Gleadell, Colin. "Ascent of a Collector." *Daily Telegraph* (21 June 2004).

Gleadell, Colin. "Prices Go Through the Roof." *Daily Telegraph* (17 May 2004): 14.

Güner, Fisun. "The Romance of Rubbish." *Metro Life* (5 April 2004): 26.

Januszak, Waldemar. "A Funny Thing Happened on the Way to the New Serpentine Show: the Gallery Got a Sense of Humour." *Sunday Times London* (22 February 2004): 8–9.

Jones, Jonathan. "Art That Would Bore a Cat." *Guardian* (19 April 2004).

Kent, Sarah. "No Laughing Matter." *Time Out London* (17–24 March 2004): 46.

Kent, Sarah. "Bad Blood." *Time Out London* (31 March–7 April 2004): 47.

Kerwin, Jessica. "The Golden Greek." *W* (1 October 2004): 364–77.

Millis, Christopher. "Garbage In . . . Art Out?" *Boston Phoenix* (14 May 2004).

"Modern Art Is Rubbish." *Boston Phoenix* (16 April 2004): 1.

Nakamura, Marie-Pierre. "Tim Noble & Sue Webster: Nos sculptures-poubelles sont la représentation romantique de notre vie de couple." *Art Actuel* (July/August 2004): 78–79.

O'Sullivan, Kevin. "Rats to Saatchi." *Daily Mirror* (22 March 2004): 20.

Renton, Andrew. "New Blood on the Walls." *Evening Standard* (24 February 2004): 41.

Robinson, Andrew. "Humanity Stakes its Claim." *Gay City* (8–14 January 2004).

"Stars & Styles, Portraits of London." *Self Service* (Spring/Summer 2004): 107, 120.

Sumpter, Helen. "Tim Noble & Sue Webster, *Modern Art Is Dead.*" *Time Out London* (21–28 April 2004): 48.

"Szene London" *Art Das Kunstmagazin* (August 2004): 40–41.

Temin, Christine. "British Artists Are Way Beyond Shocking." *Boston Globe* (28 April 2004): F1.

"Tim Noble & Sue Webster." *BH Magazine* (June 2004): 70–76.

Silver, Joanne. "Noble–Webster Show So Lovely It's Obscene." *Boston Herald* (7 May 2004): E12.

"Who Do We Admire Now?" British *Vogue* (April 2004): 135.

2003
Bowie, David. "My Favourite Piece." *Saatchi Magazine/Observer* (April 2003): 6.

Budick, Ariella. "British Artists Make Magic From Rubbish." *Newsday* (14 November 2003).

Del Drago, Elena. "Arte, arrivano i barbari." *Il Manifesto* (11 December 2003): 14.

Gilbert, Debora. "British Artists at *PS1*: Flashy Art is Entertaining." *Greenline: North Brooklyn Community News* (2–31 November 2003): 12.

Gleadell, Colin. "Shaky, Picky and Patchy." *Daily Telegraph* (10 February 2003): 18.

Leon de la Barra, Pablo. "Dirty Rough House." *Celeste* (Trimestral/Primavera 2003): 52–55.

"Noble & Webster—*One of Us.*" *Art Newspaper* (March 2003): 40.

Pownall, Elfreda. "Light Work." *Sunday Telegraph Magazine* (9 March 2003): 46–48.

Renton, Andrew. "Bright Lights, Big Sales." *Evening Standard* (18 February 2003): 51.

Roux, Caroline. "Living Rough." British *Vogue* (February 2003): 194–201.

Roux, Caroline. "Living Rough." *Vogue Nippon* (23 May 2003): 362–365.

Schmidt, Jason. "Trash and Vaudeville." *V Magazine* (May–June 2003).

"Trashed: a Post YBA Couple's Collaborative Shadow Play." *Village Voice* (19–25 November 2003).

Weber, Christa. "Lightbulb Life." *Queens Courier* (29 October–4 November 2003).

2002
Allison, Peter. "The House of the Artist." *DOMUS* (December 2002).

Baillieu, Amanda. "Mirror Mirror on the Wall." *RIBA Journal* (November 2002): 32–38.

Blow, Isabella. "Kiss My Feet. A Tribute to Manolo Blahnik." *Tatler* (February 2002).

Cargill Thompson, Jessica. "Style 50—Re-thinking Architecture." *Time Out London* (11–18 September 2002): 24–25.

Darwent, Charles. "A Ghastly Show I'm Delighted to Report." *Independent on Sunday* (19 May 2002): 10.

Gaines, Malik. "Tim Noble and Sue Webster." *Contemporary* (January 2002): 76–77.

Gether, Christian, et al. "Communicating in a Junk Culture: Tim Noble and Sue Webster: Falling Apart," *ARKEN Bulletin vol. 1,* 6–15. Arken: Arken Museum of Modern Art, 2002.

Januszak, Waldemar. "Money Where Their Mouth Is." *Sunday Times* (19 May 2002): 10–11.

Philo, Phoebe. "Another Thing I Wanted To Tell You." *Another Magazine* (Autumn/Winter 2002): 112.

Sumpter, Helen. "From Trash to Cash." *Art Review* (May 2002): 48–51.

Waldron, Glenn. "Things I Love." *i-D* (April 2002): 240–41.

2001
Byrnes, Sholto. "Webster and Noble Pass the Bucks." *Independent on Sunday* (4 March 2001): 40.

Collings, Matthew. "Art-Crazy London." *ES Magazine* (12 October 2001): 12–14.

Cumming, Tim. "Pop Goes the Easel." *Guardian* (26 March 2001): 10–11.

Fanelli, Franco. "Com'è finto il post-Uomo." *Vernissage* (November 2001): 8–4.

Fraser, Honor. "Cleaning Up." *Scotland on Sunday* (18 November 2001): 5.

Gleadell, Colin. "Artists' Colony." *Telegraph Magazine* (13 October 2001): 40–44.

Harvey, Doug. "Shadow People." *LA Weekly* (23–29 November 2001): 50.

Herbert, Martin. "Tim Noble & Sue Webster: *British Wildlife.*" *Tema Celeste* (January/February 2001): 99.

Herbert, Martin, Sarah Kent, and Martin Coomer. "Who Rules London's Art Scene?–Art's Top 25." *Time Out London* (31 January–7 February 2001): 16–17.

Johnson, Ken. "West Side: *The Armoury Show* on the Piers Just Keeps Growing." *New York Times* (23 February 2001): E33.

"Learn and Pass It On." *i-D* (November 2001): 95.

MacDonell Smith, Nancy. "Divine Collection." *Nylon* (March 2001): 196–97.

Millard, Rosie. "The Taste Makers." *Times Magazine* (6 October 2001): 24–29.

"Mister & Mistletoe." *New York Times Magazine* (23 December 2001): 44.

Rakoczy, Agnieszka. "The Power of Modern Art: *Shortcuts.*" *Cyprus Sunday Mail* (2–8 December 2001): 8–9.

Ratnam, Niru. "Listen to the Shadows." *Arena Homme+* (Autumn/Winter 2001): 360–62.

"Young Guns." *i-D* (April 2001): 76–77.

2000
Aaronovitch, David. "Brash, Innovative, My Kind of Show." *Independent* (20 September 2000): 5.

"Art or Trash." *TA NEA* (26 September 2000): 28.

Barber, Jo. "Tim's Art Is a Pile of Rubbish." *Gloucester Citizen* (21 September 2000).

Blow, Isabella. "NIE Erwachsen Werden!" German *Vogue* (November 2000): 284–88, 326.

British Wildlife." *Metro* (8 September 2000).

Buck, Louisa. "Alchemists?" *Art Newspaper* (October 2000): 43.

Callow, Claire. "*British Wildlife*." *Contemporary Visual Arts* 31: 76.

Cork, Richard "What's Cooking in Hell's Kitchen? Kitsch." *Times* (20 September 2000): 18.

Cumming, Laura. "It's Just Hell, Darling . . . " *Observer* (24 September 2000): 6.

Gerard, Jasper. "It's Absolute Rubbish, but Is It Art?" *Sunday Times* (17 September 2000): 5.

Gibbons, Fiachra. "Shock Art with Horror for All to Enjoy." *Guardian* (20 September 2000): 7.

Herbert, Martin. "Tim Noble & Sue Webster." *Time Out London* (4–11 October 2000): 52.

Hunt, David. "*I Love You*." *Time Out New York* (23–30 March 2000).

Jury, Louise, and Sholto Byrnes. "It's a Load of Rubbish, This Modern Art." *Independent on Sunday* (8 October 2000): 3.

Klinkenberg, Marty. "The Last Word in Trashy Art." *Globe and Mail* (25 March 2000).

Koroxenidis, Alexandra. "Pictures of Defiance and Charm." *Herald Tribune, Kathimerini* (25 September 2000): 6.

Lewis, Mike. "Meet the Boozing Brothers with Flare for Trouble." *Welsh Mirror* (25 April 2000): 7.

Lewisohn, Cedar. "Modern Life Is Rubbish." *Flash Art* (May–June 2000): 76–79.

Maxwell, Douglas F. "Tim Noble and Sue Webster: *I Love You*." *Review* (15 March 2000): 8.

Papadopoulou, Christy. "*Masters of the Universe* Ride the 'Crest of Chance'." *Athens News* (26 September 2000): 12–13.

Roberts, Alison. "Prada, Pop and the Pope–It's Apocalypse Now." *Evening Standard* (19 September 2000): 8–9.

Sischy, Ingrid. "Meet Britain's Latest Art Sensation." *Interview* (September 2000): 72–73, 76.

"Stop and Smell the Roses." *Interview* (October 2000): 156.

Viveros-Faune, Christian. "Diamonds in the Rubbish." *New York Press* (15–21 March 2000): 17.

Williams, Gilda. "Tim Noble & Sue Webster." *WOW* (May–July 1999): 87–88.

Vendrame, Simona. "Manichini." *Tema Celeste* (October/December 1999): 88–97.

1999
Dodd, Celia. "Art Attack." *Radio Times* (25 September–1 October 1999): 30–32.

Dunn, Joseph. "Talking Rubbish." *Sunday Times Magazine* (1 August 1999): 19.

"Eau Courante." *Numéro* (July/August 1999).

Bendle, Sherry. "*The New Barbarians*." *Big Issue* (19–25 April 1999): 28–29.

Buck, Louisa. "Look out Damien." *ES Magazine* (18 June 1999): 20–21.

Corrigan, Susan. "DUO: Two Heads are Better Than One." *i-D* (July 1999): 79–84.

Currah, Mark. "*The New Barbarians*." *Time Out London* (10 March 1999): 49.

Geraghty, Ian. "Tim Noble & Sue Webster." *Untitled* (Spring 1999): 24–25.

Januszczak, Waldemar. "Cheeky Monkeys." *Sunday Times* (21 February 1999): Culture, 10–11.

Januszczak, Waldemar. "Charlie and the Chuckle Art Factory." *Sunday Times Magazine* (3 January 1999): 29–38.

Johnston, Robert. "Most Wanted." *Sunday Times Style Magazine* (28 February 1999): 4.

"Millennium Project Artwork." *Numéro* (December 1999–January 2000): 162–63.

Shave, Stuart. "De l'or pur dans les ordures." *Numéro* (October 1999): 204–09.

Vendrame, Simona. "Manichini." *Tema Celeste* (October/December 1999): 88–97.

Williams, Gilda. "Tim Noble & Sue Webster." *Art/Text* (May–July 1999): 87–88.

"*WOW*!" *i-D* (January/February 1999): 30.

1998
Burn, Gordon. "I Want it, I Want it All, and I Want it Now." *Guardian* (7 December 1998): 2–3.

Chapman, Jake. "20 Rivington Street." *Frieze* (March/April 1998): 94–95.

Harris, Mark. "20 Rivington Street." *Art in America* (July 1998): 108.

Januszczak, Waldemar. "Out to Lunch on an Egg." *Sunday Times* (13 December 1998): 9.

Shave, Stuart. "Art as Commerce." *i-D* (August 1998): 51.

1997
Coomer, Martin. "20 Rivington Street." *Time Out London* (10–17 December 1997): 58.

Gaskin, Vivienne. "Everything Talks to Tim Noble and Sue Webster." *Everything* (February 1997): 14–16.

Williams, Gilda. "*Turning the Tables*." *Art Monthly* (March 1997): 16.

1996
"A Brush with Genius: Tim Noble and Sue Webster on Andy Warhol's *Elvis*." *Guardian* (19 November 1996): 10.
Brown, Neal. "Tim Noble and Sue Webster." *Frieze* (September/October 1996): 84–85.

Burrows, David. "*British Rubbish*." *Art Monthly* (September 1996): 47–48.

Burrows, David. "*British Rubbish*." *Variant* (Winter 1996): 16.

Collings, Matthew. "Is it Gleaming or Is it Abject?" *Modern Painters* (Winter 1996): 82.

Herbert, Martin. "*British Rubbish*." *Time Out London* (July 1996): 47.

Kent, Sarah. "No More Heroes? *The New Contemporaries*." *Time Out London* (July 1996): 42.

1995
Cork, Richard. "Summer Brings Cold Comfort (*Ideal Standard Summertime*)." *Times* (September 1995).

Dorment, Richard. "Joshua Brings Down Art's Walls." *Daily Telegraph* (2 December 1995): A3.

Gott, Richard. "Where the Art Is." *Guardian Weekend* (7 October 1995): 36–38.

Jackson, Tina. "Art Exhibitionists." *Big Issue* (September 1995): 30–32.

Stathatos, John. "*Self Storage* at Acorn Storage, Wembley." *Untitled* (Summer 1995): 22.

1994
Alberge, Dalya. "Student in Van of Motorised Art Movement." *Independent* (18 June 1994).

Blake, Peter. "The Spirit of Pop Art." *Observer Magazine* (4 December 1994): 31.

1993
Alberge, Dalya. "Artist Floats a Gut Reaction to His Critics." *Independent* (11 May 1993): 3.

Lillington, David. "Lift." *Time Out London* (December 1993): 42.

"Outside Favourites." *Time Out London* (October 1993): 16–17.

Arken Museum, Denmark
Artis-François Pinault, France
Dakis Joannou Collection, Athens
Guggenheim Museum, New York
Honart Museum, Tehran, Iran
Saatchi Collection, London
Samsung Museum, Seoul, Korea

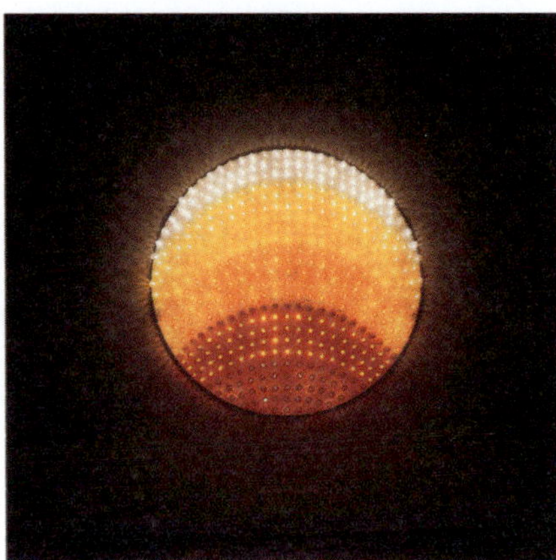

The Muthafucka, 2000
528 colored turbo caps, lamps and holders, foamex,
electronic light sequencer (24-channel fill and shimmer effect)
244 cm (diameter)

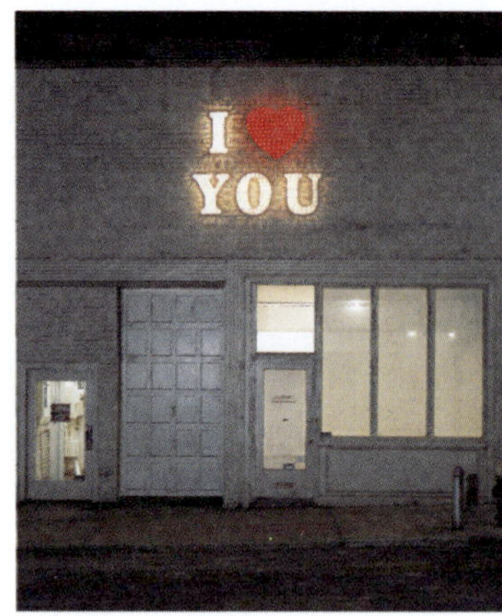

I ♥ YOU, 2000
Installation at Deitch Projects, NY
298 colored UFO reflector caps, lamps and holders, foamex, aerosol paint,
electronic light sequencer (12 x 3-channel spell, fill and shimmer effect)
180 x 8 x 160 cm

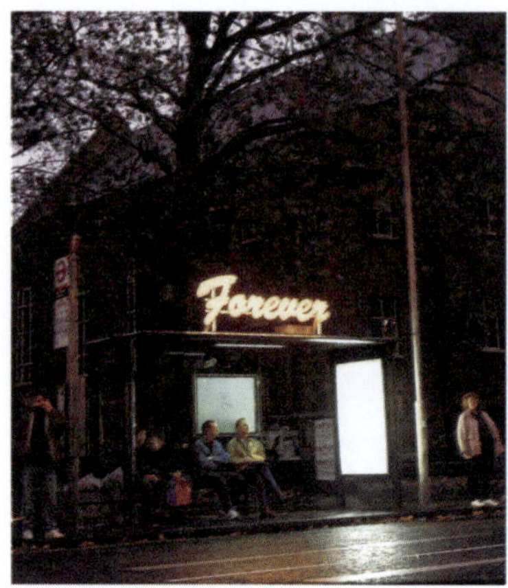

Forever, 1996
Installation, Tottenham Court Road, London
196 ice white UFO reflector caps, lamps, and holders, foamex, electronic light
sequencer (3-channel shimmer effect)
232.5 x 7 x 76.5 cm

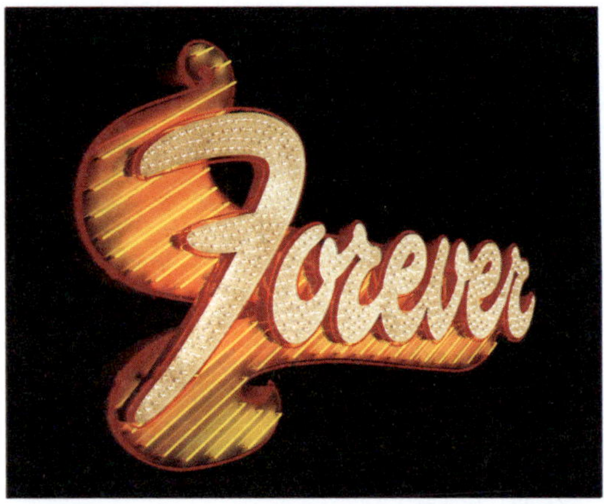

Forever, 2001 (version 3/3)
509 ice white turbo reflector caps, lamps, holders and daisy washers, ruby red
neon, 28 yellow neon strips, transformers, steel frame, painted aluminium, electronic light sequencer (28-channel scroll on/off, 7-letter spell and shimmer effect)
584 x 52 x 302 cm

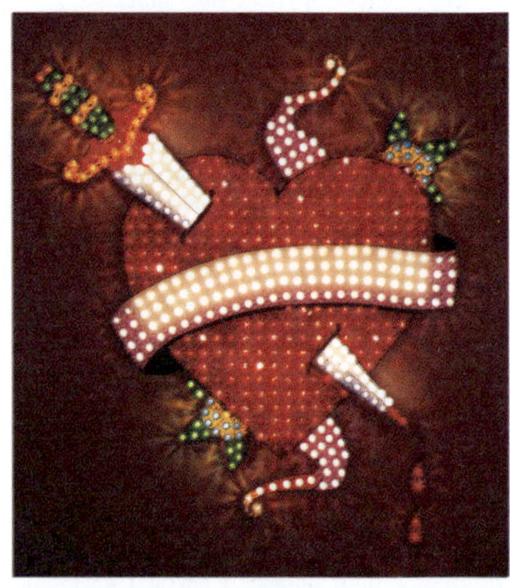

Toxic Schizophrenia, 1997
516 colored UFO reflector caps, lamps, and holders, foamex, vinyl, aerosol
paint, electronic light sequencer (51-channel multi-functional)
200 x 7 x 260 cm

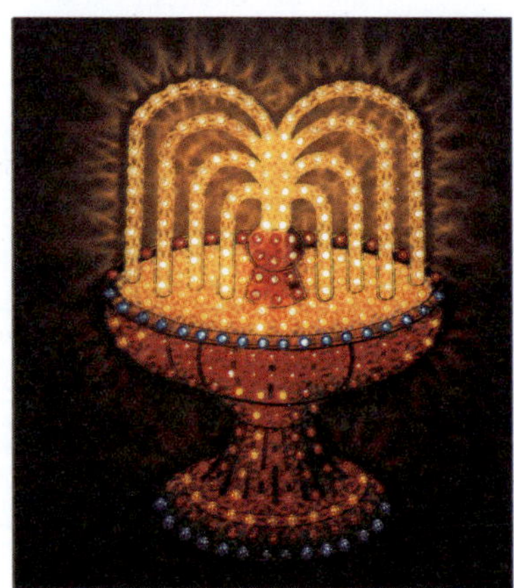

The Sweet Smell of Excess, 1998
160 white lamps, enameled steel, neon, transformers, electronic light sequencer
(3-channel bubble and chase effect)
Bottle: 208 x 63.5 cm, glass: 63.5 x 132 cm

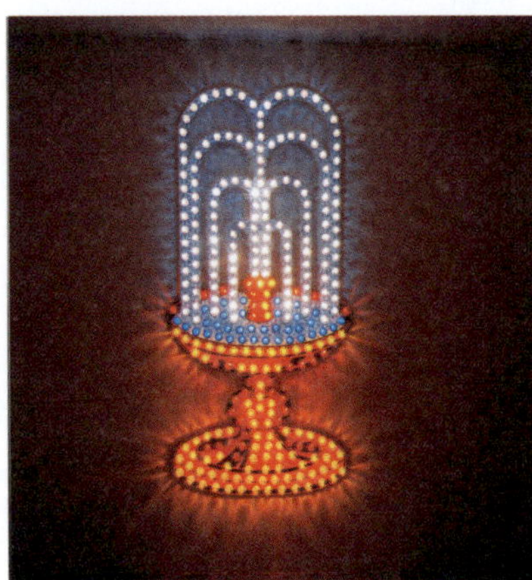

Excessive Sensual Indulgence, 1996
312 colored UFO reflector caps, lamps, and holders, foamex, vinyl, aerosol
paint, electronic light sequencer (4-channel bubble and chase effect)
88 x 7 x 187 cm

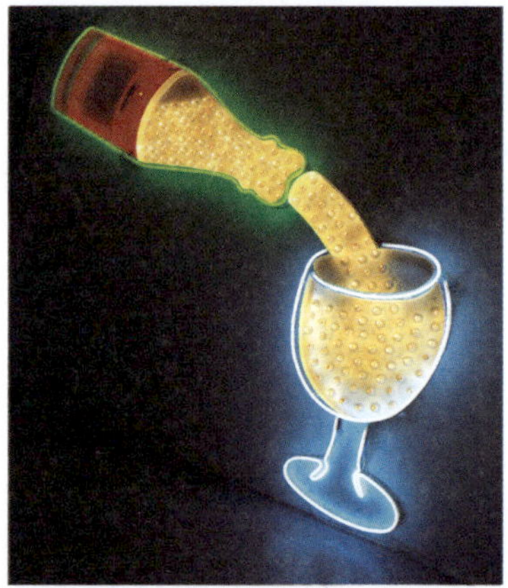

Golden Showers, 2000
294 colored UFO reflector caps, lamps, and holders, foamex, vinyl, aerosol
paint, electronic light sequencer (4-channel bubble and chase effect)
113 x 7 x 157 cm

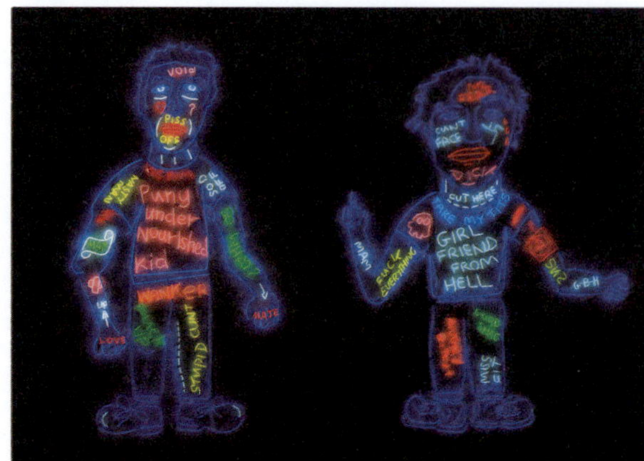

Puny Undernourished Kid & Girlfriend From Hell, 2004
Puny Undernourished Kid: 42 multicolored neon sections; *Girlfriend From
Hell*: 40 multicolored neon sections, transformers.
Puny Undernourished Kid: 180 x 4 x 284 cm
Girlfriend From Hell: 210 x 4 x 280 cm

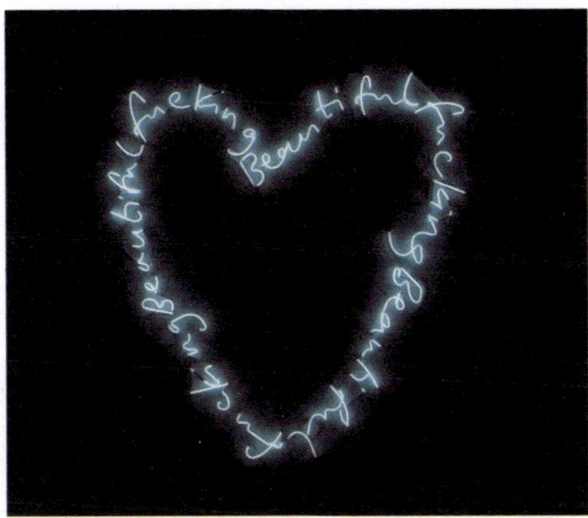

fuckingbeautiful (snow white version), 2000
8 neon sections, transformers
148 x 6.5 x 168 cm

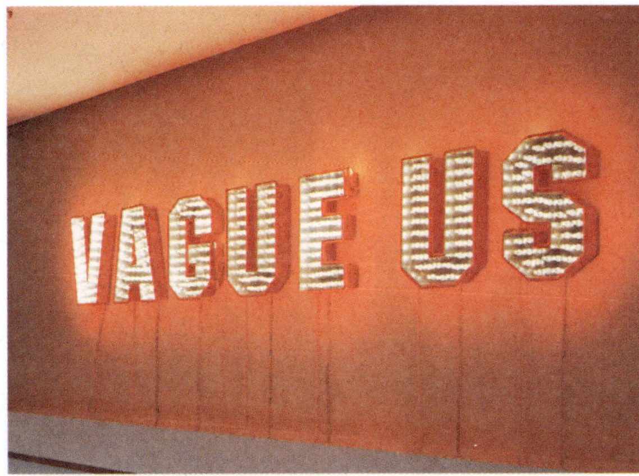

Vague Us, 1998
423 white lamps, mirror polished stainless steel, ruby red neon, transformers,
electronic light sequencer (14-channel spell and shimmer effect)
427 x 65 cm

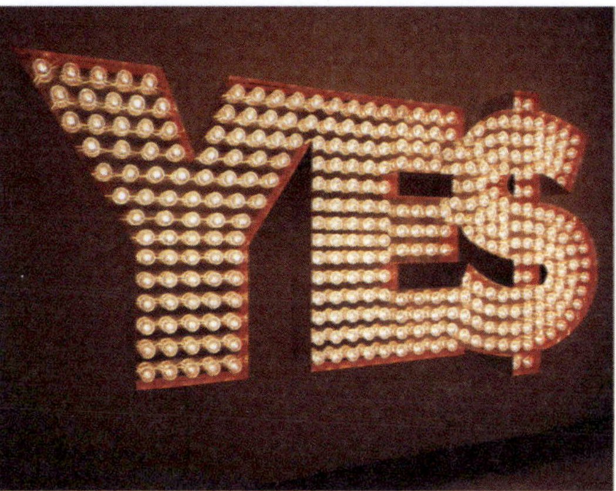

YE$, 2001
335 ice white turbo reflector caps, lamps, holders and daisy washers,
laquered brass, enameled paint, electronic light sequencer (3-channel
shimmer effect)
305 x 25.5 x 122 cm

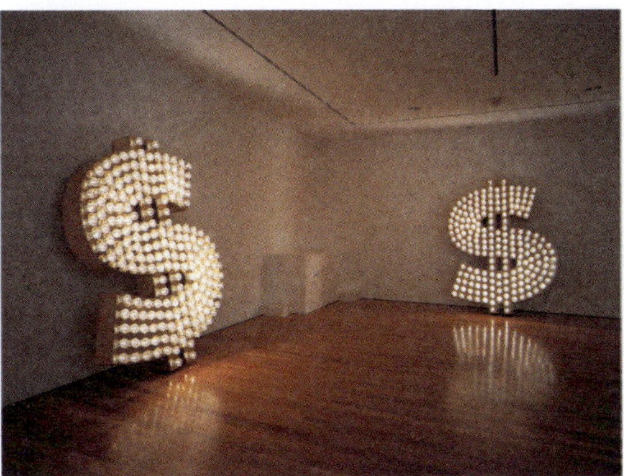

A Pair of Dollars, 2001
204 ice white turbo reflector caps, lamps, holders and daisy washers,
lacquered brass, electronic light sequencer (3-channel shimmer effect)
134 x 25 x 182 cm each

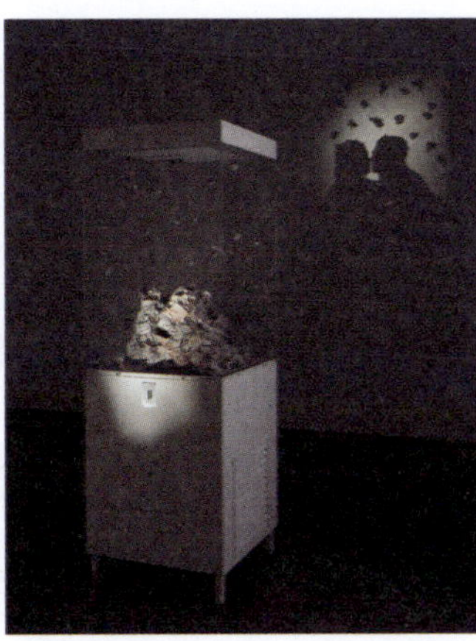

Made of Money, 2002
Sterling £5, £10, £20 and £50 notes, medium-density fiberboard, formica, per-
spex, 3 electric fans, slot machine mechanism, plastic tokens, light projector
76.3 x 76.3 x 222.5 cm

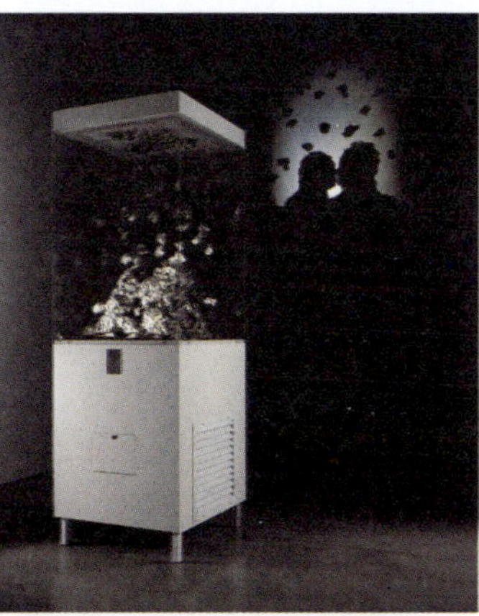

Instant Gratification, 2001
US $1 bills, bulldog clips, medium-density fiberboard, formica, perspex,
3 electric fans, slot machine mechanism, plastic tokens, light projector
76.3 x 76.3 x 222.5 cm

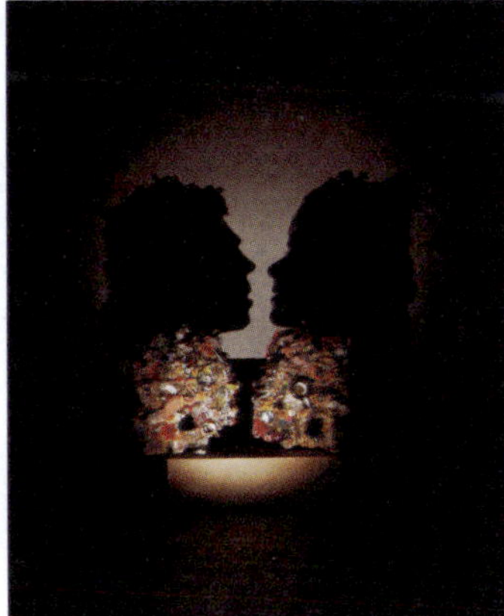

Cheap 'n' Nasty, 2000
Trash, expanding foam, medium-density fiberboard, 360-degree revolving
mechanism, light projector
275 x 104 x 152 cm

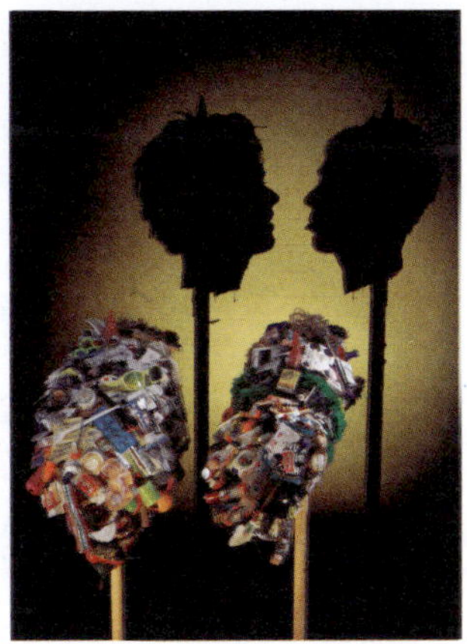

Miss Understood & Mr Meanor, 1997
Trash and personal items, wood, light projector, light sensor
70 x 60 x 140 cm

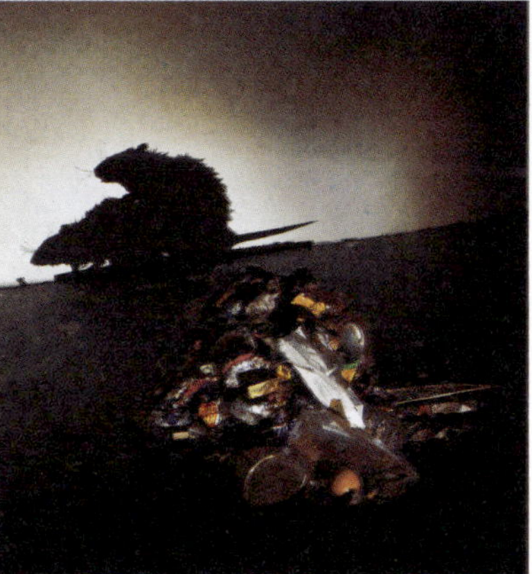

A Couple of Dirty Fucking Rats, 2000
Trash, light projector
51 x 46 x 25 cm

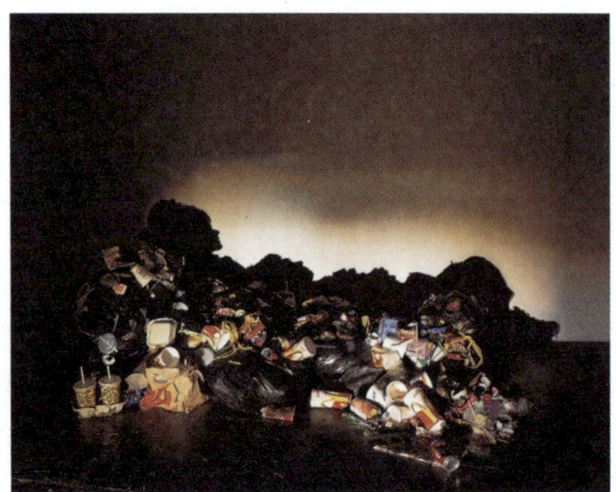

Wasted Youth, 2000
Trash, replica food, McDonald's packaging, wood, light projector
210 x 134 x 66 cm

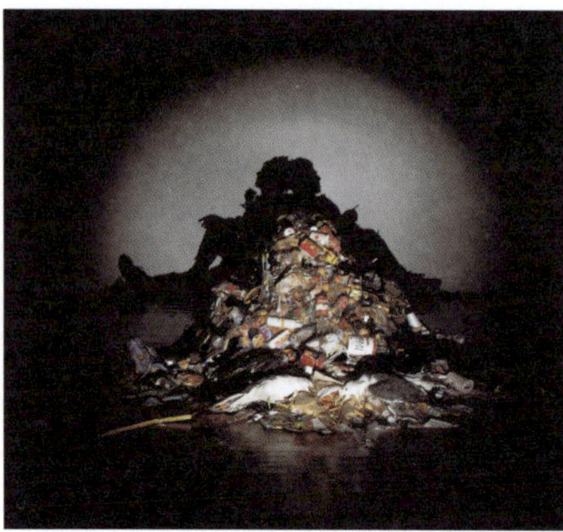

Dirty White Trash (with Gulls), 1998
6 months' worth of artists' trash, 2 taxidermy seagulls, light projector
Dimensions variable

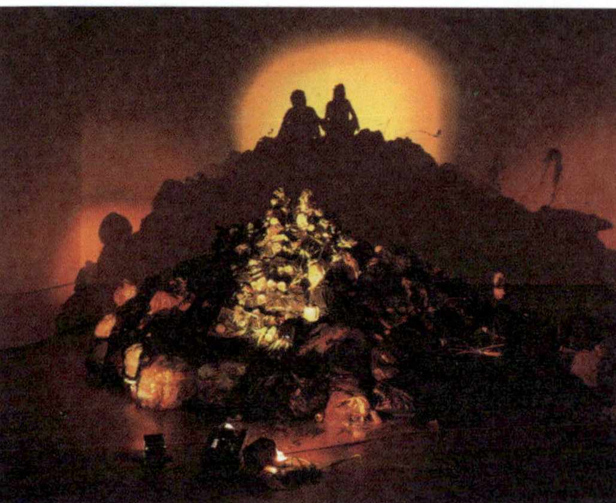

The Undesirables, 2000
Trash, electric fan, 3 light projectors and colored gels, smoke machine
Dimensions variable

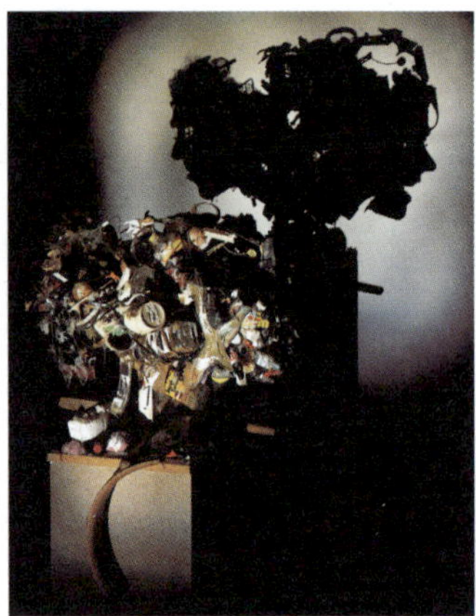

Falling Apart, 2001
Personal items trashed January–March 2001, light projector
Dimensions variable

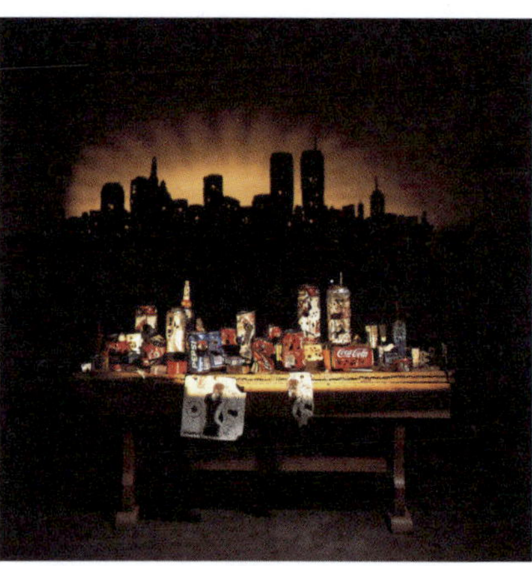

Sunset over Manhattan, 2003
Cigarette packets, tin cans shot by air gun pellets, wooden bench, light projector
110 x 31 x 75 cm

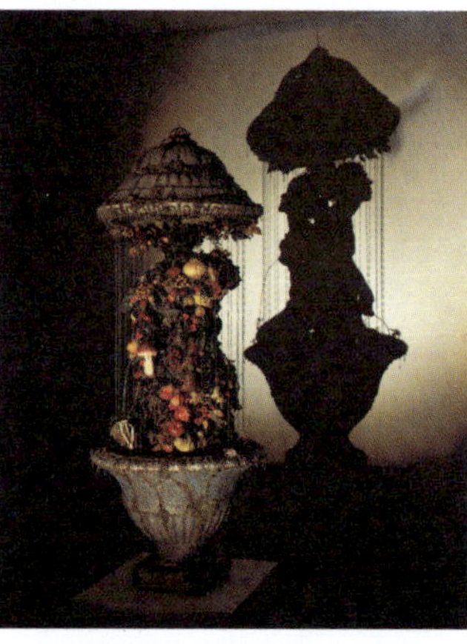

The Original Sinners, 2000
Replica fruits and berries, bark and moss, plastic ornamental bowls,
fishing wire, cooking oil, electric pump mechanism, metal, medium-density
board, light projector
60 x 60 x 200 cm

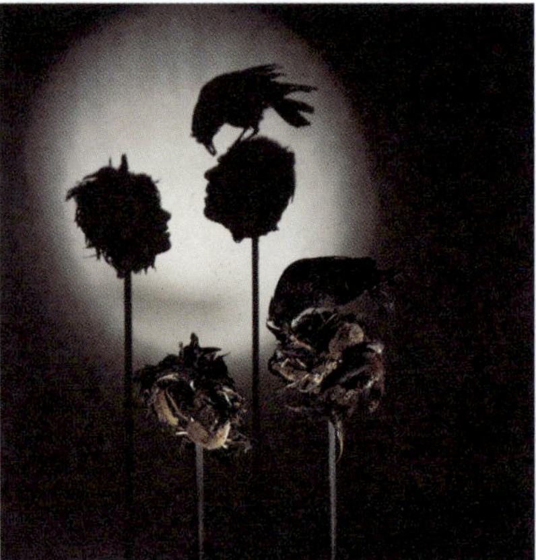

Kiss of Death, 2003
34 Taxidermy animals (6 rats, 1 mink, 8 carrion crows, 8 rooks,
11 jackdaws), animal bones, light projector, metal stand
80 x 50 x 180 cm

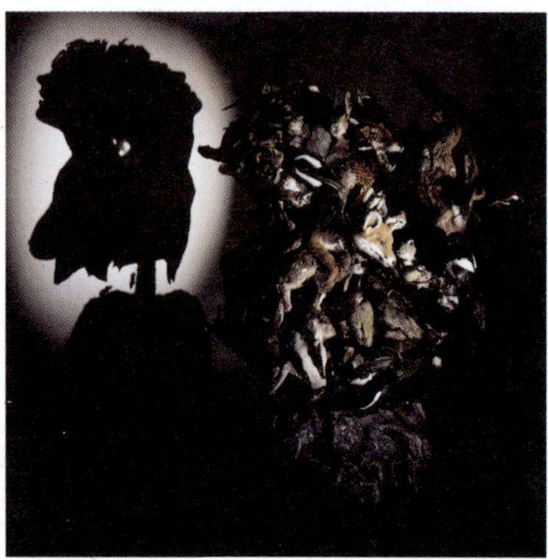

British Wildlife, 2000
88 taxidermy animals, 46 birds, 40 mammals, 2 fish, wood, polyester glass
fiber filler, moss, wire, light projector
150 x 90 x 180 cm

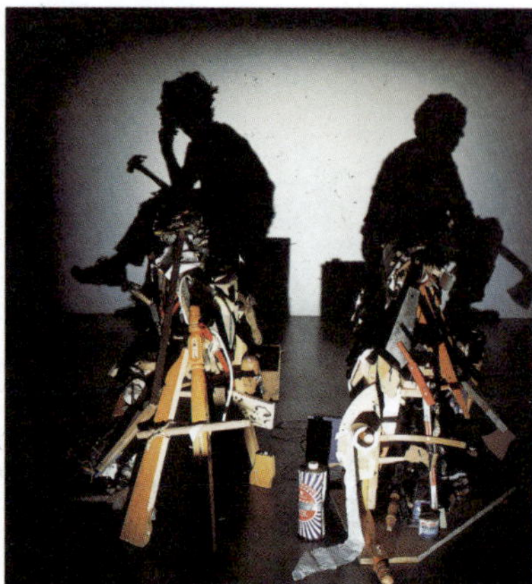

Real Life Is Rubbish, 2002
Mixed media, light projector
Dimensions variable